Your All-in-One Resource

On the CD that accompanies this book, you'll find additional resources to extend your learning.

The reference library includes the following fully searchable titles:

- *Microsoft Computer Dictionary*, 5th ed.
- *First Look 2007 Microsoft Office System* by Katherine Murray
- Windows Vista Product Guide

Also provided are a sample chapter and poster from *Look Both Ways: Help Protect Your Family on the Internet* by Linda Criddle.

The CD interface has a new look. You can use the tabs for an assortment of tasks:

- Check for book updates (if you have Internet access)
- Install the book's practice file
- Go online for product support or CD support
- Send us feedback

The following screen shot gives you a glimpse of the new interface.

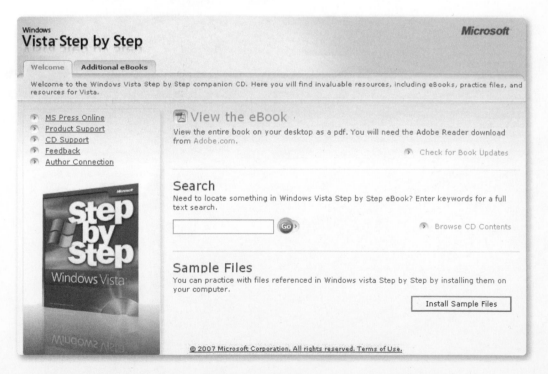

Microsoft

Microsoft® Windows® SharePoint® Services 3.0 Step by Step

Olga Londer
Bill English
Todd Bleeker
Penelope Coventry

PUBLISHED BY
Microsoft Press
A Division of Microsoft Corporation
One Microsoft Way
Redmond, Washington 98052-6399

Library of Congress Control Number: 2006940680

Printed and bound in the United States of America.

7 8 9 10 11 12 13 14 15 16 QGT 5 4 3 2 1 0

Distributed in Canada by H.B. Fenn and Company Ltd.

A CIP catalogue record for this book is available from the British Library.

Microsoft Press books are available through booksellers and distributors worldwide. For further information about international editions, contact your local Microsoft Corporation office or contact Microsoft Press International directly at fax (425) 936-7329. Visit our Web site at www.microsoft.com/mspress. Send comments to mspinput@microsoft.com.

Acquisitions Editor: Juliana Aldous Atkinson
Developmental Editor: Sandra Haynes
Project Editor: Valerie Woolley
Editorial and Production Services: Custom Editorial Productions, Inc.

Body Part No. X13-24177

Contents

Information for Readers Running Windows XP ix

Features and Conventions of This Book xii

Getting Help xv

Using the Book's CD xvii

Chapter 1   Introduction to Windows SharePoint Services 1

Chapter 2   Navigating a SharePoint Site 15

Chapter 3   Creating and Managing Sites 43

Chapter 4   Working with Lists 77

Chapter 5   Creating and Managing Libraries 133

Chapter 6   Working with Library Settings 165

Chapter 7   Working with Document Workspaces 185

Chapter 8   Working with Meeting Workspaces 203

Chapter 9   Working with Surveys and Discussion Boards 231

Chapter 10   Working with Wikis and Blogs 263

Chapter 11   Using Windows SharePoint Services with Outlook 2007 291

Chapter 12   Using Windows SharePoint Services with Excel 2007 329

Chapter 13   Using Windows SharePoint Services with Access 2007 351

Chapter 14   Using Windows SharePoint Services with InfoPath 2007 375

Chapter 15   Working with Web Parts 401

Chapter 16   Finding Information on the SharePoint Site 429

What do you think of this book? We want to hear from you!

Microsoft is interested in hearing your feedback so we can continually improve our books and learning resources for you. To participate in a brief online survey, please visit:

www.microsoft.com/learning/booksurvey/

Contents

Introduction xi

1 Introduction to Windows SharePoint Services   1

What Is Windows SharePoint Services? 2

    Team Collaboration and Sharing. 2

    Windows SharePoint Services User Permissions. 7

Versions of Windows SharePoint Services. 8

Microsoft Office Integrationwith Windows SharePoint Services. 9

Microsoft SharePoint Products and Technologies. 11

    Windows SharePoint Services and SharePoint Server 2007 11

    Windows SharePoint Services and SharePoint Designer 2007. 12

Key Points. 13

2 Navigating a SharePoint Site   15

Navigating the Home Page and the SharePoint Site. 16

Navigating the Site Hierarchy 21

Browsing Lists on a SharePoint Site 25

Browsing Document Libraries 26

Customizing the Top Navigation Area. 27

Customizing the Left Navigation Panel 30

Understanding Web Part Pages 35

Using the Recycle Bin 38

Key Points 41

What do you think of this book? We want to hear from you!

Microsoft is interested in hearing your feedback so we can continually improve our books and learning resources for you. To participate in a brief online survey, please visit:

www.microsoft.com/learning/booksurvey/

3   Creating and Managing Sites   43

Creating Sites 44

Managing Site Users and Permissions 53

Creating a Child Workspace. 60

Changing a Site's Theme 63

Saving and Using a Site Template. 65

Managing Site Features 68

Managing Site Content Syndication. 71

Deleting a Site 73

Key Points 75

4   Working with Lists   77

Discovering Default Lists in a Site. 78

Creating a New List. 83

Adding, Editing, and Deleting List Items 89

Restoring a List Item from the Recycle Bin 95

Using the Datasheet View 96

Attaching Files to List Items. 98

Adding, Editing, and Deleting List Columns 101

Sorting and Filtering a List. 110

Adding and Modifying a List View. 112

Setting Up Alerts. 117

Using Really Simple Syndication Feeds 119

Sending an E-Mail to a SharePoint List 123

Deleting a List 130

Key Points 131

5   Creating and Managing Libraries   133

Creating Libraries. 134

Creating Document Libraries. 134

Creating Form Libraries 137

Creating Picture Libraries. 141

Adding Documents. 143

Adding Pictures 145

Creating a New Folder in a Library. 145

Checking Documents In and Out from the Document Library 147

Checking Documents In and Out from the 2007 Microsoft Office Suite 149

Working with Version History 151
Deleting Documents 152
Working with Workflows 153
Using Alerts 155
Working with Offline Documents 157
Key Points 163

6 Working with Library Settings   **165**
Configuring a Library 166
Creating New Columns and Working with Content Types 169
Using Content Types and Columns 171
Creating a New View 172
Using Document Library Settings 174
Using the Document Information Panel 179
Securing a Library 179
Deleting a Library 182
Key Points 183

7 Working with Document Workspaces   **185**
Creating a Document Workspace 186
Creating a Document Workspace Within the 2007 Microsoft Office Suite 188
Accessing an Existing Document Workspace 192
Working with the 2007 Microsoft Office Suite Document
    Management Task Pane 194
Publishing a Document Back to a Document Library 198
Deleting a Document Workspace 199
Key Points 201

8 Working with Meeting Workspaces   **203**
Creating a Meeting Workspace by Using a Template 204
Creating a Meeting Workspace for a Calendar Event 207
Understanding the Home Page of a Meeting Workspace 212
Adding an Objective to a Meeting Workspace 217
Adding an Agenda to a Meeting Workspace 219
Adding an Attendee to a Meeting Workspace 221
Adding a Things To Bring List 224
Adding a Web Part to the More Page Tab 226
Key Points 229

9   Working with Surveys and Discussion Boards   **231**

  Creating a Survey. 232
  Responding to a Survey 241
  Viewing the Results of a Survey 245
  Creating and Using a Discussion Board. 250
  Enabling Discussion Board for E-Mail 256
  Viewing a Discussion Board in Outlook 2007. 258
  Key Points 261

10   Working with Wikis and Blogs   **263**

  Understanding Wikis. 264
  Creating a New Wiki Page Library 264
  Creating a New Wiki Page 269
  Linking. 271
  Versioning. 273
  Understanding Blogs 275
  Creating a Blog Site. 275
  Creating a Blog Post 278
  Adding a Blog Comment 284
  Using Really Simple Syndication Feeds 286
  Key Points 289

11   Using Windows SharePoint Services with Outlook 2007   **291**

  Connecting a SharePoint Contacts List to Outlook 2007 292
  Moving an Outlook 2007 Contact to a SharePoint Contact List 297
  Copying SharePoint Contacts into Outlook 2007 299
  Sending E-Mail by Using a SharePoint Contacts List. 302
  Viewing SharePoint Calendars Side by Side with Personal Calendars 303
  Synchronizing SharePoint Tasks List Content 305
  Managing SharePoint Alerts in Outlook 2007 308
  Creating Meeting Workspaces from Outlook 2007. .312
  Configuring an RSS Feed 317
  Work with Workflow in Outlook 2007. 322
  Key Points 327

12   Using Windows SharePoint Services with Excel 2007   329

Importing Data from an Excel 2007 Spreadsheet to a List in SharePoint 330

Using the Access Web Datasheet 333

Exporting a SharePoint List to an Excel 2007 Spreadsheet 340

Exporting an Excel 2007 Table to a SharePoint Site 344

Key Points 349

13   Using Windows SharePoint Services with Access 2007   351

Exporting Data from an Access 2007 Database to a SharePoint List 353

Importing a List to an Access 2007 Table 356

Linking an Access 2007 Table to a SharePoint List. 359

Moving Data from an Access 2007 Database to a SharePoint Site. 362

Working Offline 367

Working with Workflow 370

Key Points 373

14   Using Windows SharePoint Services with InfoPath 2007   375

Creating a Form Library from InfoPath 2007 376

Modifying an Existing Form Library. 382

Filling Out a New Form. 386

Editing an Existing Form. 387

Creating a Content Type from InfoPath 2007. 389

Associating a Content Type with a Form Library 392

Modifying a Content Type. 395

Key Points 399

15   Working with Web Parts   401

Web Parts and Web Part Pages. 402

Removing a Web Part. 405

Adding a Web Part from a Web Part Gallery 407

Customizing a Web Part by Using the Web Part Tool Pane. 414

Customizing a Home Page by Using Web Parts. 421

Creating a New Web Part Page by Using a Browser 422

Key Points 427

16   Finding Information on the SharePoint Site   429

Understanding How Search Works. 430

Executing a Search Query 432

Key Points 434

Appendix 435

Index 443

Glossary . . . . .On the CD

What do you think of this book? We want to hear from you!

Microsoft is interested in hearing your feedback so we can continually improve our books and learning resources for you. To participate in a brief online survey, please visit:

www.microsoft.com/learning/booksurvey/

Information for Readers Running Windows XP

The graphics and the operating system–related instructions in this book reflect the Windows Vista user interface. However, Windows Vista is not required; you can also use a computer running Microsoft Windows XP.

Most of the differences you will encounter when working through the exercises in this book on a computer running Windows XP center around appearance rather than functionality. For example, the Windows Vista Start button is round rather than rectangular and is not labeled with the word Start; window frames and window-management buttons look different; and if your system supports Windows Aero, the window frames might be transparent.

In this section, we provide steps for navigating to or through menus and dialog boxes in Windows XP that differ from those provided in the exercises in this book. For the most part, these differences are small enough that you will have no difficulty in completing the exercises.

Managing the Practice Files

The instructions given in the "Using the Book's CD" section are specific to Windows Vista. The only differences when installing, using, uninstalling, and removing the practice files supplied on the companion CD are the default installation location and the uninstall process.

On a computer running Windows Vista, the default installation location of the practice files is Documents\Microsoft Press\SBS_WSSv3. On a computer running Windows XP, the default installation location is My Documents\Microsoft Press\ SBS_WSSv3. If your computer is running Windows XP, whenever an exercise tells you to navigate to your Documents folder, you should instead go to your My Documents folder.

To uninstall the practice files from a computer running Windows XP:

1. On the Windows taskbar, click the **Start** button, and then click **Control Panel**.
2. In **Control Panel**, click (or in Classic view, double-click) **Add or Remove Programs**.

3. In the **Add or Remove Programs** window, click **Windows SharePoint Services 3.0 Step by Step**, and then click **Remove**.

4. In the **Add or Remove Programs** message box asking you to confirm the deletion, click **Yes**.

> **Important** If you need help installing or uninstalling the practice files, please see the "Getting Help" section later in this book. Microsoft Product Support Services does not provide support for this book or its companion CD.

Using the Start Menu

To start a Microsoft Office application, such as Microsoft Office Word, Microsoft Office Outlook, Microsoft Office Excel, Microsoft Office Access, or Microsoft Office InfoPath, on a computer running Windows XP:

● Click the **Start** button, point to **All Programs**, click **Microsoft Office**, and then click **the application you would like to start**.

Folders on the Windows Vista Start menu expand vertically. Folders on the Windows XP Start menu expand horizontally. You will notice this variation between the images shown in this book and your Start menu.

Navigating Dialog Boxes

On a computer running Windows XP, some of the dialog boxes you will work with in the exercises not only look different from the graphics shown in this book but also work differently. These dialog boxes are primarily those that act as an interface between Windows Sharepoint Services and the operating system, including any dialog box in which you navigate to a specific location. For example, here are comparisons of the ways to navigate in the Open dialog boxes from Microsoft Office client applications running on Windows Vista and Windows XP.

To navigate to the **Chapter 02 Navigating a SharePoint Site** folder in Windows Vista:

- In the Favorite Links pane, click **Documents**. Then in the folder content pane, double-click **Microsoft Press**, **SBS_WSSv3**, and double-click **Chapter 02 Navigating a SharePoint Site**.

To move back to the **Chapter 02 Navigating a SharePoint Site** folder in Windows Vista:

- In the upper-left corner of the dialog box, click the **Back** button.

To navigate to the **Chapter 02 Navigating a SharePoint Site** folder in Windows XP:

- On the **Places** bar, click **My Documents**. Then in the folder content pane, double-click **Microsoft Press**, **SBS_WSSv3**, and double-click **Chapter 02 Navigating a SharePoint Site**.

To move back to the **Chapter 02 Navigating a SharePoint Site** folder in Windows XP:

- On the toolbar, click the **Up One Level** button.

Features and Conventions of This Book

This book has been designed to lead you step-by-step through all the tasks you are most likely to want to perform in Microsoft Windows SharePoint Services 3.0. If you start at the beginning and work your way through all the exercises, you will gain enough pro- ficiency to be able to create and work with all the common types of Windows SharePoint Services files. However, each topic is self contained. If you have worked with a previous version of Windows SharePoint Services, or if you completed all the exercises and later need help remembering how to perform a procedure, the following features of this book will help you look up specific tasks:

- **Detailed table of contents.** Get an overview of which topics are discussed in which chapters.

- **Chapter thumb tabs.** Easily open the book at the beginning of the chapter you want.

- **Topic-specific running heads.** Within a chapter, quickly locate the topic you want by looking at the running head of odd-numbered pages.

- **Detailed index.** Look up specific tasks and features in the index, which has been carefully crafted with the reader in mind.

- **Companion CD.** Use to install the practice files needed for the step-by-step exer- cises, but also as a source of other useful information, including an online, search- able version of this book.

In addition, we provide a glossary of terms, located on the companion CD, for those times when you need to look up the meaning of a word or the definition of a concept.

You can save time when you use this book by understanding how the Step by Step series shows special instructions, keys to press, buttons to click, and so on.

Convention	Meaning
	This icon indicates a reference to the book's companion CD.
BE SURE TO	This paragraph preceding or following a step-by-step exercise indicates any prerequisite requirements that you should attend to before beginning the exercise, or actions you should take to restore your system after completing the exercise.

OPEN	This paragraph preceding a step-by-step exercise indicates files that you should open before beginning the exercise.
CLOSE	This paragraph following a step-by-step exercise provides instructions for closing open files or programs before moving on to another topic.
1 2	Blue numbered steps guide you through step-by-step exercises and procedures in the "Quick Reference."
1 **2**	Black numbered steps guide you through procedures in sidebars and topic introductions.
●	A single solid blue circle indicates an exercise that has only one step.
See Also	These paragraphs direct you to more information about a given topic in this book or elsewhere.
Troubleshooting	These paragraphs explain how to fix a common problem that might prevent you from continuing with an exercise.
Tip	These paragraphs provide a helpful hint or shortcut that makes working through a task easier, or information about other available options.
Important	These paragraphs point out information that you need to know to complete a procedure.
Save	The first time you are told to click a button in an exercise, a picture of the button appears in the left margin. If the name of the button does not appear on the button itself, the name appears under the picture.
Enter	In step-by-step exercises, keys you must press appear in key-shaped boxes.
Ctrl + Home	A plus sign (+) between two key names means that you must hold down the first key while you press the second key. For example, "press Ctrl + Home" means "hold down the Ctrl key while you press the Home key."
Program interface elements	In steps, the names of program elements, such as buttons, commands, and dialog boxes, are shown in black bold characters.
User input	Anything you are supposed to type appears in blue bold characters.
Glossary terms	Terms that are explained in the glossary located on the companion CD are shown in blue italic characters.

Getting Help

Every effort has been made to ensure the accuracy of this book and the contents of its companion CD. If you do run into problems, please contact the sources listed below for assistance.

Getting Help with This Book and Its Companion CD

If your question or issue concerns the content of this book or its companion CD, please first search the online Microsoft Press Knowledge Base, which provides support information for known errors in or corrections to this book, at the following Web site:

www.microsoft.com/mspress/support/search.asp

If you do not find your answer at the online Knowledge Base, send your comments or questions to Microsoft Press Technical Support at:

mspinput@microsoft.com

Getting Help with Windows SharePoint Services 3.0

If your question is about Microsoft Windows SharePoint Services, and not about the content of this Microsoft Press book, your first recourse is the Windows SharePoint Services Help system. This system is a combination of tools and files stored on your SharePoint servers when Windows SharePoint Services 3.0 was installed. If your computer is connected to the Internet, information is also available from Microsoft Office Online. There are several ways to find general or specific Help information:

- On nearly any Windows SharePoint Services browser window, you can click on the blue circle with a white question mark on it. This will display a new window where you can search for help doing tasks within the SharePoint browser interface.
- To find out about an item on the screen, you can display a ScreenTip. For example, to display a ScreenTip for a button, point to the button without clicking it.

More Information

If your question is about Windows SharePoint Services or another Microsoft software product and you cannot find the answer in the product's Help, please search the appropriate product solution center or the Microsoft Knowledge Base at:

support.microsoft.com

In the United States, Microsoft software product support issues not covered by the Microsoft Knowledge Base are addressed by Microsoft Product Support Services. Location-specific software support options are available from:

support.microsoft.com/gp/selfoverview/

Using the Book's CD

The companion CD included with this book contains the practice files you'll use as you work through the book's exercises, as well as other electronic resources that will help you learn how to use Microsoft Windows SharePoint Services 3.0.

What's on the CD?

The following table lists the practice files supplied on the book's CD.

Chapter	Files
Chapter 1: Introduction to Windows SharePoint Services	(no practice files)
Chapter 2: Navigating a SharePoint Site	Chapter02_Solution.stp, Chapter02_TravelSite.stp
Chapter 3: Creating and Managing Sites	Chapter03_Solution.stp, Chapter03_TeamMeeting.stp
Chapter 4: Working with Lists	Chapter04_Solution.stp
Chapter 5: Creating and Managing Libraries	Chapter05_Solution.stp, OakDesk.docx, pjcov.jpg
Chapter 6: Working with Library Settings	Chapter06_Solution.stp, OakChairs.docx, OakChest.docx, OakTable.docx, OakWood.docx
Chapter 7: Working with Document Workspaces	Chapter07_TeamSite.stp, Chapter07_Workspace.stp
Chapter 8: Working with Meeting Workspaces	Chapter08_Solution.stp
Chapter 9: Working with Surveys and Discussion Boards	Chapter09_Solution.stp
Chapter 10: Working with Wikis and Blogs	Chapter10_BlogSolution.stp, Chapter10_WikiSolution.stp
Chapter 11: Using Windows SharePoint Services with Outlook 2007	Chapter11_Starter.stp, Chapter11_Solution.stp

Chapter 12: Using Windows SharePoint Services with Excel 2007	Furniture_Price.xlsx, Sales_Figures.xlsx
Chapter 13: Tracking Progress on Tasks and Assignments	ExpImpWideWorldImporters.accdb, MoveWideWorldImporters.accdb
Chapter 14: Using Windows SharePoint Services with InfoPath 2007	Expense Report Template.xsn, Purchase Order Template.xsn, Chapter14_Solution.stp
Chapter 15: Working with Web Parts	Chapter15_Solution.stp
Chapter 16: Finding Information on the SharePoint Site	Chapter16_Starter.stp

In addition to the practice files, the CD contains some exciting resources that will really enhance your ability to get the most out of using this book and Windows SharePoint Services, including the following:

- *Microsoft Windows SharePoint Services 3.0 Step by Step* in eBook format
- *Microsoft Computer Dictionary*, Fifth Edition eBook
- *First Look 2007 Microsoft Office System* (Katherine Murray, 2006)
- Sample chapter and poster from *Look Both Ways: Help Protect Your Family on the Internet* (Linda Criddle, 2007)
- Windows SharePoint Services version comparison
- SharePoint products comparison
- Glossary for this book

Client Computer

To perform exercises in this book, your client computer should meet the following requirements.

- Operating System:
    - Windows Vista is recommended. However, you can use Windows XP or Windows Server 2003

- Software:

  - Microsoft Internet Explorer 6 or later. Microsoft Internet Explorer 7 is recommended.

  - Microsoft Office Word 2007, Microsoft Office Outlook 2007, Microsoft Office Excel 2007, Microsoft Office Access 2007, Microsoft Office InfoPath 2007.

- Disk space:

  - 10MB of available hard disk space for the practice files

Server Deployment

To perform exercises in this book, you should have access to Windows SharePoint Services 3.0 deployment, that can be either a single-box server installation or a farm deployment. The server should meet the following requirements.

- Operating System:

  - Windows Server 2003 SP1 or Windows Server 2003 x64 or Windows Small Business Server 2003; .NET Framework 3.0

- Software:

  - Windows SharePoint Services 3.0

> **Important** The companion CD for this book does not contain the Windows SharePoint Services 3.0 software. Windows SharePoint Services 3.0 is a part of Windows Server 2003 and is available as a free download from the Microsoft web site. Windows SharePoint Services 3.0 must be installed on your Windows Server 2003 server(s) before using this book..

Installing the Practice Files

You need to install the practice files in the correct location on your hard disk before you can use them in the exercises. Follow these steps:

1. Remove the companion CD from the envelope at the back of the book, and insert it into the CD drive of your computer.

   The Step By Step Companion CD License Terms appear. Follow the on-screen directions. To use the practice files, you must accept the terms of the license agreement. After you accept the license agreement, a menu screen appears.

> **Important** If the menu screen does not appear, click the Start button and then click Computer. Display the Folders list in the Navigation Pane, click the icon for your CD drive, and then in the right pane, double-click the StartCD executable file.

2. Click **Install Practice Files**.

3. Click **Next** on the first screen, and then click **Next** to accept the terms of the license agreement on the next screen.

4. If you want to install the practice files to a location other than the default folder (*Documents\Microsoft Press\SBS_WSSv3*), click the **Change** button, select the new drive and path, and then click **OK**.

> **Important** If you install the practice files to a location other than the default, you will need to substitute that path within the exercises.

5. Click **Next** on the **Choose Destination Location** screen, and then click **Install** on the **Ready to Install the Program** screen to install the selected practice files.

6. After the practice files have been installed, click **Finish**.

7. Close the **Step by Step Companion CD** window, remove the companion CD from the CD drive, and return it to the envelope at the back of the book.

Using the Practice Files

When you install the practice files from the companion CD that accompanies this book, the files are stored on your hard disk in chapter-specific subfolders under *Documents\Microsoft Press\SBS_WSSv3*. Each exercise in a chapter includes a paragraph that lists the files needed for that exercise and explains any preparations needed before you start working through the exercise.

Whenever possible, we start each chapter with a standard Windows SharePoint Services team site which occasionally must be a top-level team site. If you follow all the exercises in all the chapters in sequence, you do not have to start with a new team site for every chapter. You can just use the same site throughout the whole book.

However, if you choose to do exercises independently and not in sequence, there are a couple of exercises that depend on other exercises performed earlier in the book. If this is the case, we will tell you where the prerequisite exercise is located in the book, so that you can complete the prerequisite exercises. However, you may not want to do the prerequisite exercise and this is where the starter STP files will come in handy.

If you have sufficient rights, you can create a new child site (see Using the STP Site Templates) from the chapter's starter file provided on the CD ROM and installed in the practice folder for this chapter. The resulting child site will have the prerequisite exercises already completed for you. This option is for advanced users who might not want to do a prerequisite exercise from another chapter.

Exercises in some chapters use a subsite in addition to the standard team site. If this is the case, the practice folder for the chapter contains an STP file for the subsite.

All chapters, with exception of Chapter 1 and Chapter 16, have solution STP files. The solution STP files use the same titles as their corresponding chapters. Use a solution STP file for a chapter to create a new child site to see the results of exercises in this chapter.

(Optional) Using the STP Site Templates

To create a practice site for a chapter based on a site template STP file provided on the CD, perform the following steps:

OPEN the top-level SharePoint site to which you would like to upload the STP files. If prompted, type your user name and password, and click OK.

BE SURE TO verify that you have sufficient rights to upload to the site template gallery of a site collection. If in doubt, see the Appendix.

1. On the **Site Actions** menu, click **Site Settings** to display the **Site Settings** page.

2. In the **Galleries** section, click **Site templates** to display the site template gallery page.

3. In the toolbar, click **Upload** to display the **Upload Template: site template gallery** page.

4. Click the **Browse** button to display the **Choose File** dialog box.

5. Navigate to Documents\Microsoft Press\ SBS_WSSv3\Chapter XX (where XX is the chapter number), click the STP file that you want to use to create the new site, and then click the **Open** button.

6. Click the **OK** button once to complete the upload and a second time to take the default properties. The site template gallery page will redisplay.

Use the following steps to create a new child site based upon the uploaded template:

1. Browse to the SharePoint site that you'd like to be the parent of the new practice site.

2. On the Site Actions menu, click **Create** to display the **Create** page.

3. In the **Web Pages** section, click **Site and Workspaces** to display the **New SharePoint Site** page.

4. In the **Title** text box, type a logical name for the new site; you could simply provide the chapter number if you like, for example Chapter06.

5. Optionally, in the **Description** text box, type a description, fox example **SharePoint SBS Chapter 6 Practice Site**.

6. In the **URL name** text box, repeat the same name as you typed into the **Title** text box.

7. On the **Custom** tab in the **Template Selection** section, choose the name of the template that you just uploaded; for example, **Chapter 11 Starter**.

8. You can leave all the other options as their default values and click the **Create** button.

The Home page of the new practice site is displayed.

 **CLOSE** the browser.

(Optional) Removing the STP Site Templates

To remove the chapter starter and solution STPs from the site template gallery, perform the following steps:

 OPEN the top-level SharePoint site where you previously uploaded the STP files. If prompted, type your user name and password, and click OK.

BE SURE TO verify that you have sufficient rights to delete STPs from the site template gallery of a site collection. If in doubt, see the Appendix.

1. On the **Site Actions** menu, click **Site Settings** to display the **Site Settings** page.

2. In the **Galleries** section, click **Site templates** to display the site template gallery page.

3. Click the **Edit** icon to display the details for the site template that you wish to remove.

4. In the toolbar, click the **Delete Item** option to remove the site template. You will be prompted to confirm your request. Click **OK** to complete the deletion and redisplay the site template gallery.

5. Repeat the edit and delete steps to remove each site template that you no longer want available for the creation of practice sites.

 CLOSE the browser.

(Optional) Deleting a Practice Site

If you created a practice site that you no longer want, you can delete it. Perform the following steps to delete a practice site:

 **OPEN** the SharePoint site that you wish to delete. If prompted, type your user name and password, and click OK.

BE SURE TO verify that you have sufficient rights to delete a site. If in doubt, see the Appendix.

1. On the **Site Actions** menu, click **Site Settings** to display the **Site Settings** page.

2. In the **Site Administration** section, click **Delete** this site to display the **Delete This Site** confirmation page.

3. Click the **Delete** button to delete the site.

Removing and Uninstalling the Practice Files

You can free up hard disk space by uninstalling the practice files that were installed from the companion CD. The uninstall process deletes any files that you created in the chapter-specific folders while working through the exercises. Follow these steps:

1. On the Windows taskbar, click the **Start** button, and then click **Control Panel**.

2. In **Control Panel**, under **Programs**, click the **Uninstall a program** task.

3. In the **Programs and Features** window, click **Windows SharePoint Services 3.0 Step by Step**, and then on the toolbar at the top of the window, click the **Uninstall** button.

4. If the **Programs and Features** message box asking you to confirm the deletion appears, click **Yes**.

Chapter at a Glance

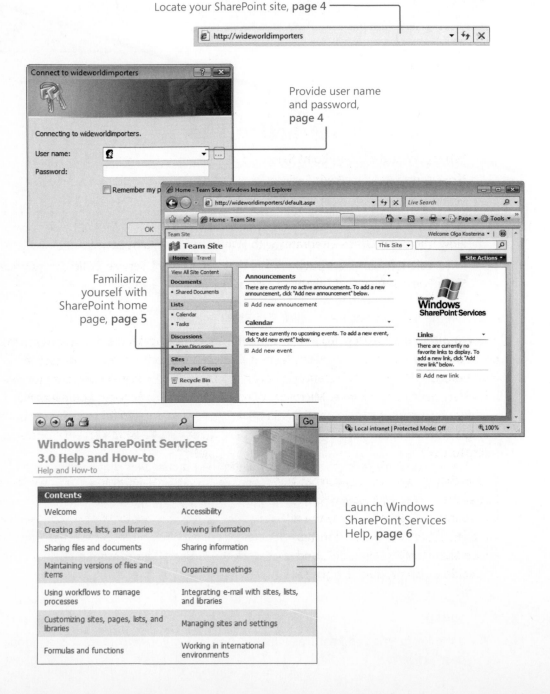

Locate your SharePoint site, **page 4**

http://wideworldimporters

Connect to wideworldimporters

Connecting to wideworldimporters.

User name:
Password:

Remember my p

OK

Provide user name
and password,
page 4

Familiarize
yourself with
SharePoint home
page, **page 5**

Home - Team Site - Windows Internet Explorer

http://wideworldimporters/default.aspx

Home - Team Site

Team Site

Welcome Olga Kosterina ▾ |

Team Site

This Site ▾

Home   Travel

Site Actions ▾

View All Site Content
Documents
• Shared Documents
Lists
• Calendar
• Tasks
Discussions
• Team Discussion
Sites
People and Groups
Recycle Bin

Announcements
There are currently no active announcements. To add a new
announcement, click "Add new announcement" below.
⊞ Add new announcement

Calendar
There are currently no upcoming events. To add a new event,
click "Add new event" below.
⊞ Add new event

Microsoft
Windows
SharePoint Services

Links
There are currently no
favorite links to display. To
add a new link, click "Add
new link" below.
⊞ Add new link

Local intranet | Protected Mode: Off   100%

Go

Windows SharePoint Services
3.0 Help and How-to
Help and How-to

Launch Windows
SharePoint Services
Help, **page 6**

Contents

Welcome	Accessibility
Creating sites, lists, and libraries	Viewing information
Sharing files and documents	Sharing information
Maintaining versions of files and items	Organizing meetings
Using workflows to manage processes	Integrating e-mail with sites, lists, and libraries
Customizing sites, pages, lists, and libraries	Managing sites and settings
Formulas and functions	Working in international environments

1 Introduction to Windows SharePoint Services

In this chapter, you will learn:

✔ What is Windows SharePoint Services.

✔ How Windows SharePoint Services enables team collaboration and sharing.

✔ What user permissions are found in Windows SharePoint Services.

✔ What differences exist between versions of Windows SharePoint Services.

✔ How Microsoft Office integrates with Windows SharePoint Services.

✔ What relationships exist between Windows SharePoint Services, Microsoft Office SharePoint Server, and Microsoft Office SharePoint Designer.

In the modern business environment, with its distributed workforce that assists customers at any time and in any location, team members need to be in closer contact than ever before. Effective collaboration is becoming increasingly more important; however, it is often difficult to achieve. Microsoft Windows SharePoint Services addresses this problem by incorporating essential collaboration and communication technologies into a single Web-based environment that integrates easily with desktop applications, such as Microsoft Office.

In this chapter, you will learn what Windows SharePoint Services is and how it works with Microsoft Office applications, providing enhanced productivity environments for users and teams. You will also learn the differences between versions of Windows SharePoint Services, as well as the relationships between Windows SharePoint Services, Microsoft Office SharePoint Server 2007, and Microsoft Office SharePoint Designer 2007 and how to decide which product is right for you.

> **Important** The exercises in this book use a fictitious business called *Wide World Importers*. In the scenarios used in the book, Wide World Importers is setting up a SharePoint environment for team collaboration and information sharing. There are three people involved in setting up and providing content for this environment: Olga Kosterina, the owner of Wide World Importers; Todd Rowe, her assistant; and Bill Malone, the head buyer.

> **Important** There are no practice files for this chapter.

What Is Windows SharePoint Services?

Windows SharePoint Services is a component of Microsoft Windows Server 2003. It is provided as a free download and gives you a powerful toolset for organizing information, managing documents, increasing the efficiency of business processes, and providing robust collaboration environments.

Windows SharePoint Services helps teams stay connected and productive by providing an infrastructure that allows easy access to the people, documents, and information they need. With Windows SharePoint Services, teams can create Web sites to share information and foster collaboration with other users. You can access content stored within a SharePoint site from a Web browser and through desktop applications, such as Microsoft Office.

> **Tip** Windows SharePoint Services, Office SharePoint Server 2007, and Office SharePoint Designer 2007 are known collectively as Microsoft SharePoint Products and Technologies.

Team Collaboration and Sharing

SharePoint sites provide places to capture and share ideas, information, communication, and documents. The sites facilitate team participation in discussions, shared document collaboration, blogging, building knowledge bases using wikis, and surveys. The document collaboration features allow for easy checking in and checking out of documents, document version control, and recovery of previous versions, as well as document-level security.

> **Tip** A *blog*, or Web log, is an online diary. A blog site allows the diarists, called bloggers, to post the articles, whereupon readers can comment on them.

Wiki (pronounced wee-kee) is a Web environment that allows Web browser users to quickly and easily add and edit text and links that appear on the Web page. The term *wiki* originates from the Hawaiian word *wikiwiki*, which means "quick." A wiki site can be used, for example, to build a knowledge base, a community resource, or an online encyclopedia.

For more information about blogs and wikis, refer to Chapter 10, "Working with Wikis and Blogs."

A SharePoint site can have many subsites, the hierarchy of which, on Web servers, resembles the hierarchy of folders on file systems—it is a tree-like structure. Similar to storing your files in folders on file systems, you can store your files within SharePoint sites. However, SharePoint sites take file storage to a new level, providing communities for team collaboration and making it easy for users to work together on documents, tasks, contacts, events, calendars, wikis, and other information. This team collaboration environment can greatly increase individual and team productivity.

The collaborative tools provided by Windows SharePoint Services are easy to use so that you can share files and information and communicate more effectively with your coworkers. You can create and use SharePoint sites for any purpose. For example, you can build a site to serve as the primary Web site for a team, create a site to facilitate the organization of a meeting, or create a wiki site to capture team knowledge. A typical SharePoint site might include a variety of useful tools and information such as shared document libraries, contacts, calendars, task lists, discussions, and other information-sharing and visualization tools.

SharePoint site users can find and communicate with key contacts and experts, both with e-mail and instant messaging. Site content can be easily searched, and users can receive alerts to tell them when existing documents and information have been changed or when new ones have been added. Custom business processes can be attached to the documents. You can customize site content and layout to present targeted information to specific users on precise topics.

In this exercise, you will locate your SharePoint site and familiarize yourself with its home page.

OPEN the browser.

BE SURE TO know the location of your SharePoint site. If in doubt, check with your SharePoint administrator.

1. In the browser **Address bar**, type the URL, or location, of your SharePoint site: http://<***yourservername/path***>.

   The *yourservername* portion of the URL is the name of the SharePoint server you will be using for the exercises in this book. The path portion might be empty or might include one or more levels in the site hierarchy on your SharePoint server.

   Important For exercises in this book, we use a site located at the server *wideworldimporters*. Its URL is *http://wideworldimporters*. However, in your environment, you will be using a different site installed on a different server. You will need to use your site location *http://<yourservername/path>* in place of *http://wideworldimporters* throughout the book.

2. If prompted, type your user name and password.

3. Click OK.

The home page of your site appears. Although it might look somewhat different than the typical SharePoint team site that Wide World Importers starts with, it is still likely to include links to a variety of information, as well as the information-sharing tools provided by Windows SharePoint Services.

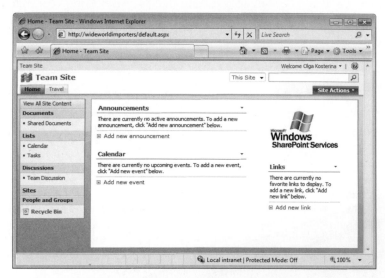

On the left side of the page, you might see links to one or more of the following: View All Site Content, Documents, Lists, Discussions, Sites, People and Groups, and Recycle Bin. The panel that contains these links is referred to as left navigation. It enables you to navigate straight to the information and tools that you require.

The area on top of the page is referred to as top navigation area. This area contains a top link bar that appears at the top of each page. It consists of several tabs with links, such as the default tab Home. It may also include other tabs with links to the subsites of this Web site; such as, for example, the second tab on the left that says *Travel*. In our example, since the Wide World Importers staff travel extensively worldwide, this is the link to a subsite that provides Wide World Importers employees with the necessary information and guidelines for arranging business travel.

On the right of the top link bar, there is a link to a menu called Site Actions. This menu provides access to various actions that allow you to change the site, including site configuration.

> **Important** Your screen might not include links to all parts of the site, such as the Site Actions link, because this is the way that security measures on your server have been set up. SharePoint site users only see the parts of the site that they can actually access: if you don't have access to a part of the site, the link to it is not displayed. To obtain additional access, contact your SharePoint administrator.

4. In the top right corner of the page, click the round Help icon with the question mark. Windows SharePoint Service 3.0 Help and How-to launches in a separate window.

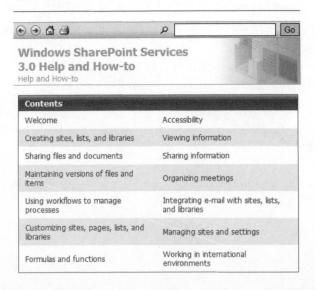

Familiarize yourself with the Help and How-to Contents, and then close the window.

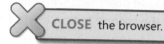 **CLOSE** the browser.

For more information on SharePoint site navigation, refer to Chapter 2, "Navigating a SharePoint Site."

Windows SharePoint Services User Permissions

In Windows SharePoint Services, access to sites is controlled through a role-based system that uses permission levels. *Permission levels* specify what permissions users have on a SharePoint site. These permissions determine what specific actions users can perform on the site; in essence, each permission level is a collection of permissions. Windows SharePoint Services has five default permission levels, as shown in the following list.

- **Read** This permission level gives read-only access to the Web site.
- **Contribute** In addition to the Read permission level, the Contribute permission level allows you to create and edit items in existing lists and document libraries.
- **Design** In addition to the Contribute permission level, the Design permission level allows you to create lists and document libraries, approve items, and edit pages in the Web site.
- **Full Control** This permission level gives full control.
- **Limited** The Limited permission level allows access to a shared resource within a site, such as a specific list, document library, folder, list item, or document, without giving access to the entire site.

> **Important** You will need Read or Contribute permission levels for most of the exercises in this book. We will instruct you to verify whether you have a sufficient permission level before introducing those exercises in which a higher level of access, such as Design or Full Control, is needed. If you are not sure what permissions are set on your SharePoint site, check with your SharePoint administrator.

For more information about permission levels, refer to Chapter 3, "Creating and Managing Sites." A full list of permissions and their associated permission levels is provided in the Appendix.

Versions of Windows SharePoint Services

The current version of Windows SharePoint Services is 3.0; we refer to this version throughout the book unless otherwise stated. Previous versions include:

- Microsoft Windows SharePoint Services 2.0
- Microsoft SharePoint Team Services

Windows SharePoint Services 3.0 provides many new, enhanced, and updated features in comparison with its predecessors. The new features include the following:

- New navigation aides, such as breadcrumbs and tree view, that enable easy, intuitive website navigation
- Blogs that enable you to maintain the online diary environment
- Wikis that enable you and your team to capture and share knowledge
- Data syndication with RSS
- Recycle Bin that allow you to restore the accidentally removed documents
- Folder and item-level access control that allows you to specify permissions on a granular level
- Rights-trimmed interface where users see only those items and links on the web-page that they can actually access
- Mobile access to your SharePoint site

In addition, Windows SharePoint Services 3.0 integration with 2007 Microsoft Office system programs has been strongly enhanced, including offline support (Office Outlook, Office Access) and content type support (Office Excel, Office PowerPoint, Office Word). Another new feature is two-way synchronization with Office Groove workspaces.

The detailed list of Windows SharePoint Services 3.0 new and improved features in comparison with the previous versions is provided in WSSVersionComparison.doc on the book companion CD.

Microsoft Office Integration with Windows SharePoint Services

Many Microsoft Office menus and features are integrated closely with Windows SharePoint Services features. You can use Windows SharePoint Services functionality not only from a browser, but also from within your Microsoft Office applications. For example, you can create a new SharePoint site and save your files to it without leaving your Microsoft Office application.

A SharePoint site's collaborative content—including documents, lists, events, calendars, task assignments, blogs, wikis, and membership rosters—can be read and edited within Microsoft Office applications.

To share a particular document, or a task, Windows SharePoint Services provides a specific site environment called a *Document Workspace*. You can create a workspace site from a Microsoft Office 2007 application or from a browser. When using Microsoft Office Word 2007, Microsoft Office Excel 2007, Microsoft Office PowerPoint 2007, Microsoft Office InfoPath 2007, and Microsoft Office OneNote 2007, users can create workspaces, post and edit documents, and assign tasks from within Microsoft Office 2007 applications while working on documents stored in SharePoint sites.

For more information about working with Document Workspaces, refer to Chapter 7, "Working with Document Workspaces."

There are different levels of integration between various versions of Microsoft Office and Windows SharePoint Services. The 2007 Microsoft Office System provides a tight, native, out-of-the box rich integration with Windows SharePoint Services, with many new and significantly enhanced features in comparison with Microsoft Office 2003. Earlier versions of Microsoft Office, such as Microsoft Office 2000 and Microsoft Office XP, also provide some integration, but it is considerably simpler and more basic.

Office 2000 provides a file save integration with Windows SharePoint Services. For example, you can open and save files stored on SharePoint sites from your Office 2000 applications and receive alerts in Microsoft Office Outlook 2000. Office XP provides additional data integration, including the ability to have interactive access to data stored on SharePoint sites. For example, you can export list data from SharePoint sites to Microsoft Office Excel 2002 and view properties and metadata for files that are stored on SharePoint sites. However, Office 2000 and Office XP are not integrated with many other features of Windows SharePoint Services. For example, you cannot use Office 2000 or Office XP applications to create workspace sites.

> **Tip** You can perform these tasks on the SharePoint site by using the browser.

Microsoft Office 2003 adds more integration features. With Office 2003, you can use Windows SharePoint Services to create documents and workspaces, organize team meetings and activities, and access and analyze data from SharePoint sites. You can also use data integration between Office 2003 and Windows SharePoint Services, moving data to and from the SharePoint site and creating databases linked to data stored on SharePoint sites.

In the 2007 Microsoft Office System, integration with Windows SharePoint Services is enhanced further. When using Office Word 2007, Office Excel 2007, Office PowerPoint 2007, Office InfoPath 2007, Office Project 2007, and Office OneNote 2007, you can directly interact with information stored in SharePoint sites without manually downloading the content. Using Word 2007, you can create and post to a blog on your SharePoint blog site. In addition, Word 2007, Excel 2007, and PowerPoint 2007 allow you to access and manage content types in document metadata in the SharePoint library.

While all 2007 Microsoft Office client applications are tightly integrated with Windows SharePoint Services, Microsoft Office Outlook 2007 provides the closest, feature-rich integration. With Office Outlook 2007, you can create and manage sites for sharing documents and organizing meetings. Outlook 2007 provides read and write access to SharePoint items such as calendars, tasks, contacts, discussions, and documents. In addition, Outlook 2007 also provides significant improvements to offline support, including the ability to check out and edit documents when offline, as well as bidirectional offline synchronization with SharePoint document libraries, discussion groups, contacts, calendars, and tasks. Other enhanced features in Outlook 2007 include roll-up views of calendars and tasks across multiple lists and sites as well as the unified view of personal and SharePoint tasks.

> **Tip** Microsoft Office Groove 2007 also enables bidirectional offline synchronization with SharePoint document libraries.

For more information about integration between Windows SharePointServices and Outlook 2007, refer to Chapter 11, "Using Windows SharePoint Services with Outlook 2007."

Microsoft SharePoint Products and Technologies

Windows SharePoint Services, SharePoint Server 2007, and SharePoint Designer 2007—known together as SharePoint Products and Technologies—facilitate collaboration both within an organization and with partners and customers. However, each of these products has a different set of capabilities.

Windows SharePoint Services and SharePoint Server 2007

As mentioned earlier, Windows SharePoint Services technology is a collection of services for Windows Server 2003 that you can use to share information and collaborate with other users. It provides a common framework for document management, a common repository for storing documents of all types, and a platform for collaboration applications.

SharePoint Server 2007 is built on top of Windows SharePoint Services. It extends Windows SharePoint Services by providing flexible organization and management tools for SharePoint sites and by making it possible for teams to publish information to the entire organization. Because SharePoint Server 2007 requires Windows SharePoint Services, all features of Windows SharePoint Services are available in SharePoint Server 2007. However, SharePoint Server 2007 provides significant additional enterprise-level capabilities, as detailed in the following list.

- **Collaboration** The collaboration components build on Windows SharePoint Services collaboration functionality to help keep teams connected and productive by providing easy access to people, documents, and information.

- **Portal** The portal components of SharePoint Server 2007 include features for designing, deploying, and managing enterprise intranet portals, corporate Internet-presence Web sites, and divisional portal sites.

- **Enterprise Search** The search components provide a consistent search experience, relevance of search results, functions to search for people and expertise, ability to index and search data in line-of-business applications, and extensibility.

- **Enterprise Content Management** Windows SharePoint Services provides core document management functionality including major and minor versioning, check-in/check-out document locking, rich descriptive metadata, workflow, content type–based policies, auditing, and role-based permissions at the document library, folder, and individual document levels. SharePoint Server 2007 builds on these capabilities to deliver enhanced authoring, business document processing, Web content management and publishing, records management, policy management, and support for multilingual publishing.

- **Business Process and Forms** This component provides a platform for rapid creation and deployment of XML-based electronic forms, centralizes form management and maintenance, and helps to extend business processes to customers, partners, and suppliers.

- **Business Intelligence (BI)** The BI features of SharePoint Server 2007 provide Web and programmatic access to published Excel spreadsheets, programmatic reuse of critical line-of-business data, and development of Web-based BI dashboards.

Depending on the components included, there are several editions of SharePoint Server 2007. These are Microsoft Office SharePoint Server 2007 editions, Microsoft Office SharePoint Server 2007 for Search editions, and Microsoft Office Forms Server editions. To decide whether you need Windows SharePoint Services by itself or an edition of SharePoint Server 2007, you need to assess how your requirements are met by the particular features and functionality of these products.

Important A detailed comparison between different editions of SharePoint Server 2007 and Windows SharePoint Services is provided in the SharePointProductsComparison.xls spreadsheet on the book's companion CD.

Windows SharePoint Services and SharePoint Designer 2007

While SharePoint Server 2007 and Windows SharePoint Services provide the technology and platform, SharePoint Designer 2007 provides the tools with which to tailor SharePoint sites. SharePoint Designer 2007, based in part on Microsoft Office FrontPage technology, provides tools for rich customization of sites, as well as the creation of reporting tools and application templates, without any coding.

Key Points

- Windows SharePoint Services provides a powerful set of tools for information sharing and document collaboration.

- SharePoint Web sites provide places to capture and share ideas, information, knowledge, communication, and documents.

- You can access content stored within a SharePoint site from both a Web browser and through desktop applications, such as Microsoft Office.

- There are varying levels of integration between different versions of Microsoft Office and Windows SharePoint Services, with Microsoft Office 2007 providing the closest integration.

- Access to a SharePoint site is controlled through a role-based system predicated on permission levels. The five default permission levels are Read, Contribute, Design, Full Control, and Limited.

- SharePoint Server 2007 is built upon Windows SharePoint Services. In addition to Windows SharePoint Services functionality, SharePoint Server 2007 provides significant additional enterprise-level capabilities including collaboration, portal, search, enterprise content management, business process and forms, and business intelligence.

- Windows SharePoint Services, SharePoint Server 2007, and SharePoint Designer 2007 are known collectively as SharePoint Products and Technologies.

Chapter at a Glance

Navigate the site content, **page 16**

Customize the top link bar, **page 28**

Customize the left navigation panel, **page 31**

Understand Web Part pages, **page 35**

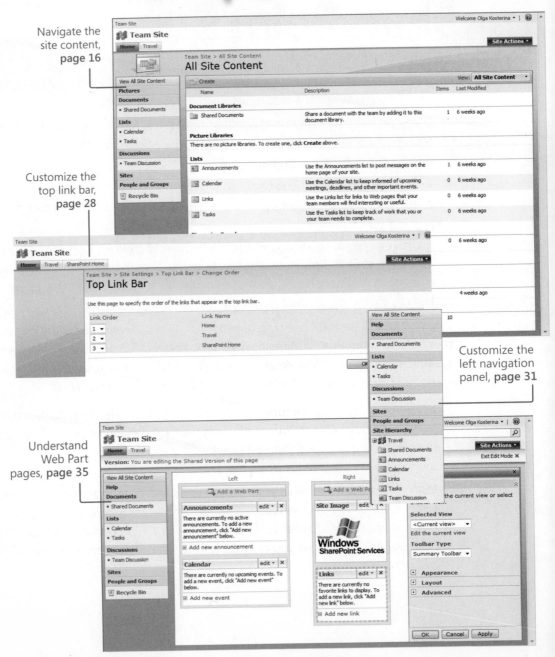

2 Navigating a SharePoint Site

In this chapter, you will learn to:

✔ Navigate the home page and the SharePoint site.

✔ Navigate the site hierarchy.

✔ Browse the lists on a SharePoint site.

✔ Browse the document libraries.

✔ Cutomize the site navigation.

✔ Use the Recycle Bin.

✔ Understand Web Part Pages.

A typical Microsoft Windows SharePoint Services Web site provides you with an infrastructure where your team can communicate, share documents and data, and work together. Different types of SharePoint sites have different infrastructures, such as a team site, a blank site, a Document Workspace, a Meeting Workspace, a blog site, and a wiki site. The team site infrastructure includes the following components.

- **Libraries** Document, picture, and form libraries are collections of files that you share and work on with your team members. A typical team site includes a built-in document library called Shared Documents. You can create your own document, picture, and form libraries when needed.

- **Lists** With SharePoint lists, you and your team members can work with structured, tabular data on the Web site. A typical team site includes four built-in lists: Announcements, Calendar, Links, and Tasks. Other lists are provided by Windows SharePoint Services that you can add to your site if required. You can also create custom lists.

- **Discussion boards** Discussion boards provide a forum where you and your team members can post comments and reply to each others' comments. By default, a typical team site comes with a built-in discussion board named Team Discussion. You can create your own discussion boards when needed.

- **Surveys** Surveys provide a way of polling team members. SharePoint sites don't have a built-in survey, but you can create your own.

- **Recycle Bin** The Recycle Bin allows you to restore items that have been deleted from the site.

In this chapter, you will learn how to navigate the SharePoint site infrastructure. You will start with the home page of a typical SharePoint site and then learn how to browse the site hierarchy. You will also learn how to navigate lists and libraries on your SharePoint site and customize navigation, as well as understand the concepts of Web Part Pages.

Important Before you can use the practice sites provided for this chapter, you need to install them from the book's companion CD to their default locations. See "Using the Book's CD" on page xix for more information.

Important Remember to use your SharePoint site location in place of *http://wideworldimporters in the exercises.*

Navigating the Home Page and the SharePoint Site

A *home page* is the main page of a SharePoint Web site; it provides a navigational structure that links the site components together. Typically, a home page of a SharePoint site has two main navigation areas: the top navigation area, which is a strip at the top of the page, and the left navigation area, which is a panel at the left of the page. The top navigation area typically provides links between sites, while the left navigation panel typically provides links within a site.

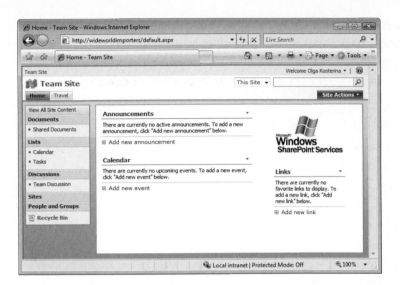

The top navigation area contains the *top link bar* which consists of the tabs displayed on all pages within the SharePoint site. The top link bar typically includes tabs with the following links.

- **Home** The Home link is usually displayed on the first tab on the left. It opens the home page for a site.

- **Links to the subsites** On a well organized site, the top link bar contains tabs with links to the subsites of the current site, such as the Travel link on the second tab in our example.

On the right side of the top link bar, you can see the Site Actions link. Clicking this link opens the Site Actions menu, which enables you to create a new list, library, discussion board, survey, Web page or site; edit site pages; and change the settings for your site. The menu options displayed in the Site Actions menu depend on the permissions that are set on the site: only options applicable to you are displayed.

For example, the Site Settings link on the Site Action menu opens the Site Settings page that enables you to administer and customize your site.

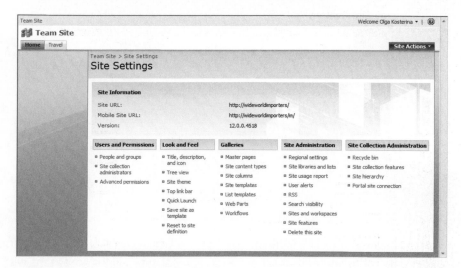

The left navigation panel typically contains the View All Site Content link, a set of *Quick Launch* links, and a Recycle Bin.

The first link in the left navigation panel is View All Site Content. The View All Site Content link opens the All Site Content page, which lists all of the libraries, lists, discussion boards, and surveys on your site. The All Site Content page also provides links to the child sites and workspaces, as well as the site's Recycle Bin. This page is your main navigational aid for the site and contains links to all major parts of the site's infrastrcuture.

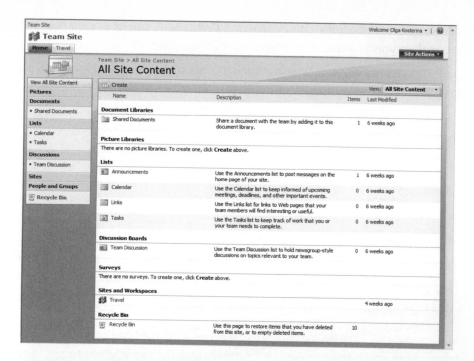

Depending on the site, the Quick Launch contains one or more links to the subsets of information contained in the All Site Content page. These subsets, referred to as views, are created by filtering the information contained within the All Site Content page. In addition to links to the the All Site Content page views, the Quick Launch contains a link to People and Groups that allows you to manage your site's permissions.

The Quick Launch can also contain links to site components created by you and your team members, such as document libraries or lists.

Typically, the Quick Launch contains the following links.

- **Documents** The Documents link opens a view of an All Site Content page displaying all document and form libraries in your site. On a typical team site, the Quick Launch also provides a second-level link to a Shared Documents library.

- **Lists** The Lists link opens a view of an All Site Content page displaying all lists in your site. On a typical team site, the Quick Launch also provides two second-level links to Calendar and Tasks lists.

- **Discussions** The Discussions link opens a view of an All Site Content page displaying all discussion boards in your site. On a typical team site, the Quick Launch also provides a second-level link to a Team Discussion board.

- **Sites** The Sites link opens a view of an All Site Content page displaying subsites to your site.

● **People and Groups** The People and Groups link opens a page that allows you to manage groups and individual users of your site.

Finally, the left navigation panel contains the link to the Recycle Bin, which opens the site's Recycle Bin.

In addition to the top and left navigation areas, the home page of a typical SharePoint team site includes views of the following lists.

● Announcements

● Calendar

● Links

● Tasks

Each of these lists is presented within its own page component called a *Web Part*. You can add items to these lists by clicking Add item within the list's Web Part.

In this exercise, you will navigate to the All Site Content page, explore its components and views, and then return to the site home page.

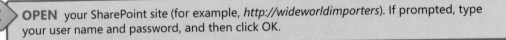

OPEN your SharePoint site (for example, *http://wideworldimporters*). If prompted, type your user name and password, and then click OK.

1. On the **Quick Launch**, click **View All Site Content**.

2. Explore the page.

   Notice that the top link bar and the Quick Launch have not changed. However, just below the top link bar and above the page title, you can see a *content navigation breadcrumb* trail showing the path to the current page from the site's home page.

Team Site > All Site Content
All Site Content

   The content navigation breadcrumb helps you keep track of where the current page is located within a SharePoint site. Components on the breadcrumb trail are links that you can click to open the corresponding pages. The last item on the breadcrumb shows the page title of the current page and is not a link.

3. Scroll down to the bottom of the page and notice all parts of the site that are listed on the All Site Content page including Document Libraries, Picture Libraries, Lists, Discussion Boards, Surveys, Sites and Workspaces, and Recycle Bin.

   You will now display this page in the Document Libraries view.

4. Scroll up to the top of the page. Open the **View** menu located on the right side of the page, and choose **Document Libraries**.

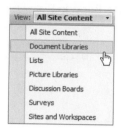

The **Document Libraries** view of the **All Site Content** page is displayed. The main part of the page lists the document libraries available on the site, including the Shared Documents library, which is present on the site by default.

You will now display the All Site Content page in the Surveys view.

5. From the **View** menu, choose **Surveys**.

The Surveys view is displayed. The main part of the page lists the surveys created on the site. The Wide World Importers site has not added a survey yet, so this page doesn't display any surveys.

6. Return to the site's home page by clicking its link on the content navigation breadcrumb that is located immediately above the **All Site Content** title.

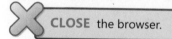

CLOSE the browser.

Navigating the Site Hierarchy

A typical SharePoint site might contains lists; document, form and picture libraries; discussion boards; surveys; and other Web pages. These items are created and maintained by Windows SharePoint Services and are linked together within the site infrastructure. In a graphical form, this site infrastructure can be represented as a tree, with the site's home page being the root of the tree.

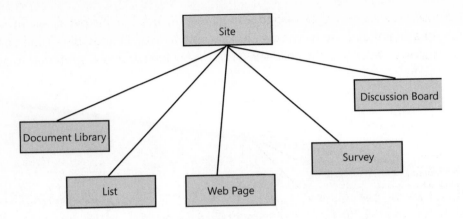

Windows SharePoint Services maintains the path in this tree structure from the site's home page to the currently displayed page. This path is shown on each page as a content navigation breadcrumb, which was introduced in the previous exercise.

In addition to its own components, such as lists and libraries, a SharePoint site can have many subsites, the hierarchy of which, on Web servers, resembles the hierarchy of folders on file systems. Sites that do not have a parent site are referred to as *top-level sites*. Top-level sites can have multiple subsites, and these subsites can have multiple subsites, proceeding downward as many levels as you need. The entire hierarchical structure of a top-level site and all of its subsites is called a *site collection*.

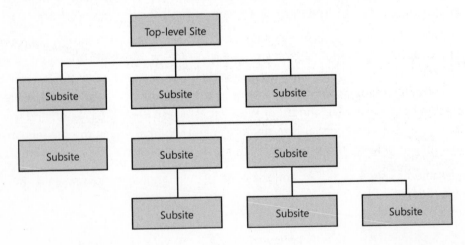

Because the subsites are contained within their parent's site, the overall hierachical structure of a SharePoint site has its own items—such as lists, libraries, discussion boards, and surveys—as well as the child sites. This overall infrastructure is referred to as a *site hierarchy*.

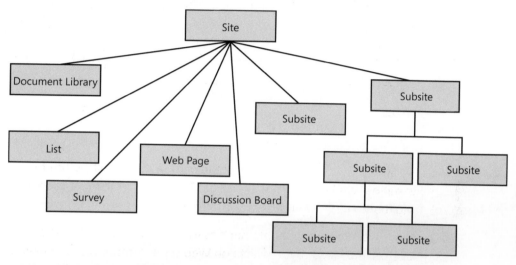

To identify the current site's position in the site collection, Windows SharePoint Services maintains a *global navigation breadcrumb* that shows the path from the top-level site to the current site. The global navigation breadcrumb is displayed on all pages at the top left of a page.

The two breadcrumb navigation trails—the global breadcrumb and the content breadcrumb—allow you to see the location of the current site within the site collection and the location of the current page within the current site. A combination of two breadcrumbs is designed so that you always know where you are within the overall hierarchy starting from the top-level site.

The last link on the global navigation breadcrumb is the same as the fist link on the content navigation breadcrumb. Clicking this link will take you to the same page as clicking the Home tab on the top link bar. The global navigation breadcrumb leads to the site identified by the Home link, and the content navigation breadcrumb starts from the page identified by the Home link..

Important If a subsite is configured to inherit a top link bar from the parent site, then the Home link points to the home page of the parent site. In this scenario, the subsite is not displayed on the global navigation breadcrumb. Instead, the global navigation breadcrumb finishes with, and the content navigation breadcrumb starts with, the parent site.

In this exercise, you will view a list of subsites to your SharePoint site, navigate the site hierarchy, and explore the navigation breadcrumbs.

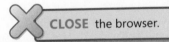

OPEN the SharePoint site in which you'd like to view the subsites. If prompted, type your user name and password, and then click OK.

BE SURE TO verify that you have sufficient permissions to view the subsites. If in doubt, see the Appendix on page 435.

1. On the **Quick Launch**, click **Sites**. The **All Site Content** page in the **Sites and Workplaces** view is displayed.

2. On the **All Site Content** page, under **Sites and Workspaces**, click a subsite where you'd like to go to. For example, on the Wide World Importers site, we will go to the **Travel** subsite.

    On the subsite's home page, in the top left corner of the page, the *global naviga-tion breadcrumb* trail is displayed. It shows where the current site is located in the site's collection, starting from the top-level site.

3. On the subsite's **home** page, on the **Quick Launch** under **Documents**, click **Shared Documents**. The **Shared Documents** library page is displayed.

    On the Shared Documents library page, notice that the global navigation bread-crumb, located at the top left of the page, hasn't changed when you moved to the Shared Documents library page from the site's home page. The reason is because you are still within the same site. However, the content navigation breadcrumb, located above the page title, has changed and is now showing the path from the site's home page to the current page.

4. Click the link on the global navigation breadcrumb that points to the parent site. You are taken back to the home page of the site where you started this exercise.

CLOSE the browser.

For more information on working with sites, refer to Chapter 3, "Creating and Managing Sites."

Browsing Lists on a SharePoint Site

SharePoint lists are Web-based, editable tables. SharePoint lists provide you and your team with the ability to work with structured data. As we have discussed, the typical team Web site provides four default lists.

- **Announcements** The Announcements list is a place to post information for the team.

- **Calendar** The Calendar list is a place to maintain information about upcoming events.

- **Links** The Links list displays hyperlinks to Web pages of interest to team members.

- **Tasks** The Tasks list provides a to-do list for team members.

> **Tip** Links to the Calendar and Tasks lists appear by default in the Quick Launch of the team site.

In addition to these default lists, you can create your own lists when necessary. When creating a new list, you can choose to place a link to this list on the Quick Launch.

For more information on working with lists, refer to Chapter 4, "Working with Lists."

In this exercise, you will view a list of all SharePoint lists that exist on your site. You will navigate to a list and then return to the home page.

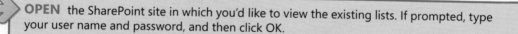

OPEN the SharePoint site in which you'd like to view the existing lists. If prompted, type your user name and password, and then click OK.

1. On the **Quick Launch**, click **Lists**.

   The **All Site Content** page is displayed in the **Lists** view. This view shows links to all existing lists in your site.

2. Click a list, such as **Announcements**.

The Announcements page appears. Notice the content navigation breadcrumb displayed above the page title and the global navigation breadcrumb displayed at the top left of the page.

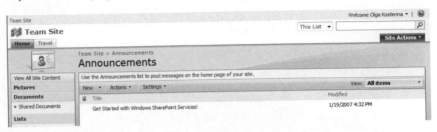

3. On the **Announcement** page, view the list items.

The team members of Wide World Importers have not put any additional announcement on this list as yet, so only the default announcement is displayed.

4. To return to the site's home page, click the **Home** tab on the top link bar.

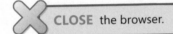 **CLOSE** the browser.

Browsing Document Libraries

A SharePoint library is, in essence, a list of files. However, SharePoint libraries not only store files, but provide a flexible collaboration environment for you and your team to work on these files.

A SharePoint library page lists each file in the library as well as its properties and provides a link to each file. By default, the team site comes with a built-in document library named Shared Documents that is listed on the Quick Launch bar.

In addition to the Shared Documents library, you can create your own document, picture, and form libraries when necessary. When creating a new library, you can choose to place a link to this library on the Quick Launch bar.

For more information on working with documents in document libraries, refer to Chapter 5, "Creating and Managing Libraries." For more information on configuring document libraries, refer to Chapter 6, "Working with Library Settings."

In this exercise, you will view a list of all SharePoint libraries that exist on your site. You will then navigate to a Shared Documents library.

 OPEN the SharePoint site in which you'd like to view the list of existing libraries. If prompted, type your user name and password, and then click OK.

1. On the **Quick Launch**, click **Documents**.

The **All Site Content** page opens in the **Document Libraries** view. This view shows links to all existing document and form libraries.

2. Click a link, such as **Shared Documents**. The **Shared Documents** page appears.

Notice the global navigation breadcrumb displayed at the top left of the page and the content navigation breadcrumb above the page title.

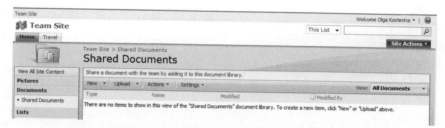

3. On the **Shared Documents** page, view the list of files in this library.

In this example, the team members of Wide World Importers have not put any documents in this library as yet.

4. To return to the site's home page, click its tab on the top link bar.

 **CLOSE** Internet Explorer.

Customizing the Top Navigation Area

In a Windows SharePoint Services site, you can customize both the top and left navigation areas. In the top navigation area, in addition to the links maintained by the Windows SharePoint Services, you can configure the top link bar to contain links of your own choosing and also select the order of their appearance in the bar. In the following exercise, you will create and position a new tab in the top link bar and then delete it.

> **OPEN** the top-level site from the address bar of your browser *http://wideworldimporters*. If prompted, type your user name and password, and click OK.
>
> **BE SURE TO** verify that you have sufficient rights to manage the site. If in doubt, see the Appendix on page 435.

1. From the **Site Actions** menu, choose **Site Settings**. The **Site Settings** page is displayed.

2. From the **Look and Feel** area, click **Top link bar.**

   The **Top Link Bar** page is displayed. It shows the links that appear in the top link bar of the site. In our example, two links are already showing: **Home** and Travel. These links represent the top-level site and the Travel subsite.

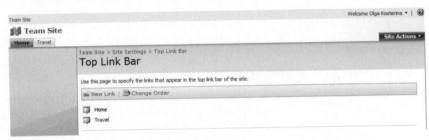

3. Click **New Link** on the toolbar to display the **New Link** page.

4. On the **New Link** page, in the **URL** area, in the **Type the Web address** box, type http://www.microsoft.com/sharepoint. Then, in the **Type the description** box type SharePoint Home

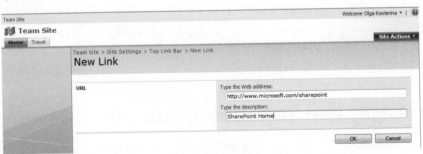

5. Click **OK** . The new link is added to the top link bar and is listed in the **Top Link Bar** page.

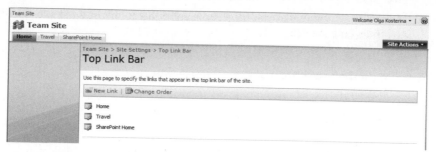

6. To test the link, click on the new tab to navigate the browser to the SharePoint Products and Technologies home page at the Microsoft Web site.

> **Important** You need Internet access to view a page at the external Web site, such as the Microsoft site.

Back

7. Click the **Back** button in the browser window to go back to the **Top Link Bar** page.

> **Tip** If you'd like the page to be open in the new browser window, you need to add a bit of JavaScript code. To edit the link you've just created, on the Top Link Bar page, click the icon to the left of SharePoint Home to display the Edit Link page. Change the Web address to *hjavascript:void window.open('http://www.microsoft. com/sharepoint')* and click OK. This case-sensitive command instructs Windows SharePoint Services to open the link in a new window but keep the current browser page where it is currently located.

You will now reorder the tabs on the top link bar.

8. In the **Top Link Bar** page, click **Change Order** on the toolbar. The **Change Order** page appears.

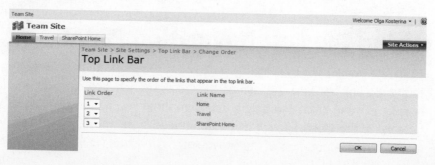

9. From the **Link Order** drop-down list to the left of the **SharePoint Home** link, choose **1**.

   The list of the links is automatically reodered. The Link Order for the Home link has been changed to 2, and the Link Order for the Travel link has been changed to 3.

10. Click **OK**. The tabs on the top link bar have been reordered, and you are taken back at the **Top Link Bar** page.

You will now delete the link from the top link bar.

11. In the **Top Link Bar** page, click the icon to the left of the link you'd like to delete, such as **SharePoint Home**.

The **Edit Link** page is displayed.

12. In the **Edit Link** page, click **Delete**. Click **OK** in the confirmation box when it appears.

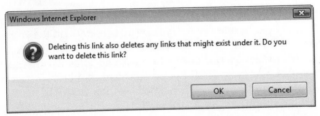

You are back at the **Top Link Bar** page. Notice that the link has been deleted.

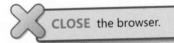 **CLOSE** the browser.

Customizing the Left Navigation Panel

There are many options available for customization of the left navigation panel. Similar to the top link bar, you can change the Quick Launch. You can add new links, edit and reorder existing links, and delete those links that you no longer require. You can even hide the entire Quick Launch if you don't need it any more. In addition, you can display a graphical representation of the site hierarchy as a tree view.

> **Important** You cannot remove the View All Site Content and Recycle Bin links from the left navigation panel.

In this exercise, you will add a link to the Quick Launch and also reorder the Quick Launch links.

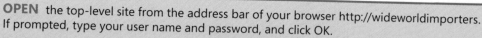

OPEN the top-level site from the address bar of your browser http://wideworldimporters. If prompted, type your user name and password, and click OK.

BE SURE TO verify that you have sufficient rights to manage the site. If in doubt, see the Appendix on page 435.

1. From the **Site Actions** menu, choose **Site Settings**.

2. In the **Site Settings** page, from the **Look and Feel** area, click **Quick Launch**. The **Quick Launch** page appears.

3. In the **Quick Launch** page, click the **New Heading** option on the toolbar.

4. In the **New Heading** page, in the **Type the Web address** box, type /_layouts/help. aspx?Key=NavBarHelpHome. Then in the **Type the description** box, type Help and click **OK**. This will create a link called Help on the Quick Launch that points to the built-in help page.

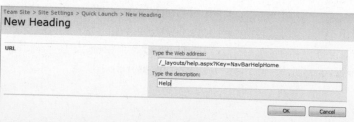

> **Tip** If you'd like to create a heading on the Quick Launch that is not a link but a section heading for a collection of links, type # in the Web address box. You can then add links to the new section using the New Link command on the Quick Launch page.

Back on the Quick Launch page, notice the Help link that appeared at the bottom of the page. You will now move the Help link to the first position on the Quick Launch.

5. Click **Change Order** on the toolbar. The **Change Order** page appears.

6. From the drop-down list to the left of the **Help** link, choose number **1**.

All of the other links are reordered.

> **Tip** Links within the sections can be reordered independently of the section headings.

7. Click **OK** to save the new order. The **Quick Launch** page appears, with the **Help** link displayed at the top.

8. Return to the site's home page by clicking the **Home** tab on the top link bar.

On the home page, the new **Help** link is displayed in the left navigation panel on top of the Quick Launch, immediately after the **View All Site Content** link.

Clicking the new **Help** link takes you to Windows SharePoint Services 3.0 Help and How-to page.

 CLOSE the browser.

While Quick Launch represents the frequently needed links, it is sometimes useful to see the full structure of the site in a graphical representation. In this exercise, you will modify the left navigation panel to display the tree view of the site's infrastructure.

 OPEN the SharePoint site in which you'd like to modify the left navigation panel. If prompted, type your user name and password, and then click OK.

BE SURE TO have permissions to manage the site. If in doubt, see the Appendix on page 435.

1. From the **Site Actions** menu, choose **Site Settings**. The **Site Settings** page is displayed.

2. Under the **Look and Feel** area, click **Tree View**.

3. On the **Tree View** page, select the **Enable Tree View** check box. Click **OK**.

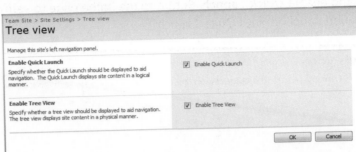

You are taken back to the **Site Settings** page.

4. Return to the site's home page by clicking the **Home** tab on the top link bar.

The left navigation panel on the home page has changed. It now displays the **Site Hierarchy**, which shows the parts of the site, as well as subsites, in a tree view. In the **Site Hierarchy**, notice the difference in the icons that represent different parts of the site's infrastructure such as the Travel subsite, the Shared Documents document library, the Announcements list, the Calendar list, the Links list, the Tasks list, and the default discussion board.

5. Using Steps 1-4 of this exercise as a guide, on the **Tree View** page, disable the **Quick Launch**. Go to the site's home page to verify that the left navigation panel displays the **Site Hierarchy** but does not display the **Quick Launch**.

You will now bring the left navigation panel back to its original configuration in which it displays the Quick Launch but does not display the Site Hierarchy.

6. Using Steps 1-4 of this exercise as a guide, on the **Tree View** page, disable the **Tree View** and enable **Quick Launch**. Return to the home page to verify that the left navigation panel displays Quick Launch.

 CLOSE the browser.

Understanding Web Part Pages

A *Web Part Page* is a special type of page on a SharePoint site that contains one or more Web Parts. A *Web Part* is an independent component that can be reused, shared, and personalized by all users who have permission to access it. Web Parts are the basic building blocks of a Web Part Page; each Web Part occupies its own rectangular area within the page.

For example, the home page of a newly created team site contains four Web Parts. Three of them display the default lists: Announcements, Calendar, and Links. The fourth Web Part displays a Windows SharePoint Services logo.

Web Part Pages often contain several Web Parts that can be connected together if necessary. By using Web Parts, you can organize disparate information and consolidate data—such as lists and charts—and Web content—such as text, links, and images—into a single Web page.

For more information on Web Part Pages, refer to Chapter 15, "Working with Web Parts."

The Links Web Part can prove to be particularly useful when you're considering making the navigation of your site easier. For example, you can add links to the Links list that are displayed within the Links Web Part.

For more information on how to add items to a list, refer to Chapter 4.

In this exercise, you will modify the title of the Links Web Part on the home page of the team site.

 **OPEN** the SharePoint site home page, such as *http://wideworldimporters*. If prompted, type your user name and password, and then click OK.

BE SURE TO verify that you have sufficient rights to modify the Web Parts. If in doubt, see the Appendix on page 435.

1. From the **Site Actions** menu, choose **Edit Page**.

   The page is displayed in the Edit mode: the Web Parts on the page are shown in the two rectangular zones with the light blue background. In addition, an orange bar is displayed on top of each Web Part.

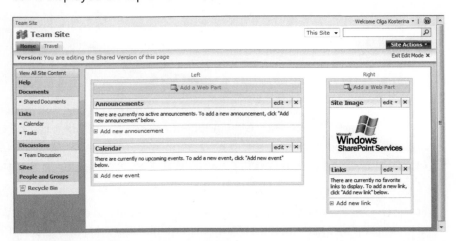

2. In the **Links** Web Part, open the **Edit** menu located at the top left of the Web Part and choose **Modify Shared Web Part**.

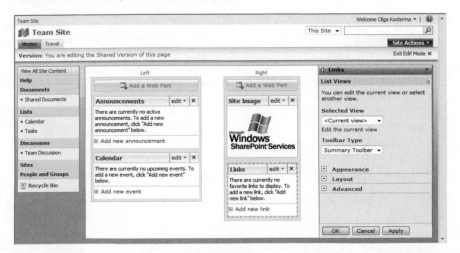

   The **Links Web Part** is displayed with the orange dashed line surrounding it. In addition, a **Web Part** tool pane is displayed on the right of the browser window.

3. In the Web Part tool pane, open the **Appearance** area by clicking a plus sign (+) to the left of it.

4. In the **Appearance** area, in the **Title** box, delete the current Web Part title **Links** and type the new title Wide World Importers Links. Leave all other settings unchanged.

5. Click **Apply**. Verify that the new title is displayed in the Web Part title bar.

6. Click **OK** in the **Web Part** tool pane to confirm that you've finished editing this Web Part.

7. At the top right of the **home** page, below the **Site Actions** menu, click **Exit Edit Mode**.

The modified Web Part is displayed on the home page.

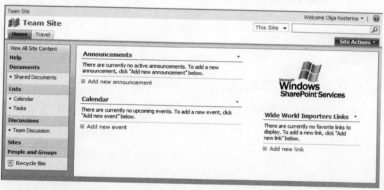

CLOSE the browser.

Using the Recycle Bin

The Recycle Bin in Windows SharePoint Services provides two-stage protection against accidental deletions. When you delete a document or other item from the Windows SharePoint Services site, it is deleted from the site and moved to the site's Recycle Bin, where it can be restored if needed. If you then delete this item from the site's Recycle Bin, it is moved to the site collection's Recycle Bin. From there, the document can be either restored to its original location or deleted.

> **Important** By default, the site's Recycle Bin holds the items for 30 days. Your SharePoint administrator can modify this setting.

In this exercise, you will delete and restore a document from the Recycle Bin.

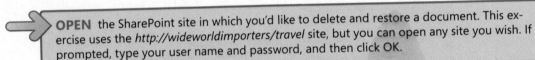

OPEN the SharePoint site in which you'd like to delete and restore a document. This exercise uses the *http://wideworldimporters/travel* site, but you can open any site you wish. If prompted, type your user name and password, and then click OK.

1. In the left navigation panel, click **All Site Content**.

2. On the **All Site Content** page, under **Document Libraries**, click the library from which you'd like to delete a document, such as **Shared Documents**.

3. On the **Shared Documents** page, hover the mouse over the document you'd like to remove. Click the down arrow to open the document menu and choose **Delete**.

4. Click **OK** in the confirmation box when it appears.

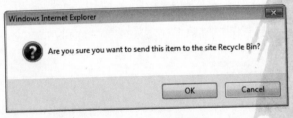

The document has been deleted from the Shared Documents library.

5. At the bottom of the left navigation panel, click **Recycle Bin**. The **Recycle Bin** page appears.

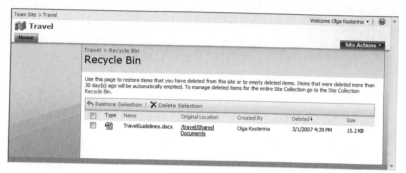

6. On the **Recycle Bin** page, select the document you have just deleted by clicking the check box to the left of the document name. Then, to restore the document to its original location, click the **Restore Selection** option on the **Recycle Bin** page toolbar.

7. Click **OK** in the confirmation box when it appears.

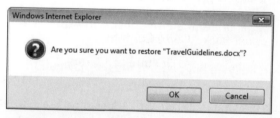

The document has been restored.

8. To navigate back to the **Shared Documents** library, return to the site's home page by using either the link on the content navigation breadcrumb or the top link bar, and then click **Shared Documents** from the left navigation panel. Verify that the document has been restored.

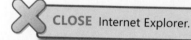

CLOSE Internet Explorer.

If an item has been deleted accidently from site's Recycle Bin, it can be restored from the Recycle Bin of the site collection. In this exercise, you will restore the document that has been removed from the site and its Recycle Bin.

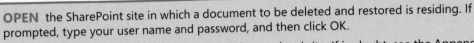

OPEN the SharePoint site in which a document to be deleted and restored is residing. If prompted, type your user name and password, and then click OK.

BE SURE TO have permissions to manage the top-level site. If in doubt, see the Appendix on page 435.

1. Using Steps 1-5 from the previous exercise as a guide, delete the document from the **Shared Documents** library, and then go to the site's **Recycle Bin** page.

2. On the **Recycle Bin** page, select the document by clicking the check box to the left of its name. Then, click the **Delete Selection** option on the **Recycle Bin** page toolbar.

3. Click **OK** in the confirmation box when it appears. The document has been removed from the site's Recycle Bin.

4. Go to the top-level site by clicking the first link on the global navigation breadcrumb.

5. On the home page of the top-level site, from the **Site Actions** menu, choose **Site Settings**.

6. On the **Site Settings** page, under the **Site Collection Administration** area, click **Recycle bin**.

7. On the **Site Collection Recycle Bin** page, in the left navigation area under **Select a View**, click **Deleted from end user Recycle Bin**.

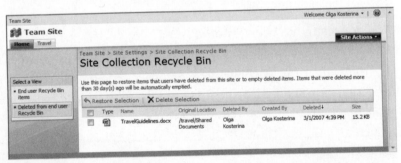

8. Select the document you have just deleted by clicking the check box to the left of the document name, and then click the **Restore Selection** option.

9. Click **OK** in the confirmation box when it appears. The document has been restored to its original location.

10. Navigate to the home page of the subsite from which the document was removed and then to the **Shared Documents** library on this subsite. Verify that the document has been restored.

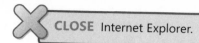

CLOSE Internet Explorer.

Key Points

- The infrastructure of a typical SharePoint team site includes the following components: document, form, and picture libraries; lists; discussion boards; surveys; and a Recycle Bin.

- A home page of a SharePoint site has two main navigation areas at the top and left of the page. The top navigation area contains the top link bar that is displayed on all pages within the site. The left navigation panel is located in the left navigation area and contains the View All Site Content link, the set of Quick Launch links, and the Recycle Bin link.

- The top navigation area typically provides navigation between the sites, while the left navigation panel provides navigation within the current site.

- Both the top link bar and Quick Launch can be customized to include the links of your choice.

- The All Site Content page that is linked from the left navigation panel displays all of the libraries, lists, discussion boards, and surveys on your site. It also provides links to the child sites and workspaces. You cannot delete the All Site Content link from the left navigation panel.

- A SharePoint site can have many subsites, the hierarchy of which, on Web servers, resembles the hierarchy of folders on file systems.

- Sites that do not have a parent site are referred to as top-level sites. Top-level sites can have multiple subsites, and these subsites can have multiple subsites, proceeding downward as many levels as you need.

- There are two navigation breadcrumbs displayed on a page: the global navigation breadcrumb, which shows the path to the current site from the top-level site, and the content navigation breadcrumb, which shows the path to the current page within the site. The first link of the content navigation breadcrumb is the same as the last link of the global navigation breadcrumb. A combination of these breadcrumbs displays the location of the current page in the overall site hierarchy.

- The home page of a typical SharePoint site contains one or more Web Parts. To assist navigation, you might consider modifying the Links Web Part.

- A Recycle Bin provides two-stage protection against accidental deletions.

Chapter at a Glance

Create new SharePoint sites, **page 44**

Create new
SharePoint
sites, page 44

Home > Create > New SharePoint Site

New SharePoint Site

Use this page to create a new site or workspace under this SharePoint site. You can specify a title, Web site address, and access permissions.

Create   Cancel

Title and Description

Type a title and description for your new site. The title will be displayed on each page in the site.

Title:
Buyers

Description:
Site for general buyer collaboration

Web Site Address

Users can navigate to your site by typing the Web site address (URL) into their

URL name:
.../sidewaldimporters/ | buyers

Out of the box Permission Levels

	Full Control	Design	Contribute	Read
Add and Customize Pages				
Add Items				
Add/Remove Personal Web Parts				
Apply Style Sheets				
Apply Themes and Borders				
Approve Items				
Browse Directories				
Browse User Information				
Create Alerts				
Create Groups				
Create Subsites				
Delete Items				
Delete Versions				
Edit Items				
Edit Personal User Information				
Enumerate Permissions				
Manage Alerts				
Manage Lists				
Manage Permissions				
Manage Personal Views				
Manage Web Site				
Open				
Open Items				
Override Check Out				
Update Personal Web Parts				
Use				
Use				
Use				
Viev				
Viev				
Viev				
Viev				
Viev				

Template:
...ration | Meetings
...ite
...ite
...ent Workspace
...e

...rmissions:
...same permissions as parent site
...unique permissions

...splay this site on the Quick Launch of the parent site?
○ No

...splay this site on the top link bar of the parent site?
○ No

...e the top link bar from the parent site?
○ No

Create   Cancel

Establish site permissions, **page 53**

Establish site
permissions,
page 53

Home > Buyers > Team Meeting > Site Settings > Site Theme

Site Theme

Use this page to change the fonts and color scheme for your site. Applying a theme does not affect your site's layout, and will not change any pages that have been individually themed.

Select a Theme

Belltown
Breeze
Cardinal
Citrus
Classic
Default Theme
Granite
Jet
Lacquer
Lichen
Obsidian
Petal
Plastic
Reflector
Simple
Verdant
Vintage
Wheat

Preview

Apply   Cancel

Theme SharePoint sites, **page 63**

Theme
SharePoint
sites, page 63

3 Creating and Managing Sites

In this chapter, you will learn to:

✔ Create sites.

✔ Manage site users and permissions.

✔ Create a child workspace.

✔ Change a site's theme.

✔ Save and use a site template.

✔ Manage site Features.

✔ Manage site content syndication.

✔ Delete a site.

Microsoft Windows SharePoint Services *sites* and workspaces are containers for *Web Parts* and the *Web pages* that contain them, lists, and document libraries. *Lists* contain structured, tabular data, while *document libraries* contain unstructured binary documents. You can use any site as a single container for your data, or you can create as many child sites as you need to make your data easier to find and manage. You will also frequently find yourself creating sites to secure a place for a given group of people to collaborate on its contents. For example, you might create a site to manage a new team or project, collaborate on a document, or prepare for and follow-up on a meeting. As a container, sites can be used to secure their contents.

As we discussed in Chapter 2, "Navigating a SharePoint Site," sites and workspaces are organized hierarchically within a *site collection*. There is always one top-level site and can optionally be one or more child sites. Typically, top-level sites are created for an entire team and therefore have many visitors (people who only read), few members (people who can create and update content), and one or two owners. But as child sites and grandchild sites are created, the total number of users typically decreases while the number of people designated as members increases.

Workspaces function just like sites except that they can be created from within Microsoft Office clients, such as Microsoft Office Word and Microsoft Office Outlook, their expected lifetime is short relative to a site, and child sites and workspaces are not allowed. Similar to clearing off a desk to work specifically on a given project, you could create a Windows SharePoint Services workspace to work on a specific document or meeting. When the given project is completed, you would likely keep the results of the project and throw away all of the other scraps. Similarly, once you are finished with a workspace, you publish the results and throw away the container.

Site templates are used in Windows SharePoint Services as a blueprint to jump-start a new site's usefulness by auto-generating the lists, document libraries, and Web pages, pre-populated with Web Parts, that will likely be most useful in a given situation. In this chapter, you will learn how to create a site using one of the site templates available from a default installation as well as the steps necessary to manage and administrate this site. You may want to differentiate a site by the way it is presented to the user, so you will also learn how to apply a *theme* to your site.

> **Important** Before you can use the practice sites provided for this chapter, you may want to install them from the book's companion CD to their default locations. See "Using the Book's CD" on page xix for more information.

> **Important** Remember to use your SharePoint site location in place of *http://wideworldimporters* in the following exercises.

Creating Sites

The catalyst for organizing your data into different site containers will often be the same catalyst for creating multiple subdirectories on the file system. You may have too much information to use a single container and still locate your information easily. If all of your files were kept in the root of the hard drive along with the operating system files and other program files, the list of files would be difficult to sort through, work with, and manage. Just as you would create subdirectories to organize your file system data, you will likely create child sites to help organize your Windows SharePoint Services data in logical ways.

The initial site created in a Windows SharePoint Services site collection is called the *top-level site*. Top-level sites are created from within *SharePoint Central Administration* because they don't have a parent site. Although the top-level site is functionally the same as its child sites, it includes administrative links on the Site Administration page to manage site collection functionality.

To create a child site, you must navigate to the New SharePoint Site page of the would-be parent site. See the Layouts Directory sidebar that follows for details on how to gain direct access to the destination directly from the browser's address bar.

Layouts Directory

The administrative pages of Windows SharePoint Services' sites are kept in a common folder called _layouts. By using the Web site address in the address bar of your browser, you can quickly navigate to administrative pages that are buried relatively deep within a site's administrative links.

The following table displays examples that are typically found on the home page of every Windows SharePoint Services site.

Web Site Address (URL)	Administrative Page
http://[site]/_layouts/viewlsts.aspx	All Site Content
http://[site]/_layouts/create.aspx	Create Page
http://[site]/_layouts/settings.aspx	Site Settings

The following table displays the same examples for a child site.

Web Site Address (URL)	Administrative Page
http://[site]/[childsite]/_layouts/viewlsts.aspx	All Site Content
http://[site]/[childsite]/_layouts/create.aspx	Create Page
http://[site]/[childsite]/_layouts/settings.aspx	Site Settings

Note that the suffix for each Web site address is the same regardless of how deeply you delve into the site hierarchy. Therefore, you can directly access the New SharePoint Site page by typing the following Web site address directly into the browser's address bar: *http://wideworldimporters/_layouts/newsbweb.aspx*.

When you initially create objects like sites, workspaces, lists, and columns in Windows SharePoint Services, you are establishing two name values: the display name, usually labeled Title or Name, and the URL name, also known as the internal name. Typically, as is the case with sites, there is an option to provide the URL name separately. Comply with the best practices outlined in the following sidebar when specifying the URL name.

Naming a URL

Follow these best practices when initially establishing a URL for objects in Windows SharePoint Services. For example, providing a URL name of Todd Rowe for a new child site would result in the following Web site address in the browser's address bar: *http://wideworldimporters/Todd%20Rowe*. Subsequently, providing a URL Name of My Cool Docs for a new document library within that site would result in the following Web site address in the browser's address bar: *http://wideworldimporters/Todd%20Rowe/My%20Cool%20Docs*. Notice that replacing the spaces with underscores improves the appearance of the Web site address: *http://wideworldimporters/Todd_Rowe/My_Cool_Docs*.

- The URL name should be descriptive, intuitive, and easy to remember.

- The URL name should be concise. There is a limit of total characters available for the entire Web site address, so you will eventually encounter problems if you consistently use long URL names.

- The URL name should not contain spaces. Spaces in the address bar are replaced with %20 and take up three characters each. Spaces also make the Web site address difficult to use in an e-mail and difficult for others to read. To reduce frustration and improve readability, an underscore can be used in place of a space.

- The URL name should be used consistently. Out of the box, tasks are found in a list called Tasks, contacts in a list called Contacts, and so on. Similarly, if you frequently create a document library to house proposals, consistently using a name such as Proposals will aid others in locating that content. Of course, you cannot have two lists with the same name in a site. Therefore, you may need to differentiate by prefixing the name, such as Customer_Proposals and Product_Proposals.

When creating a list or column, the field—generically labeled Name—is used to populate both the display name and the URL name. Because other best practices can be initiated for a specific organization, it is wise to establish your own naming conventions as early as possible. This should help prevent unintuitive, verbose, space-laden, and inconsistent objects from being created in the first place.

From the Template Selection area of the New SharePoint Site page, you can choose to initially provision your site by using one of the 10 built-in site templates. Each site template provisions lists, document libraries, and Web pages pre-populated with Web Parts that use the navigation best suited for the purpose of the site template.

Site templates are grouped under two tabs: the Collaboration tab and the Meetings tab.

The first three site templates listed on the Collaboration tab—Team Site, Blank Site and Document Workspace—all have the same latent capabilities and *Quick Launch* navigation. The *Team Site* template provisions a Shared Documents library and four lists: Announcements, Calendar, Links, and Tasks. The *Blank Site template*, as you might surmise, has no lists or document libraries and contains only the Site Image Web Part. The *Document Workspace* template provisions the same document libraries and lists as the Team Site, but makes the Shared Documents library more prominent by placing a Web Part for it on the site's default home page. It also places a Members Web Part on the default home page.

The next two site templates listed on the Collaboration tab, Wiki Site and Blog, were not available in the previous release. These two templates are new to Windows SharePoint Services; they were frequently requested additions to the list of built-in site templates.

By using the *Wiki Site* template, you can provision a container to hold primarily HTML content pages. Designated users can easily edit any content page in the site and link existing pages together or create links to new content pages. If a link is found to an uncreated page, a user can follow the link and create the page. In this way, a wiki site provides a low-maintenance way to record knowledge. Subject matter experts can capture their knowledge in context with similar knowledge. Other examples of the use of wiki sites include a list of frequently asked questions (FAQ) and their answers, idea pages, best practices or current best approach (CBA) documents, help desk or call center knowledge bases, and building an encyclopedia of knowledge. One of the initial pages in a new wiki provides good instructions on how to work with the content pages in the wiki.

Use the *Blog* template as a way to publish a type of journal. The blog owner creates posts on which other users can comment. Each post is a separate content page, and a rollup summary of these pages is typically presented in reverse chronological order (newest entries listed first) on the home page of the blog site. Blogs are commonly used as news sites, journals, and diaries. A blog focuses one or more core competencies of the author and is often used as a soapbox for the blog owner to state an opinion.

Blogs can also be used as a one-way communication tool for keeping project stakeholders and/or team members informed. Blog site content can be syndicated using an *RSS* (Really Simple Syndication) *feed*. RSS feed-aggregating software allows people to subscribe to the content they are interested in and have new and updated posts delivered to them. Using these tools, people can aggregate the content from many blogs (or any Windows SharePoint Services list) into one common reader where posts from selected authors can be sorted, filtered, and grouped. Microsoft Office Outlook 2007 can aggregate a few RSS feeds; there are also many vendors that give away or sell RSS feed–aggregating software.

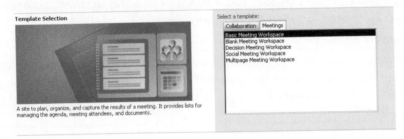

The five *Meeting Workspace* templates listed on the Meetings tab are variations on a theme. Unlike all the previously described site templates, they don't have a left navigation area. In addition to the traditional list types such as Document Library, Picture Library, Tasks, and Discussion Board, they can provision unique lists, such as Agenda, Attendees, Decisions, Objectives, and Things To Bring.

> **Tip** The 10 built-in templates are actually *configurations* of the four underlying site definitions: STS, Wiki, Blog, and MPS. Additional configurations and even alternate site definitions can be created in the underlying files by the managers of your Web servers. Built-in configurations can also be removed or altered. If you see more than two tabs, you may have Microsoft Office SharePoint Server installed and/or your company may have created their own custom templates.

You will likely focus, at least initially, on utilizing these built-in site templates. However, it is possible to save sites you create as custom site templates that you and others can choose from the Template Selection area of the New SharePoint Site page. This is done by using the Save Site As Template link in the Look And Feel area of the Site Settings page of any site. Sites saved in this way are initially only available in the same site collection in which they are saved and show up under the same tab as the site template on which they are initially based. The "Saving and Using a Site Template" section later in this chapter will explain how to copy a saved Site Template into another site collection. All alterations except security-related settings are retained on those sites provisioned by using saved custom site templates.

When creating a new site, there are two obvious permission options available. The default option, Use Same Permissions As Parent Site, checks the parent site's permission every time the user visits the child site to determine what the user is allowed to do on that site. As the permissions on the parent site change over time, the permissions on the child site also reflect those changes. The other option is to Use Unique Permissions. When you click this option as the site's creator, you are initially the only user with access to the site and are then associated with the Administrator permission level.

> **Important** If you choose Use Same Permissions As Parent Site, it is possible to have the right to create a new site but not have the right to delete it. However, if you choose Use Unique Permissions, you are the site's administrator and as such will always have the right to delete the new site.

Two other permission options are not as obvious. If you initially choose Use Unique Permissions, you are the only user with access to the site and can make any changes you wish. You can then switch to Use Same Permissions As Parent Site, whereby everyone, including you, who has access to the parent site will subsequently have access to the child site using the permissions assigned on the parent site. If you initially choose Use Same Permissions As Parent Site, the parent site's permissions will be used. Yet, if you subsequently switch to Use Unique Permissions, all of the permissions of the parent site are copied to the child site. This can save a great deal of time if most of the people who have access to the parent site also need access to the child site.

Three navigation options can be specified when creating a new site. The first two deal with the visibility of the child site being created within the navigation of the parent site. You can optionally choose to show the child site on either the Quick Launch or top link bar of the parent site. Both of these options default to Yes. Conversely, you can specify whether the top link bar of the parent site should display on the top link bar of the created child site. Again, this option defaults to Yes.

See "Using the Book's CD" on page xix for more information about using the site templates provided for each chapter in this book.

In the following exercise, you will create a child site that the buyers at Wide World Importers will use for collaboration. As a team, the buyers need a centralized place to consolidate their announcements, links, and general discussions as well as track the status of their purchases and the list of current suppliers. You will use the Team Site template to initially populate the new child site.

OPEN the top-level, would-be parent site from which you'd like to create the new site. The exercise will use the *http://wideworldimporters site*, but you can use whatever site you wish. If prompted, type your user name and password, and click OK.

BE SURE TO verify that you have sufficient rights to create a site. If in doubt, see the Appendix on page 435.

1. On the **Site Actions** menu, click **Create** to display the Create page.
2. In the **Web Pages** area, click **Sites and Workspaces** to display the New SharePoint Site page.

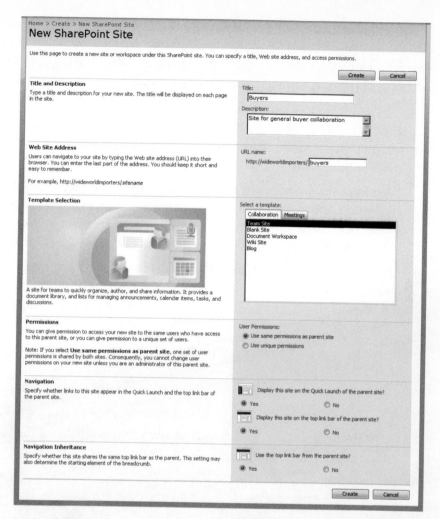

3. In the **Title** textbox, type Buyers to establish a display name for the new site.

4. In the **Description** textbox, type a description, such as Site for general buyer collaboration, to help users understand the purpose for the new site.

5. In the **URL name** textbox, type buyers for a Web Site Address.

   This determines the value in the browser's address bar that users will see when they visit the site. Refer to the Naming a URL sidebar earlier in this section for best practices regarding naming conventions.

6. On the **Template** list, click **Team Site**.

> **Tip** If you have installed the practice files from the book's CD, you will also see Wide World Importers at the bottom of the list of templates on the Collaboration tab.

7. Click the option button defining the type of permissions that you want to initially use on the site. For the Buyers site, use the default permission **Use same permissions as parent site**.

Keep the default navigation and navigation inheritance options. All of the Navigation option button options have Yes selected. In this way, both the parent site and the created child site will have navigation on the top link bar, and the parent site will also have a reference to the child site in the Quick Launch.

Create

Create

8. Click the **Create** button to create the new site with a default set of lists, document libraries, and Web pages pre-populated with Web Parts for the buyers to use on the new site.

Cancel

Cancel

> **Important** Clicking the Cancel button returns you to the Create page and will not create the site.

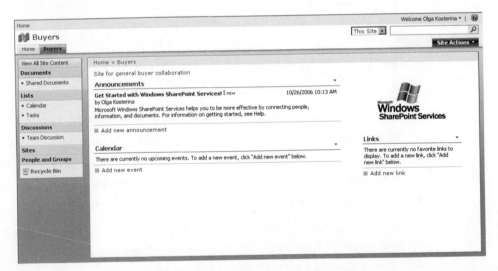

9. On the top link bar, click **Home** to return to the parent site.

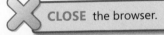 **CLOSE** the browser.

Managing Site Users and Permissions

Information in Windows SharePoint Services is secured at one of four levels.

1. Site level

2. List or document library level

3. Folder level

4. List item level

By default, all lists inherit the permissions of the site that contains them. All folders inherit the permissions of the list that contains them. All list items inherit the permissions of the folder that contains them. You can delve deeper into list, folder, and list item security in Chapter 4, "Working with Lists."

The default option, Use Same Permissions As Parent Site, checks the parent site's permission every time the user visits the child site. The Use Unique Permissions option initially provides the site's creator with sole access to the new site as its owner. When creating a new site, the Use Unique Permissions option causes the creation process to present the Set Up Groups For This Site page as the initial page.

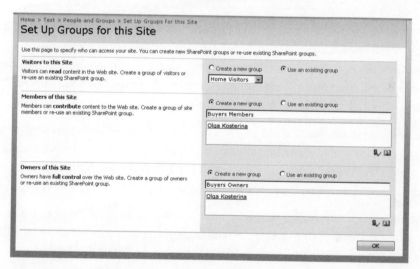

Windows SharePoint Services initially categorizes people into three groups.

1. Visitors: People or groups who only need to be able to read content on a site.

2. Members: People or groups who need to be able to create and edit content but not create lists or manage site membership.

3. Owners: People who are responsible for all aspects of managing and maintaining a site.

A site can be toggled between inherited permissions and unique permissions by clicking Advanced Permissions on the Site Settings page or by choosing People And Groups from either the bottom of Quick Launch or from the Users And Permissions area of the Site Settings page and then subsequently choosing Site Permissions from the left nav. Once on the Permissions page, choosing Inherit Permissions from the Actions menu on a site using unique permissions allows you to toggle the site to have inherited permissions. A warning dialog box will display before toggling.

Choosing Edit Permissions from the Actions menu on a site inheriting permissions allows you to toggle the site to have unique permissions. A warning dialog box will display before toggling.

A site using unique permissions has no tie to the parent site, so you are allowed to add and remove users from the site regardless of whether they have permissions on any other site. When users are added to a site, they must be either added to a *SharePoint group* or associated with at least one *permission level*.

> **Tip** SharePoint groups were called cross-site groups in the previous version of Windows SharePoint Services.

Not only can you associate individual users with permission levels, but you can also associate *Windows Groups* (*Windows NT Groups*, *Active Directory Groups,* or *Local Machine Groups*) with permission levels. This is a very practical approach to providing tight security with minimal maintenance. However, you may not have control over the Windows Groups defined in your organization.

SharePoint groups are maintained at the site collection level and represent a collection of users or groups with a defined set of one or more permission levels and a few governing attributes. When a new user or group is added to a SharePoint group, they are granted the permissions of that group in any site.

Think of permission levels as a named collection of permissions that can be assigned to SharePoint groups or users. Five permission levels are made available by Microsoft Windows SharePoint Services on every site.

1. **Read** User can view only.
2. **Contribute** User can view, add, update, and delete.
3. **Design** User can view, add, update, delete, approve, and customize.
4. **Full Control** User has full control.
5. **Limited** User has no permissions to the site in its entirety, but only to specific lists, document libraries, folders, list items, or documents when given explicit permission.

Out of the box Permission Levels

Permission	Full Control	Design	Contribute	Read
Add and Customize Pages	✓	✓		
Add Items	✓	✓	✓	
Add/Remove Personal Web Parts	✓	✓	✓	
Apply Style Sheets	✓	✓		
Apply Themes and Borders	✓	✓		
Approve Items	✓	✓		
Browse Directories	✓	✓	✓	
Browse User Information	✓	✓	✓	✓
Create Alerts	✓	✓	✓	✓
Create Groups	✓			
Create Subsites	✓			
Delete Items	✓	✓	✓	
Delete Versions	✓	✓	✓	
Edit Items	✓	✓	✓	
Edit Personal User Information	✓	✓	✓	
Enumerate Permissions	✓			
Manage Alerts	✓	✓		
Manage Lists	✓	✓		
Manage Permissions	✓			
Manage Personal Views	✓	✓	✓	
Manage Web Site	✓			
Open	✓	✓	✓	✓
Open Items	✓	✓	✓	✓
Override Check Out	✓	✓		
Update Personal Web Parts	✓	✓	✓	
Use Client Integration Features	✓	✓	✓	✓
Use Remote Interfaces	✓	✓	✓	✓
Use Self-Service Site Creation	✓	✓	✓	✓
View Application Pages	✓	✓	✓	✓
View Items	✓	✓	✓	✓
View Pages	✓	✓	✓	✓
View Usage Data	✓			
View Versions	✓	✓	✓	

Tip Permission levels were called site groups in the previous version of Windows SharePoint Services. You could also go into an advanced permissions settings page in the previous version and choose individual permissions for a user, group, or cross-site group. In Windows SharePoint Services version 3, only named permission levels can be assigned.

Although you can create your own permission levels and even alter all permission levels except for Full Control and Limited, you will likely find these built-in levels to be adequate for most business scenarios. You may want to provide all users with some level of access to the data on your site.

Tip If anonymous access has been enabled on the authentication provider in SharePoint Central Administration and has not been denied via Administration policy, anonymous users can then be granted some access to the entire site or to individual lists on a case-by-case basis. This provides the central Administrator with the option to decide whether to grant anonymous access for each Web application before its site administrators can begin to turn on this option.

> **Tip** You will also find an option to provide all authenticated users with a default level of access on each site's Add Users page. Adding users is covered later in this section.

After all users and groups are assigned to various permission levels, it is possible and even likely that someone will be associated at various levels with more than one permission level. Rather than enforcing the most restrictive permission level, all associated rights are aggregated and the cumulative list of unique rights apply. This can only be overridden by policies created in SharePoint Central Administration.

In the following exercise, you will change the permissions for a child site from inheriting permissions from its parent site to using unique permissions. You will then add users representing Wide World Importers buyers to the child site with Contribute permission.

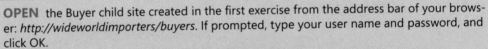

OPEN the Buyer child site created in the first exercise from the address bar of your browser: *http://wideworldimporters/buyers*. If prompted, type your user name and password, and click OK.

BE SURE TO verify that you have sufficient rights to alter the site's permissions. If in doubt, see the Appendix on page 435.

1. On the **Site Actions** menu, click **Site Settings** to display the Site Settings page.

2. In the **Users and Permissions** area, click **Advanced permissions** to display the Permission page.

   Notice that Site Permissions is selected in the left nav. This view shows the permission levels that have been assigned to the groups associated with this site. Because this child site is inheriting permissions from its parent, you see the SharePoint groups from the parent site listed.

3. On the **Actions** menu, click **Edit Permissions** to establish unique permissions for this site.

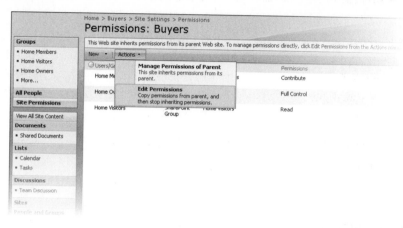

4. Click OK to confirm the change.

Notice how this page has changed. You now have check boxes next to each group, and there are additional menu options. You would select the Inherit Permissions menu option to return to using the permissions of the parent site.

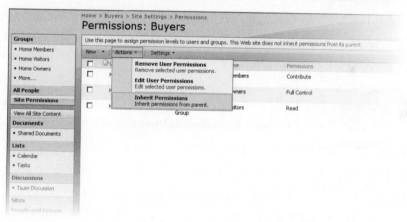

> **Important** Editing a SharePoint group affects the membership of all sites, lists, folders, and items that are using that Sharepoint group.

5. On the **New** menu, click **New Group** to display the New Group page.

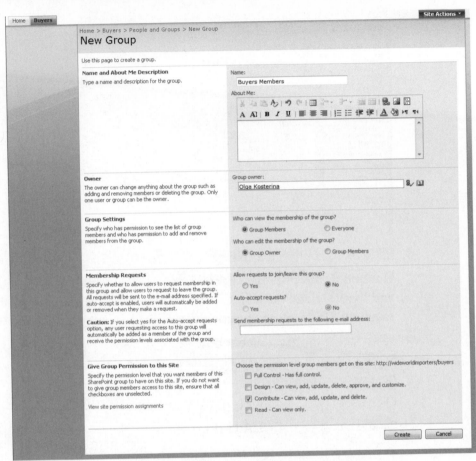

6. Type a name, such as Buyers Members, into the **Name** textbox.

7. Optionally, type a description of the new group in the **About Me** textbox.

8. Select the user or group that will own this group. It defaults to you, this example uses Olga Kosterina.

9. Leave the default settings for **Group Settings** and **Membership Requests**.

10. Select the **Contribute** permission level check box.

11. Click **Create** to add the new group to the People and Groups page for the Buyers Members SharePoint group.

Bill Malone is Wide World Importers' head buyer, so he needs to be associated with the Full Control permission level. Everyone in a Windows group called Buyers in this exercise needs to be added and associated with the Contribute permission level. All other SharePoint groups need to be removed.

12. On the **New** menu, click **Add Users** to display the Add Users - Buyers page.

Home > Buyers > Site Settings > Permissions > Add Users
Add Users: Buyers

Use this page to give new permissions.

Add Users
You can enter user names, group names, or e-mail addresses. Separate them with semicolons.

Add all authenticated users

Users/Groups:
Bill Malone

Give Permission
Choose the permissions you want these users to have. You can add users to a SharePoint group (which is already assigned to a permission level), or you can add users individually and assign them to a specific permission level.

SharePoint groups are recommended as they allow for ease of permission management across multiple sites.

Give Permission
○ Add users to a SharePoint group
  Home Members [Contribute]
  View permissions this group has on sites, lists, and items...
● Give users permission directly
  ☑ Full Control - Has full control.
  ☐ Design - Can view, add, update, delete, approve, and customize.
  ☐ Contribute - Can view, add, update, and delete.
  ☐ Read - Can view only.

OK   Cancel

13. In the **Users/Groups** text area, type the name of a user to whom to grant Full Control. This exercise uses Bill Malone.

14. Select the **Give users permission directly** option button.

15. Select the **Full Control** check box. If e-mail has been enabled for your SharePoint installation, you can optionally send a message to Bill notifying him that he now has Full Control of this site.

16. Click **OK** to add the user's (e.g., Bill's) permissions to the site.

17. On the **New** menu, click **Add Users** to display the Add Users - Buyers page.

18. In the **Users/Groups** text area, type the name of a group to whom to grant Contributor permissions. This exercise uses Buyers.

> **Important** Typically, you add users and Windows groups by using a format such as domainname\username or domainname\groupname, but your computer name cannot be anticipated here. Fortunately, Windows SharePoint Services searches your computer for users and Windows groups that match even if the proper naming convention isn't provided.

19. Select the **Add users to SharePoint Group** option button.

20. From the drop-down list, click **Buyers Members [Contribute]**.

21. Click **OK** to add the permissions for the group (e.g., Buyers Windows) to the SharePoint group.

22. On the left nav, click **Site Permissions** to return to the Permissions page.

23. Select the check boxes beside all three parent site SharePoint groups. On the **Actions** menu, click **Remove User Permissions**.

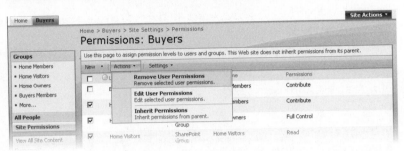

24. In the confirmation dialog box, click **OK** to apply the change. Clicking **Cancel** would discard the removal request.

> **Tip** It is wise to associate every user in the various child sites in a site collection with at least the Reader permission level in the top-level site. Users will be unable to use custom site templates and list templates imported into a site collection unless they are associated with one of the built-in permission levels in the top-level site.

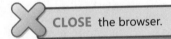 **CLOSE** the browser.

Creating a Child Workspace

Windows SharePoint Services makes it easy to navigate from parent site to child site. Because the Buyer child site was created with navigational links on both the top link bar and Quick Launch, navigating to the child site from the top-level site is easy. Simply click the link on the Buyers tab. However, how would you find the Buyers child site if this navigation wasn't included? In the following exercise, you will create a Meeting Workspace as a child site of the Buyers child site. Because you must already be in a site to create a child site, you will first see how to navigate to the Buyers child site. You will then view the site hierarchy of the entire site collection from the top-level site.

OPEN the top-level site from the address bar of your browser: *http://wideworldimporters*. If prompted, type your user name and password, and click OK.

BE SURE TO verify that you have sufficient rights to create a new site. If in doubt, see the Appendix on page 435.

1. On the top of the left nav, click **View All Site Content** to show all lists, document libraries, sites, and workspaces that have been created on the All Site Content page of this site.

2. In the **Sites and Workspaces** area near the bottom of the page, click **Buyers** to navigate to the child site. This link would appear even if there wasn't a link to this child site in the top link bar or Quick Launch.

> **Tip** Alternatively, you can type the entire site hierarchy directly into the browser's address bar. This may seem a bit odd at first, but Microsoft Internet Explorer learns the places that you type often, which can be a real time saver instead of clicking through the user interface. To see the child sites of the current site, complete the current site's Web site address with /_layouts/mngsubwebs.aspx.

3. On the **Site Actions** menu, from the **Buyers** site, click **Create** to display the Create page.

4. In the **Web Pages** area of the **Create** page, click **Sites and Workspaces**.

5. As in the earlier example, type a **Name** and **URL name**, such as Team Meeting and TeamMeeting, respectively. Remember to follow the best practices found in the Naming a URL sidebar earlier in this chapter concerning naming conventions.

6. Optionally, in the **Description** textbox, type a description, such as Site for monthly team meeting details, to help users understand the purpose for the new site.

7. In the **Template Selection** area, click the **Meetings** tab. Then, on the **Template** list, click **Basic Meeting Workspace**.

8. Keep the default permissions that are set on **Use same permissions as parent site**.

9. Keep the default navigation and navigation inheritance options.

10. Click **Create** to create and display the new Meeting Workspace.

Notice how Meeting Workspaces differ in appearance from team sites. The Quick Launch is gone. An additional set of Page tabs display above the Web Parts. Add Pages and Manage Pages options are shown on the Site Actions menu.

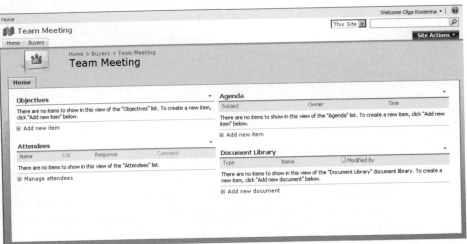

11. On the global nav at the top left corner of the page, click **Home** to return to the top-level site.

12. To see the entire hierarchy of child sites, on the **Site Actions** menu, click **Site Settings** to display the Site Settings page.

13. On the **Site Settings** page, in the **Site Collection Administration** area, click **Site hierarchy** to display the Site Hierarchy page.

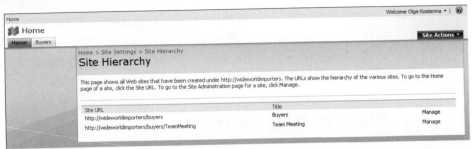

This page shows you all of the flattened out, fully qualified child sites in the entire hierarchy. You can click on the site name to display the site or click on the Manage link to display the Site Administration page for the associated child site.

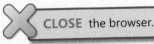

CLOSE the browser.

Changing a Site's Theme

These blue SharePoint sites are OK initially, but they eventually blur together and start to look too "SharePointy." Thankfully, Windows SharePoint Services provides us with the ability to apply themes to our sites. Themes can radically affect display items such as colors, graphics, text, banners, and borders. Numerous built-in themes are available from which to choose.

> **Tip** With Microsoft Office SharePoint Designer, you can gain even more control over how themes are applied to your site. You can choose to apply a theme to only specific pages or even create your own custom themes.

Each Windows SharePoint Services site can have its own theme, or you can set several sites to all have a common theme so that they are visually related.

Perhaps the buyers at Wide World Importers want to theme their Team Meeting child site so that it stands out from the other sites. In this exercise, you will navigate to the Team Meeting site and apply a theme.

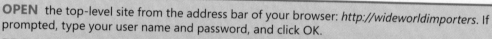

OPEN the top-level site from the address bar of your browser: *http://wideworldimporters*. If prompted, type your user name and password, and click OK.

BE SURE TO verify that you have sufficient rights to set a site's theme and view the site hierarchy. If in doubt, see the Appendix on page 435.

1. On the **Site Actions** menu, click **Site Settings** to display the Site Settings page.

2. In the **Site Collection Administration** area, click **Site hierarchy** to display the Site Hierarchy page.

3. Click the **Manage** link to the far right of the **Site URL** (http://wideworldimporters/buyers/TeamMeeting) for the **Team Meeting** child site's Site Settings page to display.

4. In the **Look and Feel** area, click **Site theme** to display the Site Theme page.

5. On the **Select a Theme** list, click **Breeze**.

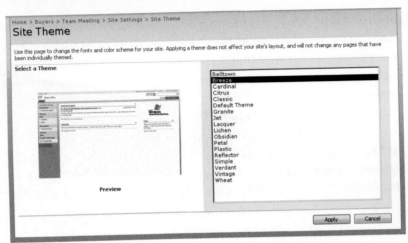

6. Click **Apply** to save the theme choice of the Meeting Workspace and redisplay the Site Settings page.

7. From the **breadcrumb** just above the large Site Settings words near the top of the page, click **Team Meeting** to display the newly themed home page of the Team Meeting site.

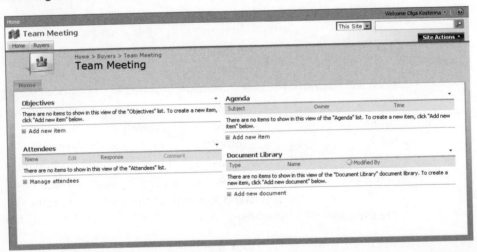

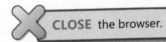 **CLOSE** the browser.

Saving and Using a Site Template

After working with a site, you may want to save it just the way it is so that it can be recreated over and over again. Windows SharePoint Services facilitates this activity by allowing anyone with a Design permission level to save a site as a custom template. Custom templates provide a way of packaging up a set of changes to an existing site definition and making that package available as a template for new sites or lists. These custom templates behave in much the same way as built-in templates do in that they provision lists, document libraries, and Web pages pre-populated with Web Parts that are best suited for the purpose of the template. In fact, everything in a site except security-related information is saved in a custom site template, including its theme and navigation. You can even optionally retain the data in all of the site's lists and document libraries.

> **Tip** The STP files on this book's CD that are used to re-create the solutions for each chapter are actually custom site templates saved to a file.

> **Important** By default, there is currently a 10-MB limit on the total size of any custom template. An administrator with console access to the Web servers can increase this capacity to as much as 500 MB.

Every custom template is based on an underlying site definition and saved as a file in the *site collection site gallery* document library in the root of the site collection. Once saved, a custom site template is made immediately available throughout the entire site collection in which it is saved. When creating a new child site, any user associated with one of the default permission levels (excluding the Limited permission level) in the top-level site can see the saved custom site template as an option in the Template Selection area of the New SharePoint Site page. To use a custom site template when creating a new top-level site from SharePoint Central Administration, it must be placed into the *central template gallery* by using a command line tool on the Web server rather than simply placing it in the site collection site gallery.

Let's assume that the unique look that the buyers of Wide World Importers created for their Team Meeting site has caught on and they want to be able to use it repeatedly. In the following exercise, you will save the Team Meeting site as a custom site template and then use it to create another meeting site as a child of the Buyers child site.

OPEN the Team Meeting site from the address bar of your browser: *http://wideworldim-porters/buyer/TeamMeeting.* If prompted, type your user name and password, and click OK.

BE SURE TO verify that you have sufficient rights to save a site template and create a new site. If in doubt, see the Appendix on page 435.

1. On the **Site Actions** menu, click **Site Settings** to display the Site Settings page.

2. In the **Look and Feel** area, click **Save site as template** to display the Save Site as Template page.

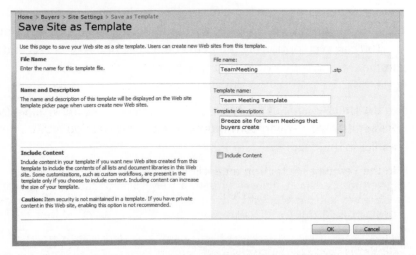

3. In the **File name** textbox, type TeamMeeting to establish a name for the STP file.

4. In the **Template title** textbox, type Team Meeting Template to establish the name that will display as a choice in the list of templates on the Template Selection page.

5. In the **Description** textbox, type a description, such as Breeze site for team meetings that the buyers created, to help site creators understand the intended purpose of the custom site template.

6. Click **OK** to save the custom site template in the site collection site template gallery and display the Operation Completed Successfully page.

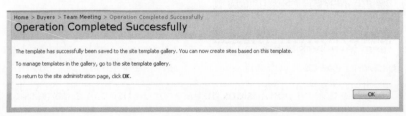

> **Tip** If you want to see where the custom site template is placed, you can click on the site template gallery link on the Operation Completed Successfully page.

7. Click **OK** to acknowledge the page and redisplay the Site Settings page.

8. On the top link bar, click **Buyers** to display the Buyers child site.

9. On the **Site Actions** menu, click **Create** to display the Create page.

10. In the **Web Pages** area, click **Sites and workspaces** to display the New SharePoint Site page.

11. In the **Title** textbox, type Important Meeting to establish a display name for the new site.

12. In the **Description** textbox, type a description, such as Site for that important meeting, to help users understand the purpose for the new site.

13. In the **URL name** textbox, type ImportantMeeting as the Web site address. Remember the naming conventions listed in the Naming a URL sidebar presented earlier in this chapter.

14. In the **Template Selection** area, click the **Custom** tab.

    The Team Meeting Template is now available in the Template list. Also note that the description given to the custom site template is displayed below the image.

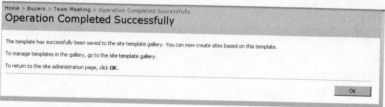

15. On the **Template** list, click **Team Meeting Template**.

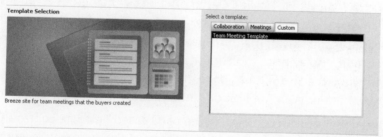

16. Keep the default permissions that are set on **Use same permissions as parent site**.

17. Keep the default navigation and navigation inheritance options.

18. Click the **Create** button to create and display the new Meeting Workspace. The new Important Meeting site will be identical to the original Team Meeting site.

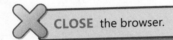

CLOSE the browser.

Managing Site Features

Features are a new concept in this version of Windows SharePoint Services. They provide activatable chunks of functionality that developers and administrators can make available at one of four scopes.

1. **Farm level** These Features are activated for all sites in the entire Windows SharePoint Services farm and are managed by central administrators.

2. **Web Application level** These Features are activated for all sites where the Web address is the same. For instance, all sites that start with http://wideworldimporters would be managed under the same Web Application. These Features are also managed by central administrators.

3. **Site Collection level** These Features are activated only for sites within a given site collection. Management of these Features is accomplished from the top-level site of the site collection and is typically distributed to department-level administrators.

4. **Site level** These Features are activated only for the site in which the activation is performed. Management of these Features may be done by anyone with Administrator privileges on the site.

Features can encapsulate any combination of the following types of functionality.

- Add or remove links (called Custom Actions) in numerous locations around the Windows SharePoint Services user interface. These locations include the Site Actions menu, any of the drop-down menus on any list or document library, the new/edit/display page toolbar for any list item, the smart menu on any list item in a list view, the Site Settings page, the Content Type Settings page, and either the Operations or Web Application settings pages in Central Administration.

- Override specific rectangles on the page called delegate controls. This can include an additional page header at the very top of the page (this is empty on all pages by default), links in the global navigation at the top right of the page, a replacement search box, or any number of other controls that your development staff creates.

- Register a computer program that converts documents from one format to another when uploaded to a document library.

- Add new application and administration Web pages or any other physical document including site and list templates, images, or other needed technical files.

- Define the style and behavior of a new list of your choice from the Create page.

- Create a new list for you.

- Define a new Site Column that could be used in lists, document libraries, or content types.

- Define an entire content type that could subsequently be associated with a list or document library.

- Add a custom workflow that could dictate the order of tasks that must be accomplished for a list item to move from one state to another.

- Register a computer program that runs custom code when you interact with items in a list or document library. Adding new items, modifying an existing item, checking out, checking in, or even undoing a checkout of an item or deleting are all examples of interactions that can cause this custom code to run.

A Feature must be installed in a scope on your Windows SharePoint Services farm where you can see it before you begin working with it. In the following exercise, you will work with a site Feature called Team Collaboration Lists, which is one of the two visible Features installed by default in a Windows SharePoint Services installation. The other is a site collection Feature called Three-State Workflow.

> **Important** Microsoft Office SharePoint Server installations include many more Features, but they are beyond the scope of this book.

OPEN the top-level site from the address bar of your browser: *http://wideworldimporters*. If prompted, type your user name and password, and click OK.

BE SURE TO verify that you have sufficient rights to manage Features. If in doubt, see the Appendix on page 435.

1. On the **Site Actions** menu, click **Site Settings** to display the Site Settings page.

Deactivate

2. In the **Site Collection Administration** area, click **Site collection features** to see that the Three-state workflow Feature has already been activated in this site collection. Notice that the Status is Active and there is a Deactivate button.

3. On the **Site Actions** menu, click **Create**. Notice all of the different kinds of lists and document libraries that can be created from this page. This Create page will be contrasted with a modified Create later in this exercise.

4. On the **Site Actions** menu, once again click **Site Settings** to display the Site Settings page.

5. In the **Site Administration** area, click **Site features** to see that the Team Collaboration Lists Feature has already been activated in this site. Again, notice that the Status is Active and there is a Deactivate button.

6. Click **Deactivate**. A warning screen is shown to confirm that you really want to de-activate this Feature.

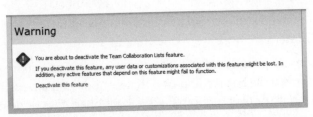

> **Warning**
>
> ⚠ You are about to deactivate the Team Collaboration Lists feature.
>
> If you deactivate this feature, any user data or customizations associated with this feature might be lost. In addition, any active features that depend on this feature might fail to function.
>
> Deactivate this feature

7. Click the **Deactivate this feature** link to confirm this action.

8. On the **Site Actions** menu, again click **Create**. All of the lists and document libraries that were previously there have been removed from this page, leaving only a few non-list options under the Web Pages group.

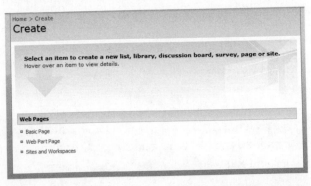

> Home > Create
> **Create**
>
> **Select an item to create a new list, library, discussion board, survey, page or site.**
> Hover over an item to view details.
>
> **Web Pages**
> ▫ Basic Page
> ▫ Web Part Page
> ▫ Sites and Workspaces

9. On the **Site Actions** menu, click **Site Settings** one last time.

10. In the **Site Administration** area, click **Site features**.

11. To the right of the **Team Collaboration Lists** Feature, click **Activate** to add all of the collaboration lists back to the Create page.

12. Optionally, on the **Site Actions** menu, click **Create** again to see that the lists and document libraries have been restored.

 CLOSE the browser.

Managing Site Content Syndication

Really Simple Syndication (RSS) is a standard way to make emerging content available to readers of a Windows SharePoint Services list or document library. Once a reader subscribes to an RSS feed (the XML emitted from a Web request), he can use an RSS aggregator running on his desktop to check for new or modified content as often as he chooses.

> **Tip** Office Outlook 2007 can be used as an aggregator. This topic is discussed in Chapter 11, "Using Windows SharePoint Services with Outlook 2007." Harvard Law also has a list of third-party RSS aggregators: *http://blogs.law.harvard.edu/tech/directory/5/aggregators*.

The aggregator gathers all updates into a common pool of data that can be searched, sorted, filtered, and grouped by the aggregator as directed. Windows SharePoint Services can provide list data in RSS 2.0 format. RSS content is sometimes described as being "pulled" by the subscribers, for they can easily unsubscribe from a feed at any time. This can be a fabulous way to roll up data entered into a SharePoint list. By default, every Web application in Windows SharePoint Services is configured to allow RSS for all site collections they contain.

Site collection administrators can specify whether RSS feeds are allowed on lists in the sites within the site collection; they are allowed by default. Each site can then subsequently specify whether RSS feeds are allowed on lists in the site; they are also allowed by default. If sites do allow feeds, several attributes can be optionally defined that will be included in every feed. In the following exercise, you will verify that RSS is allowed on both the site collection and the top-level site and specify the optional attributes. Consuming the RSS feed for a given list will be covered in Chapter 4.

 OPEN the top-level site from the address bar of your browser: *http://wideworldimporters*. If prompted, type your user name and password, and click OK.

BE SURE TO verify that you have sufficient rights to administrate a site. If in doubt, see the Appendix on page 435.

1. On the **Site Actions** menu, click **Site Settings** to display the Site Settings page.

2. In the **Site Administration** area, click **RSS** to display the RSS page.

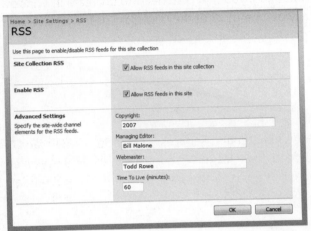

If you are on the top-level site of the site collection, as in this example, and you are a site collection Administrator, you see the Allow RSS Feeds In This Site Collection check box in the Site Collection RSS area. Unchecking this check box grays out the options in the Enable RSS area, and no sites in this collection can allow RSS feeds. Leave this check box checked in this exercise.

All sites have the Allow RSS Feeds In This Site check box in the Enable RSS area. If this check box is unchecked, no lists in this site are allowed to provide their data in the form of an RSS feed. As with the first check box, leave this checkbox checked in this exercise.

3. In the **Copyright** textbox, enter 2007.

4. In the **Managing Editor** textbox, enter Bill Malone.

5. In the **Webmaster** textbox, enter Todd Rowe.

6. Leave the **Time to Live** textbox at **60** minutes. This instructs the aggregator to wait at least this long before checking for updates. A shorter period will increase the frequency a site could get requests from aggregators, while a longer duration can help to diminish aggregator requests.

7. Click **OK** to commit these changes.

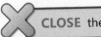 **CLOSE** the browser.

Deleting a Site

When you create something, you may also need to uncreate it. Windows SharePoint Services automatically generates all of the necessary user interface elements to create, review, update, delete, manage, and restore your sites.

> **Tip** You can restore a site from a Recycle Bin up to 30 days, by default, after it has been deleted.

There will be times when you want to remove a site that you either created in error or no longer need. In fact, the creator of the Important Meeting child site at Wide World Importers had a change in priorities and no longer needs the site. Therefore, in this exercise, you will delete the Important Meeting child site from the Buyers child site.

OPEN the Buyer site from the address bar of your browser: *http://wideworldimporters*. If prompted, type your user name and password, and click OK.

BE SURE TO verify that you have sufficient rights to delete a site. If in doubt, see the Appendix on page 435.

1. On the **Site Actions** menu, click **Site Settings** to display the Site Settings page.

2. In the **Site Administrations** area, click **Sites and workspaces** to display the Sites and Workspaces page.

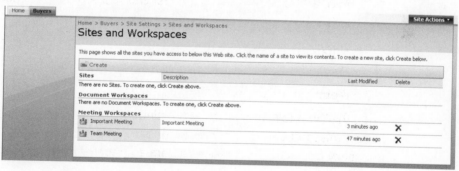

Delete icon

4. To the far right on the **Important Meeting** line, click the **Delete** icon to begin the site deletion process and display the Delete Web Site page.

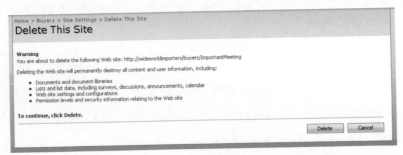

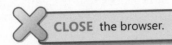

Delete

5. Click the **Delete** button to confirm the deletion request.

6. Click **OK** to confirm, complete the deletion process, and return to the Sites and Workspaces page.

   The Important Meeting site is no longer displayed.

> **Tip** It is also possible to delete the site that you are in by clicking Delete This Site in the Site Administration area of any site's Site Settings page. This is the only way to delete a top-level site without removing the entire site collection. Windows SharePoint Services will also prevent you from deleting a parent site that still contains child sites.

CLOSE the browser.

Key Points

- Sites are containers for lists, document libraries, and Web pages pre-populated with Web Parts.

- The initial site created in a Windows SharePoint Services site collection is called the top-level site.

- To create a child site, you must navigate to the New SharePoint Site page.

- Don't use spaces in site names, and keep them short and intuitive.

- Sites are easy to create and secure.

- Only after a site is using unique permissions can you manage its users and SharePoint groups.

- Permission levels are a named collection of permissions.

- All associated permissions are aggregated and the cumulative list of unique permissions apply.

- Each site can have its own theme.

- Sites can be saved as custom templates and immediately be used to create other clone sites in a site collection.

- Some installed Features can be activated at the Site Collection level, while others can be activated on a site-by-site basis.

- Sites can allow or disallow RSS feeds on the lists contained within them.

- Deleting a site sends it to the Recycle Bin in Windows SharePoint Services, from where it can be restored.

Chapter at a Glance

View existing site content, page 82

Create new lists and libraries, page 83

Use list actions, page 101

View list items in the datasheet view, page 96

Create new list views, page 110

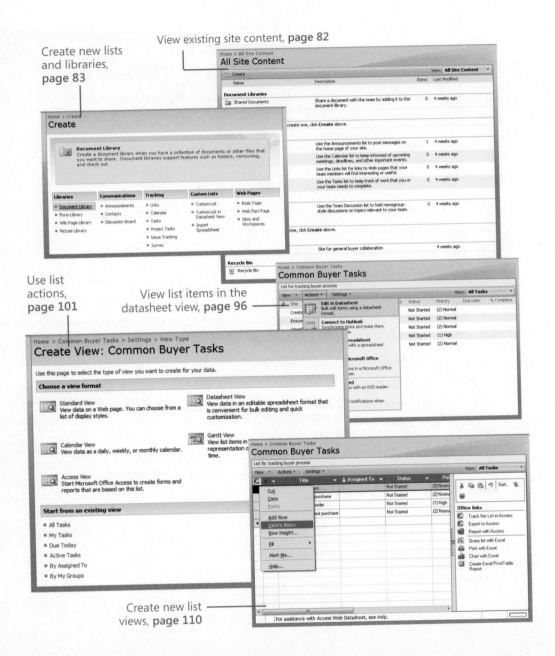

4 Working with Lists

In this chapter, you will learn to:

- ✔ Discover default lists in a site.
- ✔ Create a new list.
- ✔ Add, edit, delete and restore list items.
- ✔ Use Datasheet view.
- ✔ Attach files to list items.
- ✔ Add, edit, and delete list columns.
- ✔ Sort and filter a list.
- ✔ Add and modify a list view.
- ✔ Set up alerts.
- ✔ Use RSS feeds.
- ✔ E-mail-enable a list and library.
- ✔ Delete a list.
- ✔ Restore a list.

You can think of the *lists* found in Microsoft Windows SharePoint Services as spreadsheets that you and your coworkers can simultaneously use on the Internet. SharePoint lists represent editable, Web-based tables that facilitate concurrent, multi-user interactions against a common, centralized, extensible set of columns and rows. They empower you to provision your own repositories of structured information in which *list items* behave like rows consisting of self-labeled *columns*. All of the Web pages needed to create, review, update, delete, and manage a list and its data are automatically and dynamically generated by Windows SharePoint Services.

> **Tip** Unstructured information is typically stored as a document with associated columns in a document library. Document libraries are discussed at length in Chapter 5, "Creating and Managing Libraries," and Chapter 6, "Working with Library Settings."

In this chapter, you will discover the default lists that already exist on your site, create new lists, and alter existing lists. Depending on the site template that you initially create, some lists (such as Announcements, Events, and Links) may be provisioned when the site is created and you need only to begin using them. Yet, there will come a time when the lists that are auto-provided do not quite meet a need. Therefore, this chapter explores the Web pages that allow you to not only alter existing lists, but create your own custom lists.

> **Important** Before you can use the practice sites provided for this chapter, you need to install them from the book's companion CD to their default locations. See "Using the Book's CD" on page xix for more information.

> **Important** Remember to use your SharePoint site location in place of *http://wideworldimporters* in the following exercises.

Discovering Default Lists in a Site

Many default lists are included with Windows SharePoint Services. When you need to create a list, you can use the default *list templates* by using the Create option from the Site Actions menu to generate a new list with a static set of predefined columns. Later in this chapter, we'll explore how additional columns can be added and how most default columns can be altered or deleted, even after data have been entered into a list. The list templates built into Windows SharePoint Services are described in the following table.

 Meeting Workspaces   Team Sites, Wikis, Blogs

Icon	List Template	Site Type	Description
	Agenda		Create an Agenda list when you want to outline the meeting topics, who will cover them, and how much time each presenter is allotted.
	Announcements		Create an Announcements list when you want a place to share news, status, and other short bits of information.
	Calendar		Create a Calendar list when you want a calendar-based view of upcoming meetings, deadlines, and other important events. You can share information between your Calendar list and Microsoft Office Outlook.

	Contacts		Create a Contacts list when you want to manage information about people with whom your team works with, such as customers or partners. You can share information between your Contacts list and Office Outlook.
	Custom		Create a Custom list when you want to specify your own columns. The list opens as a Web page and allows you to add or edit items one at a time.
	Custom list in Datasheet view		Create a Custom list when you want to specify your own columns. The list opens in a spreadsheet-like environment for convenient data entry, editing, and formatting. It requires Microsoft Office Access on the client and ActiveX control support.
	Decisions		Create a Decisions list when you want to keep track of all decisions made at the meeting. Attendees and others can then review the results of the meeting.
	Discussion Board		Create a discussion board when you want to provide a place for newsgroup-style discussion. Discussion boards provide features for managing discussion threads and ensuring that only approved posts appear.
	Document Library		Create a document library when you have a collection of documents or other files that you want to share. Document libraries support features such as folders, versioning, and check out.
	Form Library		Create a form library when you have XML-based business forms, such as status reports or purchase orders, that you want to manage. These libraries require an XML editor, such as Microsoft Office InfoPath.
	Import Spreadsheet		Import a spreadsheet when you want to create a list that has the same columns and contents as an existing spreadsheet. Importing a spreadsheet requires Microsoft Office Excel.
	Issue Tracking		Create an Issue Tracking list when you want to manage a set of issues or problems. You can assign, prioritize, and follow the progress of issues from start to finish.
	Links		Create a Links list when you have links to Web pages or other resources that you want to share.
	Objectives		Create an Objectives list when you want to let your attendees know your goals for the meeting. Every meeting should begin with a purpose in mind.

	Picture Library		Create a picture library when you have pictures you want to share. Picture libraries provide special features for managing and displaying pictures such as thumbnails, download options, and a slide show. Pictures can even be edited using a built-in ActiveX control.
	Project Tasks		Create a Project Tasks list when you want a graphical view (a Gantt Chart) of a group of work items that you or your team needs to complete. You can share information between your Project Tasks list and Outlook.
	Survey		Create a survey when you want to poll other Web site users. Surveys provide features that allow you to quickly create questions and define how users specify their answers.
	Tasks		Create a Tasks list when you want to track a group of work items that you or your team must complete.
	Text Box		Create a text box when you want to insert custom text into the meeting, such as instructions or motivational quotes.
	Things To Bring		Create a list of things that attendees should bring to be prepared for the meeting such as notebooks, handouts, or something to eat.
	Wiki Page Library		Create a wiki page library when you want to have an interconnected collection of wiki pages. Wiki page libraries support pictures, tables, hyperlinks, and wiki linking.

As discussed in Chapter 3, "Creating and Managing Sites," Windows SharePoint Services will provision some of these lists for you when you create a new site depending on which site template you use.

- The three collaboration sites provision lists as follows.
    - The *Blank Site* template has no lists or document libraries.
    - Both the *Team Site* template and *Document Workspace* template provision a Shared Documents library and four lists: Announcements, Calendar, Links, Tasks, and a Team Discussion board. We will discuss Document Workspaces in detail in Chapter 7, "Working with Document Workspaces."

- The *Blog* site template provisions a picture library called Photos and five lists: Categories (Custom list), Comments (Custom list), Links, Other Blogs (Links list), and Posts (Custom list).

- The *Wiki* site template only provisions a single wiki page library called Wiki Pages.

- The *Meeting Workspace* templates all provision unique lists such as Agenda, Attendees, Decisions, Objectives, and Things To Bring. We will discuss Meeting Workspaces in detail in Chapter 8, "Working with Meeting Workspaces."

In the following exercise, you will first browse to the lists created for the Wide World Importers' top-level site. Subsequently, you will browse to the Create page to see the list templates available when you create a new Team Site.

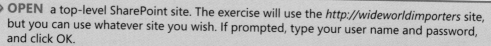

OPEN a top-level SharePoint site. The exercise will use the *http://wideworldimporters* site, but you can use whatever site you wish. If prompted, type your user name and password, and click OK.

BE SURE TO verify that you have sufficient rights to browse the site and create lists. If in doubt, see the Appendix on page 435.

1. In the left navigation panel, click **View All Site Content** to display the All Site Content page.

This team site has one default document library called Shared Documents; four default lists: Announcements, Calendar, Links, and Tasks; and a discussion board called Team Discussion. The bottom of this page also lists any immediate child sites and the Recycle Bin (discussed later in this chapter).

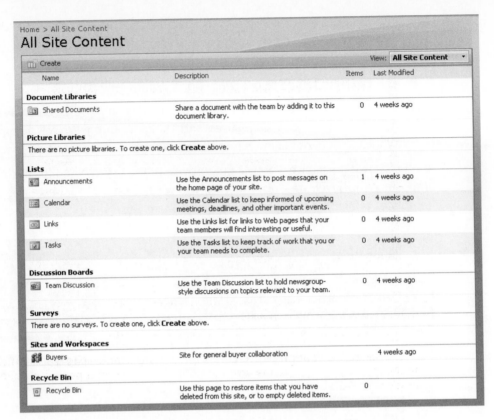

2. On the toolbar, click **Create** to display the Create page.

Tip Don't be confused by the naming convention here. The names of list templates are identical to the names of the default lists generated by Windows SharePoint Services; however, they are radically different things. Each list template shown on the Create page could be used to create one or more uniquely named instances in the All Site Content page. For example, the Announcements list template was used to create the Announcements list, but the resulting list could have been called something entirely different, such as Sales Notices. The names do not have to be identical.

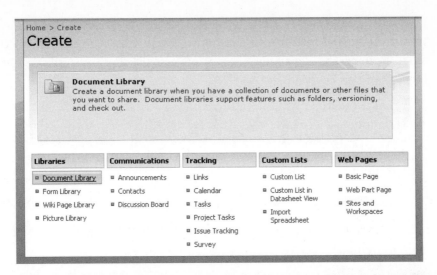

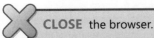 **CLOSE** the browser.

> **Tip** Because the Windows SharePoint Services administration pages are now security trimmed, you wouldn't see the first four columns on the Create page if you didn't have permission to create a list.

Creating a New List

The first step in creating a new list is to ask yourself: "What kind of information do I want to gather/display?" The answer to this question will help you determine which list template to choose. Perhaps you want to start with a list that is close to your end goal and then add, delete, and alter the default columns to provide the solution you are trying to achieve. For example, if you are planning to collect information such as names and addresses, you can choose the Contact list template to create your initial list and then modify it. Perhaps you want to start with a bare-bones list and build it entirely from scratch. In that case, you would likely choose the Custom List list template to create your initial list.

> **Tip** If the list items in the list you want to create always begin with a document, consider using a document library instead of a list. Document libraries are discussed at length in Chapters 5 and 6.

In the following exercise, you will create a list for the buyers at Wide World Importers to track the status of tasks involved in the buying process. This task list will be based on the Tasks list template. Once the list is created, you will alter the display name so that it displays Common Buyer Tasks.

OPEN the SharePoint site where you would like to create the new list. The exercise will use the *http://wideworldimporters* site, but you can use whatever site you wish. If prompted, type your user name and password, and click OK.

BE SURE TO verify that you have sufficient rights to create lists. If in doubt, see the Appendix on page 435.

1. On the **Site Actions** menu at the top right of the page, click **Create** to display the list templates on the Create page.

   > **Tip** Oddly, a Meeting Workspace doesn't have a Create option on the Site Actions menu. Therefore, you must click the list name in one of the Web Parts on the home page, then click View All Site Content in the left navigation panel, and then click Create on the toolbar.

2. In the **Tracking** group, click **Tasks** to display the New List page.

   You will use this page to create a task list based on the Tasks list template. You can name your new task list anything you want.

   > **Tip** There is no restriction to the number of copies of any list template that you can create in a site. You can create as many task lists as you like.

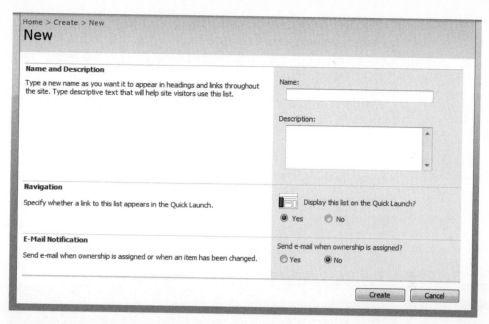

3. In the **Name** textbox. type BuyerTasks to establish a display name for the new list.

Because there is no textbox with which to provide the URL name, this textbox also supplies the value that Windows SharePoint Services uses for the internal names.

> **Important** When you initially create a list in Windows SharePoint Services, you are establishing two name values: the display name, usually labeled Name or Title, and the URL name, also know as the internal name. However, only the display name can be changed after the item is created. When the URL name cannot be set on a Windows SharePoint Services Create page, the display name (usually labeled Title) is used to populate both names.

> **Tip** Best practices to follow when initially naming a list in Windows SharePoint Services include the following: The initial name should be descriptive, intuitive, and easy to remember. The initial name should be concise. The initial name should not contain spaces. The initial name should be consistently used throughout the site. More details about these naming recommendations and the reasons they are needed can be found in the Naming a URL sidebar in Chapter 3.
>
> Your organization may also have specific naming conventions that you will want to follow.

4. In the **Description** textbox, type the description List for tracking buyer process to help users understand the purpose for the new list.

5. Check that the option indicating whether you want to see this new list on the Quick Launch is selected. This is a default setting.

> **Tip** Again, Meeting Workspaces are different. Because there isn't a Quick Launch on the home page, the Quick Launch option is not presented. Instead, there is an option to Share List Items Across All Meetings in a series.

Create

6. Click the **Create** button to complete the list creation. The BuyerTasks default list view page (AllItems.aspx) is displayed.

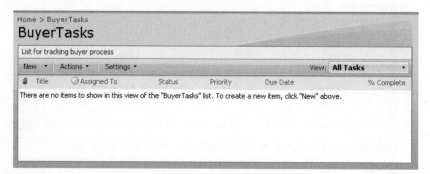

7. Go to the Home page of the site by clicking a link to it on the breadcrumb or top link bar, The new BuyerTasks list is now showing in the Quick Launch.

Because this list was named without a space, it would be useful to change the display name so that it has a space in it. The remainder of this exercise demonstrates that revisions to the list name only impact the display name and not the URL name.

8. On the **Quick Launch**, click **BuyerTasks** to redisplay the BuyerTasks default list view page.

9. On the **Settings** menu, click **List Settings** to display the Customize BuyerTasks page.

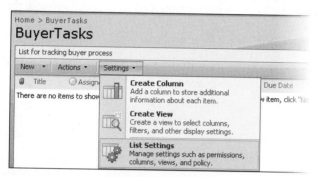

10. In the **General Settings** area, click **Title, description and navigation** to display the List Settings: BuyerTasks page.

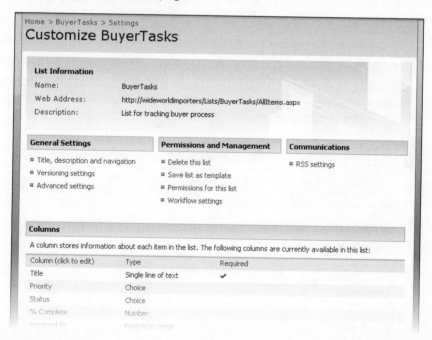

11. Replace the BuyerTasks text by typing Common Buyer Tasks (with spaces) into the **Name** textbox.

Save

Save

12. Click the **Save** button to save the change and display the Customize Common Buyer Tasks page.

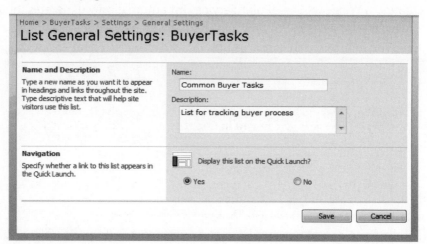

13. On the breadcrumb, click **Common Buyer Tasks** to display the Common Buyer Tasks default list view page.

The bold title near the top of this page and all other pages associated with this list now reflects the modified display name. However, you can see that the browser's address bar still reflects the initial name (internal name) given to this list. To change the name in the address bar requires Microsoft Office SharePoint Design or Microsoft Office SharePoint Server.

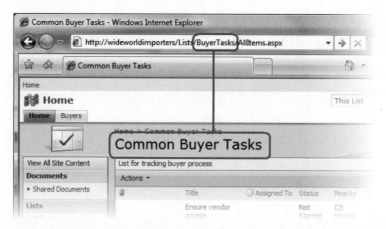

14. Go to the Home page of the site by clicking a link to it on the breadcrumb or top link bar. The Quick Launch shows the new display name.

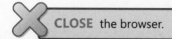
CLOSE the browser.

Adding, Editing, and Deleting List Items

Creating a Windows SharePoint Services list automatically generates the pages needed to view the list as a whole, view a list item, add a new list item, and edit an existing list item. The interface also provides options to delete a list item and subscribe to an *alert* for the list or list item, as well as other options, such as importing and exporting list items.

Subscribing to an alert is briefly covered later in this chapter, while importing and exporting of list items is covered in Chapter 10, "Working with Wikis and Blogs."

> **Tip** While some lists only have a single view when initially created, multiple *list views* are generated when a new Task list is created. The Common Buyer Tasks list was created using the Tasks list template that has the following five list views: All Tasks (default), Active Tasks, By Assigned To, By My Groups, Due Today, and My Tasks.

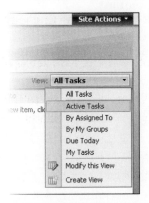

You can navigate to a list's default list view page by clicking the list's name in the Quick Launch or clicking the link at the top of any List View Web Part for that list.

In this exercise, you will add several Task list items for the buyers at Wide World Importers to use in their buying process, modify one of the list items, and delete another. Todd Rowe would also like to get their Public Workshops onto the calendar. Therefore, you will add one recurring event to the Events list.

> **OPEN** the SharePoint site where you would like to create the new list. The exercise will use the *http://wideworldimporters* site, but you can use whatever site you wish. If prompted, type your user name and password, and click OK.
>
> **BE SURE TO** verify that you have sufficient rights to create lists. If in doubt, see the Appendix on page 435.

1. On the **Quick Launch**, click **Common Buyer Tasks** (created in the last section) to display the Common Buyer Tasks default list view page.

2. On the toolbar, click **New** to display the Common Buyer Tasks: New Item page.

3. In the **Title** textbox, type **Create vendor SharePoint list**.

4. Leave the default values for the **Priority**, **Status**, and **% Complete** fields.

5. In the **Description** textbox, type **List for vendors to submit products offered this year**.

6. From the **Start Date** textbox, delete today's date.

7. Leave the **Due Date** textbox empty.

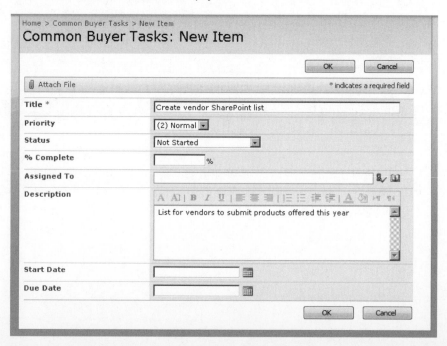

OK

8. Click the **OK** button to save the list item and redisplay the Common Buyer Tasks default list view page.

! NEW

The newly created list item shows in the body of the page. A small image with an exclamation mark and the word NEW displays to the right of the Title text, indicating that this list item was recently created.

9. Using Steps 2-8 as a guide, create list items using the values in the following table.

Title	Description
Ensure vendor access	Ensure vendor has access to add a list item for each product line offered.
Identify products to purchase	Identify which vendor products to purchase.
Generate purchase order	Use Microsoft Word mail merge to generate a purchase order from the filtered list.
Notify Receiving about purchase	Notify Receiving about the anticipated arrival of vendor products.

> **Tip** When you need to create several items for a list, creating one item at a time can become tedious. It is possible to create multiple list items using a Datasheet view. This option is covered briefly in the following section and in detail in Chapter 12, "Using Windows SharePoint Services with Excel 2007."

Todd suggests that generating the purchase should be changed to a high-priority task. You will now edit the "Generate purchase order" list item to implement this suggestion.

10. Hover over the **Generate purchase order** list item and click the down arrow to display the smart menu (called an edit control block or ECB).

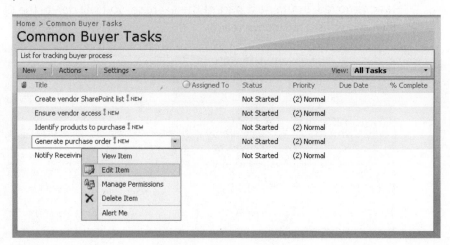

11. On the smart menu, click **Edit Item** to display the Common Buyer Tasks: Generate purchase order Edit page.

12. Change the **Priority** field from (2) Normal to **(1) High** and click **OK** to save the change and redisplay the default list view page.

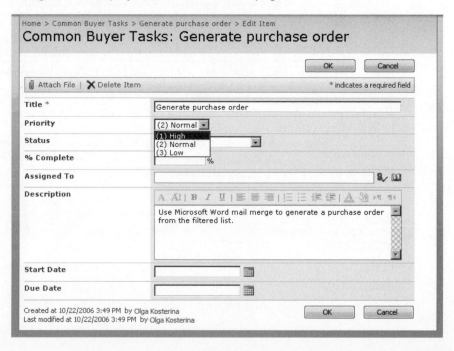

Todd also suggests that creating the vendor SharePoint list is only done when a new vendor is established rather than at each buying cycle. He therefore wants the task removed. In the next part of the exercise, you will delete the Create vendor SharePoint list task from the list.

13. Hover over the **Create vendor SharePoint list** list item and click the down arrow to display the smart menu. On the smart menu, click **Delete Item** to remove the list item. You will be prompted to confirm the deletion.

> **Tip** Once a list item is deleted, it is moved into the site's Recycle Bin. Working with the Recycle Bin will be covered in the next section.

14. Click **OK** to confirm the deletion and redisplay the default list view page.

To add a recurring Public Workshop to the Events list, you must first navigate to the Events list.

15. At the top of the **left navigation panel**, click **View All Site Content** to display the All Site Content page.

16. In the **Lists** area, click **Calendar** to display the Calendar list.

17. On the toolbar, click **New** to display the Calendar: New Item page.

18. In the **Title** textbox, type Public Workshop.

19. Leave the default value for the **Begin** date. Change the time to **5 PM**.

20. Leave the existing value in the **End** date (it can be left blank). Change the time to **6 PM**.

The monthly meeting will last one hour.

21. In the **Description** textbox, type Each month we will present another topic to the public.

22. Select the **Recurrence** check box named **Make this a repeating event**.

The page will post back and many user interface changes will occur when Recurrence is selected.

23. Select the **Monthly** option. Note that the pattern changes.

24. In the **Pattern** area, select **The first Tuesday of every month(s)** option by choosing options from the drop-down lists and populating the textbox. (Note that the first Tuesday may not fall until the next month.)

25. Leave the default values for all other fields.

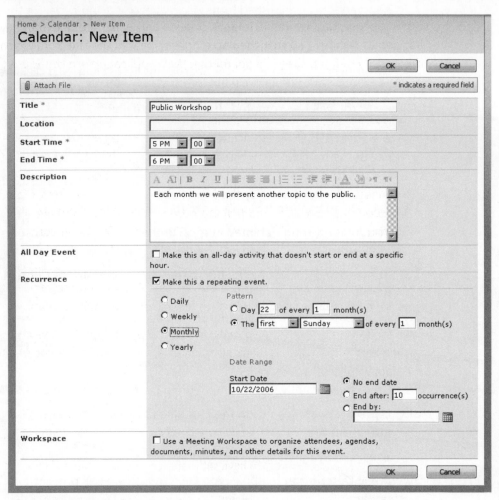

26. Click **OK** to save the list item and redisplay the Calendar default list view page.

CLOSE the browser.

Restoring a List Item from the Recycle Bin

When documents, list items, folders, or even entire lists are deleted, they are simply flagged as removed so that they no longer appear in the site from which they were deleted. By default, sites in a SharePoint Web application are configured to display the deleted item in the site's Recycle Bin for 30 days. If the user hasn't restored the deleted item in that time period, it is then permanently expunged from the database. If the user empties their Recycle Bin before the 30 days have elapsed, the deleted item is still available to a site collection administrator from the site collection's Recycle Bin. However, the total size of the deleted items must remain below a given percentage (50% by default) of the total size that a site is allowed to consume (the site quota). If a deleted item exceeds the configured size allowed by the SharePoint central administrator for sites in the Web application, the items deleted first are purged even if 30 days have not elapsed so as to make room for the newly deleted item. In this way, SharePoint central administrators can make disaster recovery plans based on the Recycle Bin's allowable total maximum size. Of course, SharePoint central administrators can set the number of days that Recycle Bins retain deleted items, ranging from the default 30 days to some other specific number of days to "never retain deleted items" to "never remove deleted items."

In the following exercise, Todd realizes that the Create Vendor SharePoint List task that he deleted in the previous exercise was a mistake. He visits the Recycle Bin and restores the data without anyone's help.

OPEN the SharePoint site where the list item was deleted in the last exercise. The exercise will use the *http://wideworldimporters* site, but you can use whatever site you wish. If prompted, type your user name and password, and click OK.

BE SURE TO verify that you have sufficient rights to create lists. If in doubt, see the Appendix on page 435.

1. In the left navigation area, click **Recycle Bin** to display the site Recycle Bin page.

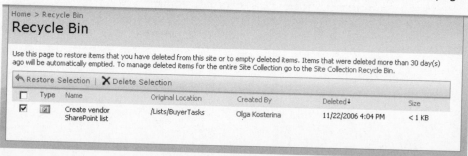

2. Select the check box to the left of the **Create vendor SharePoint list** list item.

3. From the toolbar, click **Restore Selection** to restore the list item.

4. Click **OK** to confirm the restoration and redisplay the Recycle Bin page.

5. Go to the Home page of the site by clicking a link to it on the breadcrumb or top link bar.

6. On the **Quick Launch**, click **Common Buyer Tasks** to display the Common Buyer Tasks default list view page.

   The Create vendor SharePoint list list item is once again visible in the list view.

 CLOSE the browser.

Using the Datasheet View

If you have installed Microsoft Office Access 2007, you can use an optional Datasheet view of the list that can be a tremendous productivity boost. Creating one item at a time requires several clicks and can become tedious. Datasheet view presents all of the list items in a list within a grid, which facilitates editing across the entire table. Drop-down lists, check boxes, and column edits are all still maintained. Therefore, using Datasheet View is a lot like editing a table in Office Access. You can use your cursor keys or your mouse to move from cell to cell to make changes to any row in the list. When you move off of a row, the changes are saved automatically. The last row in Datasheet view is used to add additional list items to the list. Change from Standard view to Datasheet view by choosing Edit In Datasheet from the Actions menu.

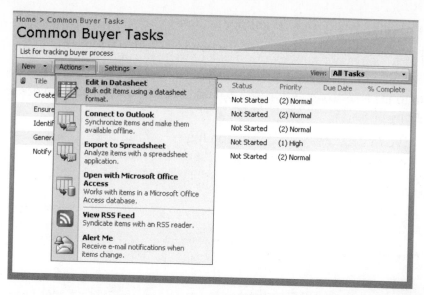

An entire task pane on the right edge of the Datasheet view enables powerful integration between Windows SharePoint Services, Office Excel, and Access.

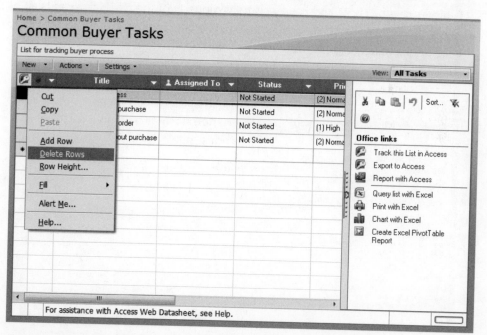

Datasheet view is covered in depth in Chapter 12, "Using Windows SharePoint Services with Excel 2007."

Attaching Files to List Items

Occasionally, you might want to attach one or more documents to a list item. By default, all lists in Windows SharePoint Services allow attachments. However, if every list item always has one and only one document, reconsider the use of a list and opt for a document library instead.

> **Tip** It is possible to disable attachments to list items. To do this, choose List Settings from the Settings menu, click Advanced settings, and finally select the Disabled option in the Attachments area.

Home > Common Buyer Tasks > Settings > Advanced Settings

List Advanced Settings: Common Buyer Tasks

Content Types

Specify whether to allow the management of content types on this list. Each content type will appear on the new button and can have a unique set of columns, workflows and other behaviors.

Allow management of content types?

○ Yes   ⦿ No

Item-level Permissions

Specify which items users can read and edit.

Note: Users with the Manage Lists permission can read and edit all items. Learn about managing permission settings.

Read access: Specify which items users can read

⦿ All items
○ Only their own

Edit access: Specify which items users can edit

⦿ All items
○ Only their own
○ None

E-Mail Notification

Send e-mail when ownership is assigned or when an item has been changed.

Send e-mail when ownership is assigned?

○ Yes   ⦿ No

Attachments

Specify whether users can attach files to items in this list.

Attachments to list items are:

⦿ Enabled
○ Disabled

Folders

Specify whether the "New Folder" command appears on the New menu. Changing this setting does not affect existing folders.

Display "New Folder" command on the New menu?

○ Yes   ⦿ No

Search

Specify whether this list should be visible in search results. Users who do not have permission to see these items will not see them in search results, no matter what this setting is.

Allow items from this list to appear in search results?

⦿ Yes   ○ No

[OK]   [Cancel]

In the following exercise, you will create a simple Microsoft Office Word document to simulate a purchase order and attach it to an existing list item in the Common Buyer Tasks list.

OPEN the SharePoint site where the Common Buyer Tasks list was created. The exercise will use the *http://wideworldimporters* site, but you can use whatever site you wish. If prompted, type your user name and password, and click OK.

BE SURE TO verify that you have sufficient rights to create lists. If in doubt, see the Appendix on page 435.

1. Open **Microsoft Word**.

2. In the new document, type Purchase Order.

3. On the **File** menu, select the **Save As** option. Save the document to the **Documents** folder on your hard drive as WideWorldPurchaseOrder.docx.

> **Tip** You can save documents directly to a document library by specifying the HTTP location in place of the hard drive, such as *http://wideworldimporters/Shared Documents/*. Only saved documents can be attached to list items as attachments.

4. Close **Microsoft Word**.

5. In the browser on the **Quick Launch**, click **Common Buyer Tasks**. The Common Buyer Tasks default list view page is displayed.

6. Hover over the **Generate purchase order** list item, click the down arrow to display the smart menu, and click **Edit Item** on the smart menu to display the Common Buyer Tasks: Generate purchase order Edit page.

7. On the toolbar, click **Attach File** to display the Add Attachments page.

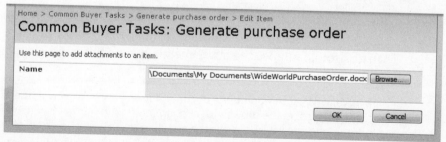

8. Click **Browse...** to display the Choose File dialog box.

> **Tip** When using the Choose File dialog box, you may need to navigate to Documents to find the WideWorldPurchaseOrder.docx that you created earlier in this chapter. Alternatively, in the Name textbox, you can type the location of the document to attach.

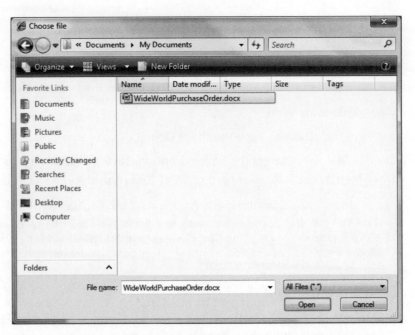

Open

9. Choose **WideWorldPurchaseOrder.docx**. Click the **Open** button, or double-click the document to open it.

Once chosen, the location of the selected document is displayed in the Name textbox on the Add Attachments page.

10. Click **OK** to attach the document to the list item.

The Common Buyer Tasks: Generate purchase order Edit page is displayed, and the attachment is listed at the bottom of the page. It also presents a Delete link that can be used to remove the attachment any time this page is displayed.

> **Important** At this point, the document is only associated with the list item in memory. Closing the browser or clicking any link to navigate anywhere else, including returning to the list, abandons the attachment. You must click OK to save the attachment's association with this task. Also, no warning that the attachment will be permanently lost is provided if the Delete link is clicked. The attachment's association to this task is simply removed, and file removal is made permanent when you click OK.

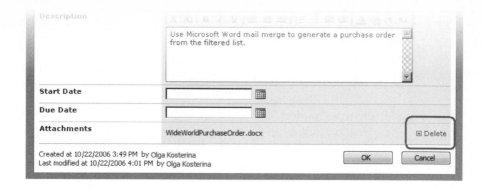

Attachment

11. Click **OK** to complete the process of attaching the document to the list item. The default list view page is displayed once again.

Each list item in the list that has one or more attachments will display with an attachment icon in the leftmost column.

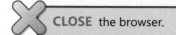

CLOSE the browser.

Adding, Editing, and Deleting List Columns

The list templates provided by Windows SharePoint Services are a great way to generate a list with very little effort. However, should you need to customize the templates, Windows SharePoint Services allows you to add, edit, and delete columns.

There are a plethora of column types available when you want to extend a list with an additional column. Once you name your new column, you need to select one of the column types displayed in the following table.

Column Type	Used to	Options	Edit Using
Single Line Of Text	Enter a word or freeform phrase up to 255 characters.	● Required ● Maximum Number Of Characters ● Default Value	Single-line textbox
Multiple Lines Of Text	Optionally enter freeform prose, including formatted text.	● Required ● Number Of Lines To Display (default 6) ● Type Of Text ● Allow Changes Or Append ● Default Value	Multiple-line text-box with toolbar to edit text
Choice	Select one or more from static list.	● Required ● List Of Choices ● Display Choices ● Allow 'Fill-In' Choices ● Default Value	Drop-down list, option buttons, or group of check boxes
Number	Enter a number.	● Required ● Minimum And Maximum Values ● Number Of Decimals ● Default Value ● Show As Percentage	Single-line textbox
Currency	Enter a monetary value.	● Required ● Minimum And Maximum Values ● Number Of Decimals ● Default Value ● Currency Format	Single-line textbox
Date And Time	Enter date and/or time-of-day.	● Required ● Date Format ● Default Value ● Calculated Value	Date textbox with popup calendar and drop-down lists for hours and minutes
Lookup	Select one list item from a list in the site.	● Required ● Get Information From ● In This Column	Dropdown list
Yes/No	Enter true or false.	● Default Value	Single check box

Person Or Group	Select one or more users.	● Required ● Allow Multiple Selections ● Allow Selection Of People/ Groups ● Choose From All Users/ SharePoint Group ● Show Field	Textbox with Check Names icon
Hyperlink Or Picture	Enter a link to a page or picture.	● Required ● Format URL As	Single-line textbox
Calculated	Calculate information from columns on this list, columns on another list, dates, or numbers using standard mathematical operators.	● Formula ● The Data Type Returned From This Formula Is	Single-line textbox

After a column has been added, it is possible to make changes to it. You can change the display name, but the internal name cannot easily be changed. Most other column options can be changed even after data has already been entered into the list. If changing an option will potentially result in the loss of information, Windows SharePoint Services w prompts you to confirm the change before proceeding.

> **Tip** You can also change a field from "not required" to "required" after data has already been entered into the list. The underlying data is not affected unless someone attempts to edit an existing record. The new required rule is enforced, and the list item cannot be saved without providing a value in the Required column.

Most columns in the list can be deleted. However, all lists have at least one column that cannot be removed. For instance, the Title column is used to show the smart menu, so it can be renamed but not deleted. Certain lists also prevent the deletion of columns so that the list can display properly or integrate with the Microsoft Office suite properly. For example, the Assigned To, Status, and Category columns of any list based on the Issues list template cannot be deleted, and all of the default columns in any list based on the Calendar list template cannot be deleted.

Other columns that are automatically created and populated for each list item cannot be changed: ID, Created, Created By, Modified, and Modified By. The ID column ensures that the list item is unique in the list. It contains a sequential number beginning with 1 and increments by 1 for each new list item. Windows SharePoint Services automatically captures when the list item was Created, who it was Created By, when it was last Modified, and who it was last Modified By. Initially, the Created and Modified columns are equal, as are the Created By and Modified By columns.

This Windows SharePoint Services release introduces a new kind of column that can be added to the list called a *site column*. These columns are typically defined once by an administrator and represent a common set of data used across multiple lists. They are stored at the site level in a *site column gallery*, but the collective site columns in all of the galleries in the current site's parentage can be used on a list or *content type* in this site. Thus, an administrator could define a site column in the top-level site for users in all sites in the site collection to use. Site columns provide two very valuable enhancements over regular list columns.

1. Administrators can change site columns at any time, and the change can be pushed down to all content types and lists that have used that site column within a given site collection.

2. Because site columns define a common set of data, lists that contain multiple content types can sort, filter, and group the disparate list items using their common site columns.

In the following exercise, you will enhance the Common Buyer Tasks list by adding a Sequence column, adding a Date Completed site column, editing the Priority column to include an additional option, and deleting the % Complete column. Finally, you will change the order of the columns on the New, Display, and Edit pages to show the Description column immediately after the Title column.

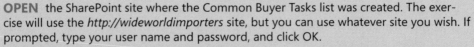

OPEN the SharePoint site where the Common Buyer Tasks list was created. The exercise will use the *http://wideworldimporters* site, but you can use whatever site you wish. If prompted, type your user name and password, and click OK.

BE SURE TO verify that you have sufficient rights to manage the list. If in doubt, see the Appendix on page 435.

1. On the **Quick Launch**, click **Common Buyer Tasks** to display the Common Buyer Tasks default list view page.

2. On the **Settings** menu, choose **List Settings** to display the Customize Common Buyer Tasks page.

3. Near the bottom of the **Columns** area, click **Create column** to display the Common Buyer Tasks: Add Column page.

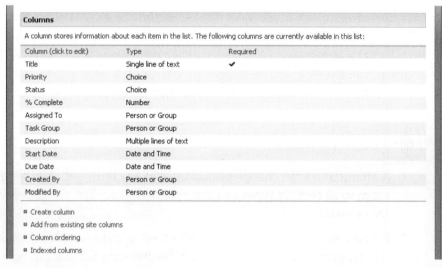

Columns

A column stores information about each item in the list. The following columns are currently available in this list:

Column (click to edit)	Type	Required
Title	Single line of text	✔
Priority	Choice	
Status	Choice	
% Complete	Number	
Assigned To	Person or Group	
Task Group	Person or Group	
Description	Multiple lines of text	
Start Date	Date and Time	
Due Date	Date and Time	
Created By	Person or Group	
Modified By	Person or Group	

▫ Create column
▫ Add from existing site columns
▫ Column ordering
▫ Indexed columns

4. In the **Column name** textbox, type Sequence.

5. On the list of column types, click **Number** (notice all of the other options described earlier in this section).

6. In the **Description** textbox, type Used to order tasks.

7. Leave the default values for the rest of the column's settings.

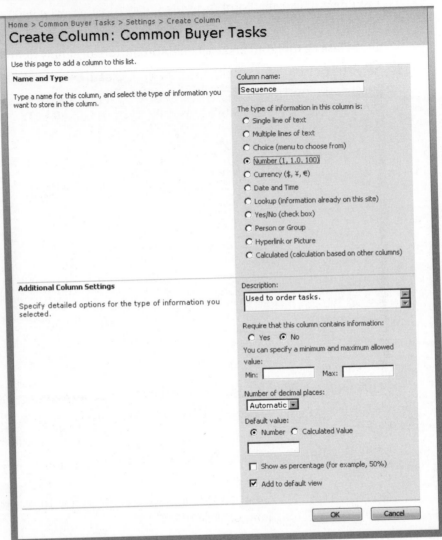

8. Click **OK** to finish adding the Sequence column to the list. The Customize Common Buyer Tasks page is displayed.

   Todd Rowe would like to see a column added to track the date that each task is completed.

9. In the **Columns** area, click **Add from existing site columns** to display the Add Columns from Site Columns: Common Buyer Tasks page.

10. On the **Select site columns from** drop-down list, click **Core Task and Issue Columns** to filter the list of Available site columns to just a handful of task-oriented site columns.

Add

11. Click **Date Completed** and click the **Add** button, or simply double-click **Date Completed** to move it to the Columns to add list.

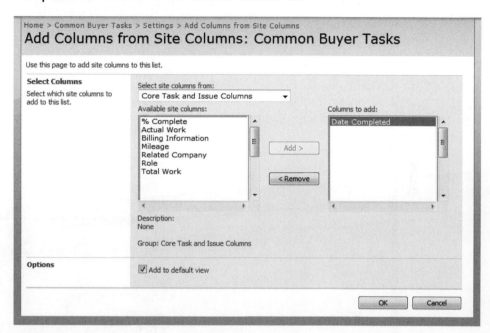

12. Click **OK** to add the column to the list and redisplay the Customize Common Buyer Tasks page.

Some tasks are commonly very low on the task list, and the buyers want to add an option in the Priority column to reflect this. They typically use Medium rather than Normal to rank their tasks and would like to allow people to type in priorities other than High, Medium, Low, or Very Low.

13. In the **Columns** area, click **Priority** to edit the settings for the existing column using the Common Buyer Tasks: Change Column page.

14. In the **Additional Column Settings** area, type (4) Very Low as the last line in the **Type each choice on a separate line** textbox to add an additional option to the drop-down list.

15. Edit the values in the **Type each choice on a separate line** textbox, replacing (2) Normal by typing with (2) Medium in the second line. This will alter the options that will be available in the Priority drop-down list during data entry.

> **Tip** Any list items that previously had the (2) Normal option chosen need to manual-
> ly change to the new option, (2) Medium. Also, when leaving the Choice textbox, the
> Default value changes to the first choice—(1) High in this case. If you want the Default
> value to remain the second option, you must type (2) Medium into the Default value
> textbox. For this exercise, you can use the default (1) High.

16. In the **Allow 'Fill-in' choices** column, click **Yes** to allow values that are not included
in the column's list of choices to be entered.

> **Tip** Optionally choose to display the choices using Radio buttons or Checkboxes.
> Choosing Checkboxes will allow multiple values to be selected.

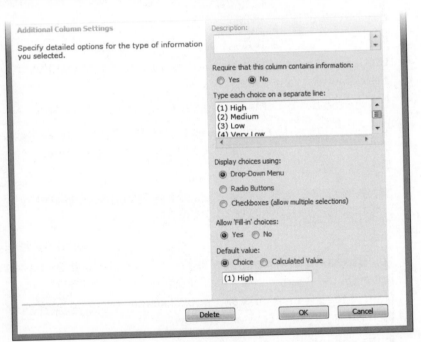

17. Click **OK** to save changes to the Priority column. The Customize Common Buyer
Tasks page is displayed.

The buyers don't plan on using the % Complete column, and it can therefore be
deleted. In the next part of the exercise, you will delete this column from the list.

18. In the **Columns** area, click **% Complete** to delete the existing column using the
Common Buyer Tasks: Change Column page.

19. At the bottom of the page, click **Delete** to initiate deletion of the % Complete column from the list and display the deletion confirmation dialog box.

20. Click **OK** to finish deleting the % Complete column. The Customize Common Buyer Tasks page is displayed.

When creating or editing list items, the buyers would like to show the Description column immediately after the Title column. In the next part of the exercise, you will change the order of the columns in the list.

21. In the **Columns** area, click **Column ordering** to display the Common Buyer Tasks: Change Field Order page.

22. To the right of the **Description** column on the **Position from Top** drop-down list, click **2** to change the sequence of the fields displayed on the New, Display, and Edit pages so that the Description column comes immediately after the Title column. The column is instantly moved to the second position.

23. Click **OK** to save the sequence change. The Customize Common Buyer Tasks page is displayed.

24. In the breadcrumb at the top of the page, click **Common Buyer Tasks** to return to the default list view page.

25. On the toolbar, click **New** to display the Common Buyer Tasks: New Item page.

26. On the modified **Common Buyer Tasks: New Item** page, verify that the order of the columns has changed and the Description column comes immediately after the Title column.

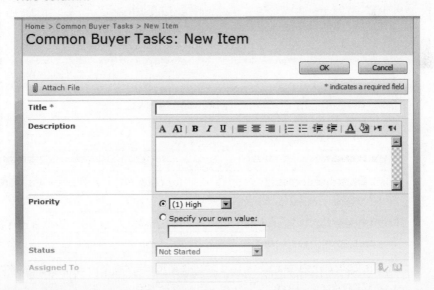

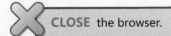

CLOSE the browser.

Sorting and Filtering a List

As the list grows, it eventually becomes difficult to see the entire list on a single page. To this end, Windows SharePoint Services provides built-in sorting and filtering capabilities. On any standard list view page, individual column headers can be used to alphabetically sort the entire list by first ascending and then descending order.

Filtering on the list view page works similarly to the way that an Excel AutoFilter works. Filtering is enabled on the top-right corner of every column, and a unique list of the values for each column is generated and presented as a drop-down list above that column. Filters are cumulative but temporal; the next time a list view is chosen, its settings, including filters, will be applied to the list regardless of what was previously chosen for a given column.

> **Tip** In Datasheet view, sorting and filtering are available from the drop-down arrow also located on the top-right corner of every column.

In this exercise, you will sort and filter the Common Buyer Tasks list.

OPEN the SharePoint site where the Common Buyer Tasks list was created. The exercise will use the *http://wideworldimporters* site, but you can use whatever site you wish. If prompted, type your user name and password, and click OK.

BE SURE TO verify that you have sufficient rights to view the list. If in doubt, see the Appendix on page 435.

1. On the **Quick Launch**, click **Common Buyer Tasks** to display the Common Buyer Tasks default list view page (in Standard view).

2. Edit each list item as indicated in the following table.

Title	Sequence
Ensure vendor access	1
Notify Receiving about purchase	2
Identify products to purchase	3
Generate purchase order	4

3. From the **All Items** list view, hover over the **Sequence** column and wait for about one second.

   The column is immediately underlined and a tool tip appears that reads Sort by Sequence.

↑
Ascending Sort

↓
Descending Sort

4. Click the **Sequence** column. A down arrow icon displays to the right of the column name, and the list items will display in ascending numerical order.

5. Click the **Sequence** column again. An up arrow icon displays to the right of the column name, and the list items will display in descending numerical order.

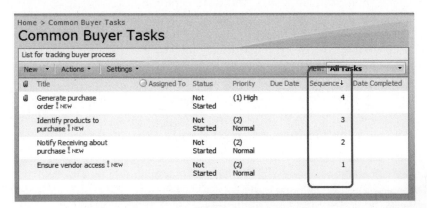

> **Tip** Clicking on another column will abandon the sort on the current column. You must use a list view to sort more than one column.

6. Next, hover over the **Priority** column and click the smart menu icon to show the sorting and filtering options for this column. Filtering is significantly improved since the previous release. The page does not reload, therefore saving time for you, the network, and the SharePoint servers. Only the unique values for this column are retrieved. The previous release was very inefficient; not only was all data for the page retrieved again, but the unique values for every visible column in the current list view were also retrieved even though you were only attempting to filter the Priority column.

Smart Menu

7. On the smart menu, click **(1) High** for **Priority**, and the page immediately redisplays the filtered list with only those list items that are set to a high priority.

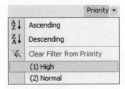

Filtered

The Filtered icon displays to the right of each column that has an applied AutoFilter.

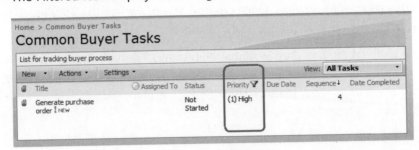

8. To return to a full list, from the list view drop-down list at the top right of the list, choose either one of the list views (including the current list view) or the **Clear Filter from Priority** option on the smart menu of the **Priority** column.

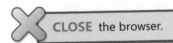 **CLOSE** the browser.

Adding and Modifying a List View

Sorting and filtering directly on the columns of a list view only result in a temporal view; that is, the sort and filter is not remembered the next time this list view is used. However, you can define new list views to provide a named definition of how the information in the list is displayed. List views define which columns to show in a list and in what sequence these columns are displayed. The sequence is defined from left to right. List views can also define the order of rows to be presented, which rows to reveal, and how the list items will be grouped, totaled, styled, and paginated. List views can be created using one of the starter views defined in the following table.

Icon	Starter View	Description
	Standard view	View data in a standard table; easily switch to Datasheet view.
	Datasheet view	View data in an editable spreadsheet; easily switch to Standard view.
	Calendar view	View data in a calendar format; easily switch from day view to week view to month view.
	Gantt view	View list items in a Gantt chart to see a graphical representation of how a team's tasks relate over time.
	Access view	Start Access to create forms and reports that are based on this list.
	An existing view	New to this release, base your new list view on an existing list view already defined on this list.

Every time a new list view is created for a specific list, it begins as either a starter view or a copy of an existing view. Once created, it is placed on the list view drop-down list with the other list views at the top right of the list.

Two kinds of list views are available: Public and Personal. Public list views can be seen by everyone viewing the list, whereas Personal list views can only be viewed by the creator. Only users with manage list permissions can create Public list views. Everyone can create their own Personal list views on a list.

In this exercise, you will create a Public list view called High Priority Tasks so that buyers can see only those tasks that are currently set to a (1) High priority, along with their current status. You will use the Datasheet view starter so that all list items can be easily updated simultaneously.

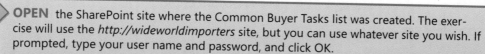

OPEN the SharePoint site where the Common Buyer Tasks list was created. The exercise will use the *http://wideworldimporters* site, but you can use whatever site you wish. If prompted, type your user name and password, and click OK.

BE SURE TO verify that you have sufficient rights to manage the list. If in doubt, see the Appendix on page 435.

1. On the Quick Launch, click **Common Buyer Tasks** to display the Common Buyer Tasks default list view page (in Standard view).

2. From the bottom of the list view drop-down list, click **Create View** to display the Create View: Common Buyer Tasks page. A Create View option in the Settings menu for the list also displays the same page.

3. At the bottom of the page, click **Create a new view** to display the Common Buyer Tasks: Create View page.

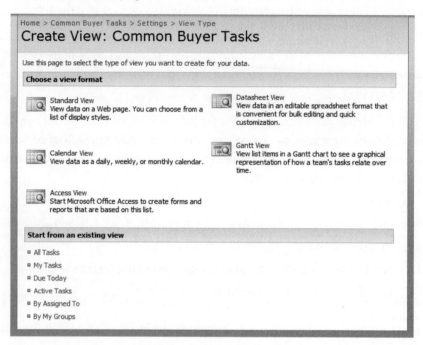

4. Click **Datasheet View** so that the new list view will have an editable spreadsheet as its default view and to display the Common Buyer Tasks: Create View page.

5. In the **View Name** textbox, type HighPriorityTasks.

6. Verify that **Create a Public View** is checked.

7. Uncheck all check boxes in the **Display** column except the **Title (linked to item with edit menu)** and **Status** columns.

The Title column is currently set to 20 and the Status column is currently set to 4. Therefore, the Title column will display before the Status column.

> **Tip** Three Title columns are listed in the Columns area. They all represent the same value, but each is displayed in a special way. The selected Title column, Title (linked to item with edit menu), not only shows the text value of the Title column, but also includes a smart menu that can be accessed by hovering over the text and clicking on the emergent drop-down list. Whereas the Title column named Title (linked to item)—currently unselected and at the bottom of the Columns area—simply presents the text value in the Title column as a link to the View page for each list item. Finally, the actual Title column, also currently unselected, is just like any other column: it only displays the text captured for the Title column for each list item.

8. On the **First sort by the column** drop-down list in the **Sort** area, click **Sequence** to order the list using the value in the Sequence column. It is OK to sort by a column that is not included in the view.

   By default, the list is in ascending order.

9. On the **Show the items when column** drop-down list in the **Filter** area, click **Priority** to set up the row filter.

10. For the **filter** condition, leave **is equal to** as the selected option.

11. In the textbox just below the filter condition, type (1) High.

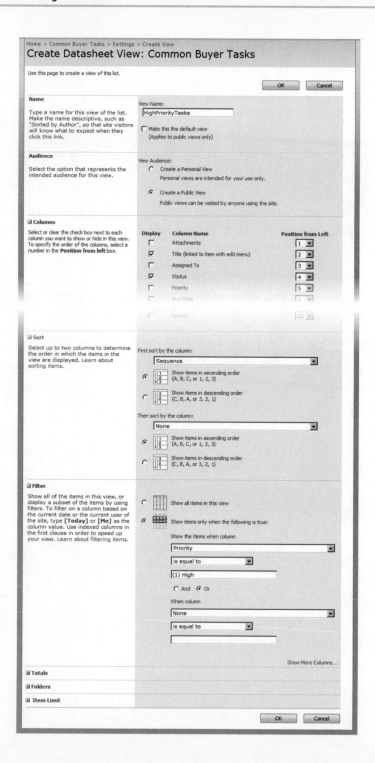

12. Click **OK** to save the list view and display the Common Buyer Tasks using the new view.

    Now that the list view is created, you can go back and change the display name.

13. In the list view drop-down at the top-right corner of the list, click **Modify this View** to display the Common Buyer Tasks: Edit View page.

14. In the **View Name** textbox, replace HighPriorityTasks with High Priority Tasks (with spaces) to change the name that is displayed at the left of the list view page.

    Notice that the name of the page shown in the address bar of the browser can optionally be edited, too.

15. Click **OK** to save the change and redisplay the Common Buyer Tasks list.

16. On the breadcrumb at the top of the page, click **Common Buyer Tasks** to return to the default list view page for the list.

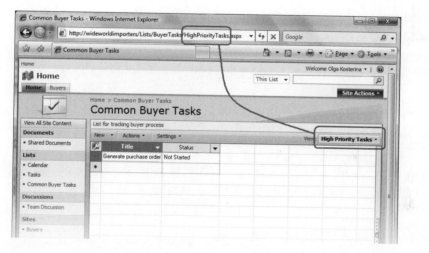

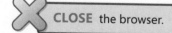
CLOSE the browser.

Setting Up Alerts

Windows SharePoint Services includes a handy feature that sends an e-mail notification whenever changes are made to content in a site, including changes made to list items in a list. The setup for an e-mail notification is called an alert. No alerts are set up automatically, so you must sign up for the alerts that you want.

Alerts are quite easy to set up. Every list in a Windows SharePoint Services site displays an Alert Me option on the Actions menu. Clicking this option allows you to subscribe to a list-level alert. You also find a similar Alert Me option on the smart menu for each list item in every list and on the toolbar when viewing any list item. As you might suspect, this option allows you to subscribe to a list item–level alert.

Alerts specify to whom the alert will be sent and the kind of changes and frequency for which the alert will be sent. By default, the alert is sent to the e-mail address of the user setting up the alert. If no e-mail address has been established for the authenticated user, an e-mail prompt is generated in the Send Alerts To area. Once provided, the address will be remembered for subsequent subscriptions.

When setting up alerts, you have a choice as to the type of change about which you want an alert to be initiated. List-level alerts allow subscriptions for All Changes To Any List Item Changes or, alternatively, for New Items Are Added Only, Existing Items Are Modified Only, or Items Are Deleted Only. If you wish to see added and changed items but not deleted items, you need to set up two alerts. List item–level alerts, on the other hand, are only fired when that item changes because you can only set up this alert once the list item already exists, and a deletion is considered a change to the list item.

> **Tip** Document libraries support the additional ability to set up alerts when Web discussion updates occur. Document libraries are discussed in Chapters 5 and 6.

You must specify a filter concerning when to send alerts; the default is when anything in a list changes. Different lists have different filters. The Task list that you are working with has the following filters.

- Anything Changes,
- A Task Is Assigned To Me,
- A Task Becomes Complete,
- A High Priority Task Changes,
- Someone Else Changes A Task Assigned To Me,
- Someone Else Changes A Task,
- Someone Else Changes A Task Created By Me,
- Someone Else Changes A Task Last Modified By Me,
- Someone Changes An Item That Appears In The Following View (choose a list view).

You must also specify the alert frequency. Three choices exist for any type of alert.

1. Send e-mail immediately
2. Send a daily summary
3. Send a weekly summary

Choosing to receive an alert immediately actually queues the notice to be sent as soon as the next job runs once the alert is triggered. By default, the alert job runs every five minutes but could be configured by your administrator to wait as long as 59 minutes. The daily and weekly summaries store all changes made to the list or list item and send a summary at the end of the period chosen. By default, daily summary alerts are generated at midnight each night, and weekly summary alerts are generated at midnight every Sunday night.

> **Tip** Administrators of the Windows SharePoint Services environment can establish quotas for the total number of alerts to which any user can subscribe. By default, this quota is set to 50. This number can be changed or even set to unlimited. Alerts can also be turned off entirely.

You can view and manage all of the alerts that you previously set up by using the View My Existing Alerts On This Site link at the top of the New Link page. From here, you can use the toolbar to Add Alert to any list in the site or Delete Selected Alerts.

> **Important** Alerts must be manually deleted when users are removed from a site or their alerts will be orphaned. Also, when users set up alerts for themselves, they will continue to receive them even when they are removed from access to the list. It is important to delete these alerts to prevent unauthorized users from accessing site and user information.

Using Really Simple Syndication Feeds

By default, Really Simple Syndication (RSS) 2.0 is automatically allowed and configured on all lists in all site collections for all Web applications in Windows SharePoint Services version 3. Chapter 3 describes how to configure RSS syndication from the Site Administration area of the Site Settings page. If RSS is not enabled for the Web application, all RSS links described in the following exercise will not be displayed.

In the following exercise, you will view the contents of the Buyer's list and learn how to modify the RSS settings in a list.

OPEN the SharePoint site where the Common Buyer Tasks list was created. The exercise will use the *http://wideworldimporters* site, but you can use whatever site you wish. If prompted, type your user name and password, and click OK.

BE SURE TO verify that you have sufficient rights to manage the list. If in doubt, see the Appendix on page 435.

1. On the **Quick Launch** , click **Common Buyer Tasks** to display the default list view page of the Common Buyer Tasks list. If you didn't create the Common Buyer Tasks list, you can use any list to complete this exercise.

2. On the **Settings** menu, choose **List Settings**.

3. From the **Communications** area, click **RSS settings** to display the Modify List RSS Settings page.

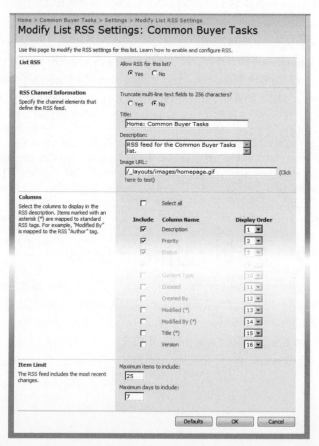

By default, Allow RSS for this list? is set to Yes in the List RSS area. Even though this example recommends no changes to the default settings, we will explain all of the available options.

4. In the **RSS Channel Information** area, leave the default values for the four fields.

The Truncate multi-line text fields to 256 characters? is set to No, so all text is sent to everyone that subscribes to the feed. If you anticipate a great deal of data in the feed but the first few sentences are all that most people need to read, you want to change this option to Yes. Anyone viewing the feed item has the option to browse the entire contents. Title, Description, and Image URL are used as part of the feed details.

Check boxes selected in the Columns area indicate that the contents of those fields are also included in the feed details. Select or deselect columns at will. This example uses the default columns.

The Item Limit area helps control the cost to your site's bandwidth and your farm's network when thousands of people subscribe to hundreds of lists and come to the site every hour (60 minutes is the default Time To Live set in the RSS settings on the Site Settings page for each site) to check for updates. The Maximum items to include field indicates how many list items to include in the feed, and the Maximum days to include field indicates how long a list item should be included. This example includes up to 25 items for any items modified in the last week (7 days). The default value for Maximum items to include is 25, and the default value for Maximum days to include is 7.

As you might suspect, clicking the Defaults button resets the page to the values provided when the list was first established.

5. Click **OK** to save any changes made to these values. Click **Cancel** to abandon any changes and return to the List Settings page.

6. Using the breadcrumb at the top of the page , return to the default list view of the list.

7. On the **Actions** menu, choose **View RSS Feed** to display the feed page.

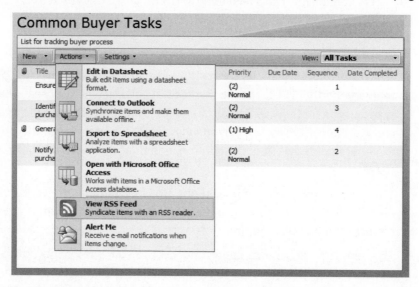

The resulting page isn't much to look at or interact with, but viewing it in the browser is not the intent of the page. The Web address in the browser can be used in your aggregator to view the contents of this list offline, or you can click the Subscribe to this feed link.

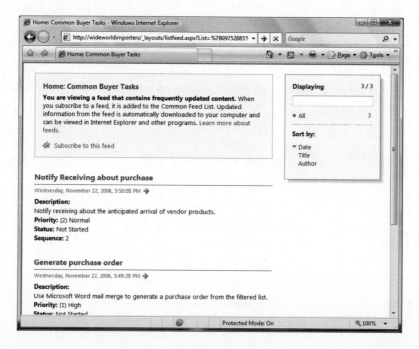

> **Tip** Consuming an RSS feed using Microsoft Office Outlook 2007 is covered in Chapter 11. It is also possible to aggregate feeds using Internet Explorer 7.

In the top-right corner of the browser page, you can search the feed by simply typing your search terms into the textbox. The feed will automatically refresh whenever you stop typing for more than one second.

Clicking All will return to showing all items in the feed and not all items in the list.

It is also possible to sort the feed by clicking on the Date, Title, or Author fields. To reverse the sort from ascending to descending, click the field a second time.

8. At the top of the feed page, click the **Home: Common Buyer Tasks** link to return to the list.

 CLOSE the browser.

Sending an E-Mail to a SharePoint List

Windows SharePoint Services allows list managers to assign an e-mail address to some of the out-of-the-box lists that can be created from the Create page. Once configured, you can send an e-mail to the list. At first blush, e-mailing a Windows SharePoint Services list seems like an odd thing to do; yet, consider the following ways that this capability could be used.

- You are on an airplane working with an Office Word document. When you are finished, you e-mail the document to a specific document library. This e-mail sits in your outbox until the next time you connect to the Internet, at which time it is automatically sent to the document library. When Windows SharePoint Services receives the document, it is inserted into the document library for you.

- An e-mail distribution group is set up that includes all of the members of your team. The e-mail address of a discussion board is also included in the distribution group. Every message sent to the group is also inserted into the list. When team members visit the Windows SharePoint Services site that contains the list, they see the entire conversation that took place via email. They can even use the list to reply to the messages posted to the list.

Enabling a discussion board for e-mail is covered in Chapter 9, "Working with Surveys and Discussion Boards."

The following table differentiates between those lists that can and cannot be e-mail enabled in Windows SharePoint Services (lists are in alphabetical order).

E-mail-Enabled Lists	Lists That Are Not E-mail Enabled	
Announcements	Agenda	Project Tasks
Blog Posts	Contacts	Survey
Calendar	Custom List	Tasks
Discussion Board	Decisions	Text Box
Document Library	Issue Tracking	Things To Bring
Form Library	Links	Wiki Page Library
Picture Library	Objectives	

Before this e-mail feature can be used, the Windows SharePoint Services farm administrator must configure the Web application for outgoing e-mail. This can be done from the Incoming E-Mail Settings link in the Topology And Services area on the Operations tab in SharePoint 3.0 Central Administration. The screen looks like the following image.

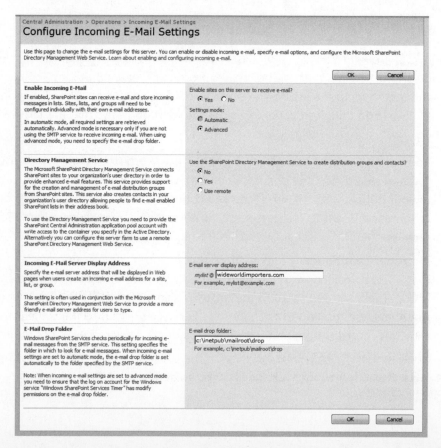

In the following exercise, you will create a new e-mail-enabled picture library so that customers can e-mail pictures to you of potential product offerings. You will subsequently review the generated incoming e-mail settings. You will also update the incoming e-mail settings of an existing Announcements list so that people can e-mail general corporate announcements to the list. Once configured, you will e-mail each of these lists and review the results.

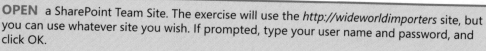

OPEN a SharePoint Team Site. The exercise will use the *http://wideworldimporters* site, but you can use whatever site you wish. If prompted, type your user name and password, and click OK.

BE SURE TO verify that you have sufficient rights to browse the site and create lists. If in doubt, see the Appendix on page 435.

1. On the **Site Actions** menu at the top right of the page, choose **Create** to display the list templates on the Create page.

2. In the **Tracking** group, click **Picture Library** to display the New List page.

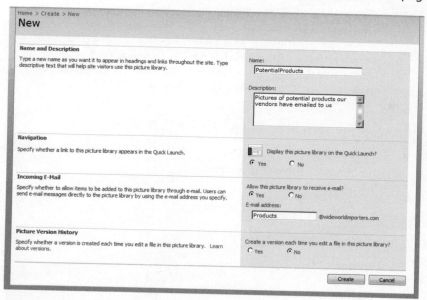

3. In the **Name** textbox, type PotentialProducts to establish a display name for the new list.

Because there is no textbox to provide the URL name, this textbox also supplies the value that Windows SharePoint Services uses for the internal names.

4. In the **Description** textbox, type the description Pictures of potential products our vendors have emailed to us to help others understand the purpose for the new list.

5. Check that the option indicating that you want to **Display this picture library on the Quick Launch** is selected. This is a default setting.

6. The **Allow this picture library to receive e-mail** option is initially set to No. Change this setting to **Yes**. If this option is not available, a SharePoint administrator in SharePoint 3.0 Central Administration has either not configured SharePoint for incoming e-mail or has disabled incoming e-mail for your lists.

7. Enter an **E-mail address**, such as Products@wideworldimporters.com.

   Of course, you only provide the part of the e-mail address that precedes the "at" sign (@). Take note of the entire e-mail address displayed on the screen, and use the address you see instead of Products@wideworldimporters.com for the rest of this exercise.

   > **Important** If the incoming e-mail settings for your Windows SharePoint Services farm have been configured to use the SharePoint Directory Management Service, any e-mail address you choose will be created for you in a designated Active Directory location. However, if the farm has not been configured to use the SharePoint Directory Management Service, an e-mail account for every e-mail address you choose must be established before messages sent to that account arrive at the list.

8. Leave the **Version** setting with the default value.

9. Click **Create** to complete the list creation. The PotentialProducts default list view page (AllItems.aspx) is displayed.

10. On the **Settings** menu, choose **Picture Library Settings** to see the auto-configured settings for this new list.

11. From the **Communications** area, click **Incoming e-mail settings**. Once again, if this option is not available, a SharePoint administrator needs to configure the farm for incoming e-mail in SharePoint 3.0 Central Administration.

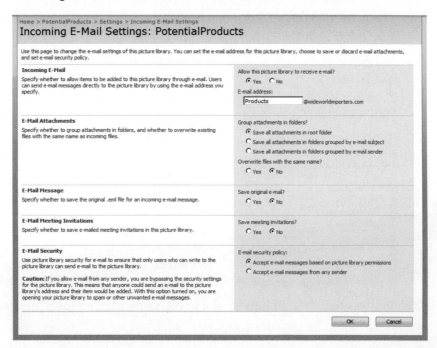

The options here are fairly easy to understand. For this exercise, you do not need to change any of them. Simply notice that the picture library has been configured to receive e-mail by using the e-mail address that you suggested. All e-mail attachments sent to the picture library are saved into the root of the library, but do not overwrite any files. If a duplicate is sent, the file is suffixed with an incremental counter (just like the file system). It does not save the original e-mail attachment. However, if this option is set to Yes, the e-mail is simply saved as a document attachment to the list item. If someone sends a meeting invitation to this list, it is ignored. Finally, only people with the ability to create new items in the list are allowed to send e-mail to the list; all other e-mail is ignored.

12. Click **Cancel** to continue.

13. From the **Lists** area of the **Quick Launch**, click **Announcements** to navigate to the Announcements list.

14. On the **Settings** menu, choose **Picture Library Settings**.

15. From the **Communications** area, click **Incoming e-mail settings** to alter the settings to allow e-mail announcements to be sent to this list.

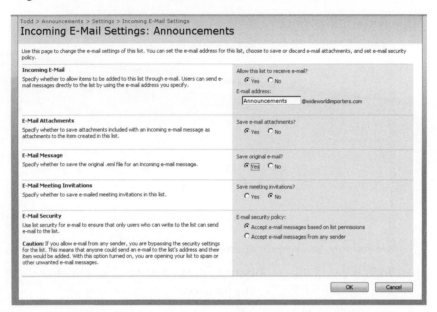

16. Set the **Allow this picture library to receive e-mail** to **Yes**.

17. Enter an **E-mail address**, such as Announcements@wideworldimporters.com.

With the exception of attachments, the remainder of the settings are the same for a list as they are for a picture library. E-mail attachments sent to a library actually become list items. Therefore, you can choose what folder to put them into and whether to overwrite existing documents. E-mail attachments sent to a list simply become list item attachments, so they can either be attached or unattached to the list item—hence the diminished options for e-mail attachments on a list.

18. Change **Save original e-mail** to **Yes** and leave all other options set to their default values.

19. Click **OK** to save the changes.

20. Open **Outlook 2007** and send one e-mail with a picture attachment to the **Products** e-mail setup and a second e-mail with an optional attachment to the **Announcements** e-mail setup mentioned earlier in this exercise.

21. Browse back to the **PotentialProducts** list to see that the picture attached to the list has been added to the picture library.

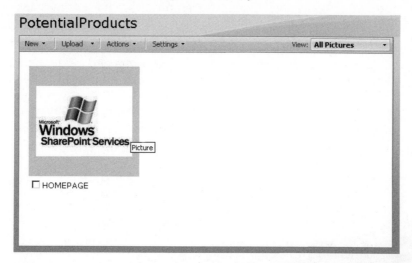

22. Browse back to the **Announcements** list to see that the second e-mail that was sent has been added to the list as well.

23. Open the announcement to see that the subject, body, and original message have all been captured on the announcement.

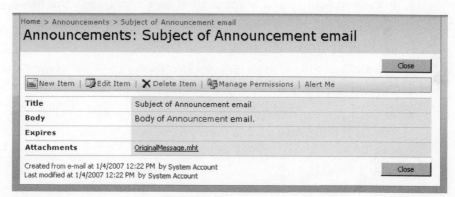

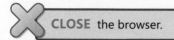 **CLOSE** the browser.

Deleting a List

It is important to know how to get rid of an obsolescent list or perhaps one created in error. Unlike the previous release, deleting a list only marks it as being removed. It doesn't permanently remove the list from the database, and all the list items contained within it, even though no longer visible, are safely retained inside the list in the site's Recycle Bin.

That said, the buyers at Wide World Importers are happy with their new Common Buyer Tasks task list and no longer need the Tasks task list that was created when the site was originally provisioned. In this exercise, you will delete the surplus list.

OPEN the SharePoint site where the Common Buyer Tasks list was created. The exercise will use the *http://wideworldimporters* site, but you can use whatever site you wish. If prompted, type your user name and password, and click OK.

BE SURE TO verify that you have sufficient rights to delete the list. If in doubt, see the Appendix on page 435.

1. On the **Quick Launch**, click **Tasks** to display the Tasks default list view page.

2. On the **Settings** menu, choose **List Settings** to display the Customize Tasks page.

3. In the **Permissions and Management** area, click **Delete this list**. The Are you sure you want to send this list to the site Recycle Bin? dialog box is displayed.

4. Click **OK** to confirm the deletion.

   The All Site Content page is displayed. The list is longer shown on the All Site Content page or the Quick Launch.

5. At the bottom of the **Quick Launch**, click the **Recycle Bin** link. The deleted list is shown. You can now restore the list if you wish to do so.

CLOSE the browser.

Key Points

- Lists are like editable, Web-based tables.

- List templates can be used to generate a new list with a static set of default columns. There are 21 built-in, default list templates: Agenda, Announcements, Calendar, Contacts, Custom List, Custom List in Datasheet View, Decisions, Discussion Board, Document Library, Form Library, Import Spreadsheet, Issue Tracking, Links, Objectives, Picture Library, Project Tasks, Survey, Tasks, Text Box, Things To Bring, and Wiki Page Library.

- Create lists in Windows SharePoint Services by using descriptive, easy to remember, consistent names.

- One or more documents can optionally be attached to a list item.

- Windows SharePoint Services allows you to add, edit, and delete the columns in any list.

- List views define how list items in the list are displayed. Lists can be sorted and filtered manually or through the use of named list views.

- Public list views can be viewed by anyone, whereas Personal list views can only be viewed by their creator.

- Some lists and libraries can be configured to receive e-mail.

- Deleting a list moves it and all of its list items to the site Recycle Bin.

Chapter at a Glance

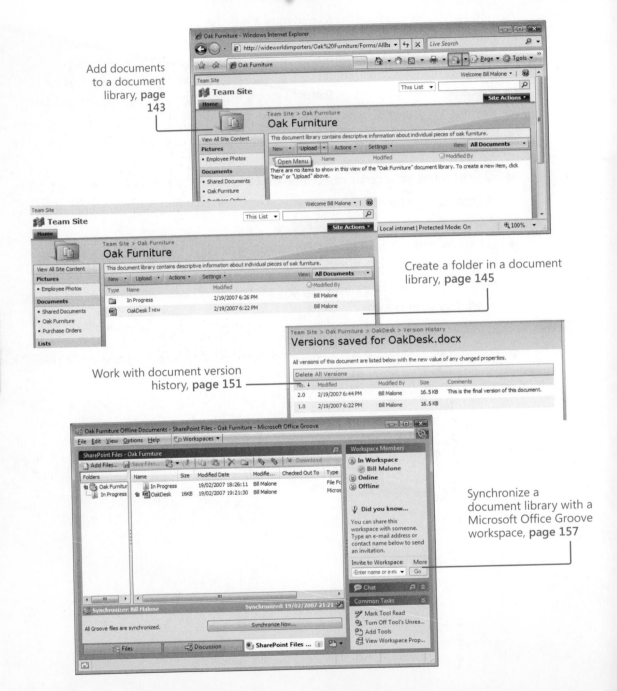

Add documents to a document library, **page 143**

Create a folder in a document library, **page 145**

Work with document version history, **page 151**

Synchronize a document library with a Microsoft Office Groove workspace, **page 157**

5 Creating and Managing Libraries

In this chapter, you will learn to:

✔ Create libraries.

✔ Add documents.

✔ Add pictures.

✔ Create a new folder in a library.

✔ Check documents in and out from the document library.

✔ Check documents in and out from the 2007 Microsoft Office suites.

✔ Work with version history.

✔ Create and configure a workflow.

✔ Use a workflow.

✔ Work with offline documents.

✔ Synchronize documents with a Microsoft Office Groove workspace.

✔ Delete and restore documents.

✔ Use alerts.

One of the most compelling features that Microsoft Windows SharePoint Services provides is libraries. Libraries are a great place to store documents or forms. In the business world, being able to work with documents quickly and effectively is of paramount importance. In previous chapters, you learned that lists are an effective way to work with all types of data; libraries function similarly for documents and forms, such as Microsoft Office Word documents. Using SharePoint document libraries, you can filter and group documents as well as view metadata for documents stored in the library.

In this and the following chapter, you will learn how to work with documents in Windows SharePoint Services. This chapter focuses on creating libraries, adding documents and pictures to them, and working with documents in document libraries. In Chapter 6, "Working with Library Settings," we will focus on modifying and configuring document libraries. You will use the libraries and views created in this chapter's exercises to complete the exercises in Chapter 6.

> **Important** Before you can use the practice sites provided for this chapter, you need to install them from the book's companion CD to their default locations. See "Using the Book's CD" on page xix for more information.

> **Important** Remember to use your SharePoint site location in place of *http://wideworldimporters* in the following exercises.

Creating Libraries

You can use **document libraries** to store your documents on a SharePoint site rather than on your local computer's hard drive so that other employees can find and work with them more easily. Libraries are used to store files whereas lists are used to store other types of content. Like lists, libraries contain metadata that allow you to filter, sort, and group items in the libraries easily.

Creating Document Libraries

When you create a new SharePoint site, a generic document library called Shared Documents is created for you. Because this library lacks a descriptive name, you should create new libraries for a particular business category or subject instead. In the examples used in this book, Bill Malone of Wide World Importers could create a document library for documents describing different types of art that the company carries or one for company newsletters. You want to make sure that the name of a document library is descriptive and that each library has a specific topic to make it easier to find documents. Storing all documents together in the Shared Documents—or any—document library defeats the purpose of using SharePoint sites to make information easier to locate.

In the following exercise, you will open your SharePoint site and create a new document library called Oak Furniture.

OPEN the SharePoint site in which you'd like to create a document library. If prompted, type your user name and password, and then click OK.

BE SURE TO verify that you have sufficient rights to create a document library. If in doubt, see the Appendix on page 435.

1. On the **Site Actions** menu, click **Create**. The Create Page page appears.

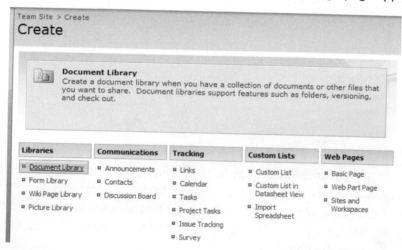

2. In the **Libraries** column, click **Document Library**. The New Document Library page is displayed.

3. In the **Name** box, type the name that you want to give the document library, for example Oak Furniture.

4. In the **Description** box, type the description of the document library, for example, This document library contains descriptive information about individual pieces of oak furniture.

5. In the **Document Version History** area, under **Create a version each time you edit a file in this document library?**, select the **Yes** option.

Leave all other areas of the page at their default settings. You have entered all of the necessary information to create a document library.

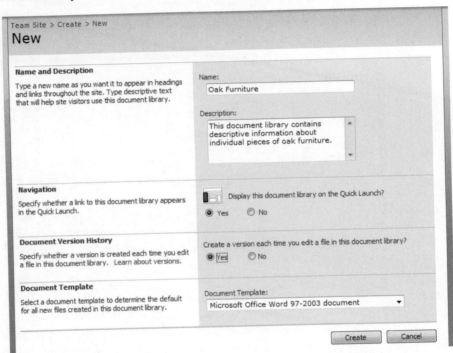

6. Click the **Create** button.

The new Oak Furniture document library appears.

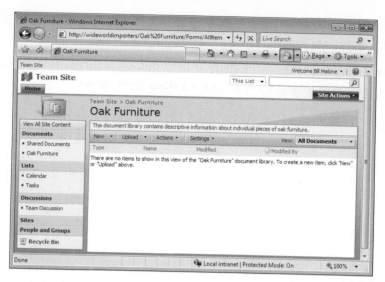

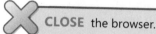 **CLOSE** the browser.

Creating Form Libraries

Form libraries function similarly to document libraries, but they store specific types of documents— forms—and have enhanced integration with Microsoft Office InfoPath, such as allowing you to create form libraries from Office InfoPath. Chapter 14, "Using Windows SharePoint Services with InfoPath 2007," discusses in detail how Windows SharePoint Services and InfoPath work together.

Forms are a more structured type of information. They contain a set of fields that are filled out in a uniform manner. Form libraries are excellent repositories for structured documents, such as Purchase Orders or Vacation Requests. To obtain the full benefit of form libraries, you must use InfoPath for designing and filling out forms.

The following exercise walks you through creating a new form library by using Windows SharePoint Services. In this exercise, you will open the SharePoint site and create a new form library called Purchase Orders. You will then associate a Purchase Order form template with that library so that, when someone fills out the form, they are presented with the standard Purchase Order form.

Note that this is a long series of steps to perform, so please keep in mind that you will be accomplishing the following tasks.

● Creating a new form library

● Associating a new form with the form library

● Setting this form as the primary form that is invoked when the New Form command is invoked

OPEN the SharePoint site in which you'd like to create a form library. If prompted, type your user name and password, and then click OK.

BE SURE TO have Microsoft Office InfoPath 2007 installed.

BE SURE TO verify that you have sufficient rights to create a form library. If in doubt, see the Appendix on page 435.

1. From the **Site Actions** menu, click **Create**. The Create Page page appears.

2. In the **Libraries** column, click **Form Library**. The New Form Library page appears.

3. In the **Name** box, type Purchase Orders.

4. In the **Description** box, type Contains purchase orders

   You have entered all of the necessary information to create a form library.

5. Click **Create**.

   The form library is created, and you are taken to the new Purchase Orders form library. At this point, if you click New Document you will be presented with a blank form. You still need to associate a necessary form template with the newly created library. To associate a form template with a form library, it is necessary to create a new content type as the default selection when the New button is created.

6. From the **Site Actions** menu, click **Site Settings**.

7. Under **Galleries**, click the **Site Content Types** link. The Site Content Types Gallery appears.

8. Click **Create**.

9. In the **Name** input box, type Purchase Orders.

10. On the **Select Parent Content Type From:** drop-down list, click **Document Content Types**.

11. On the **Parent Content Type:** drop-down list, click **Form**. Leave the rest of the page at the default settings.

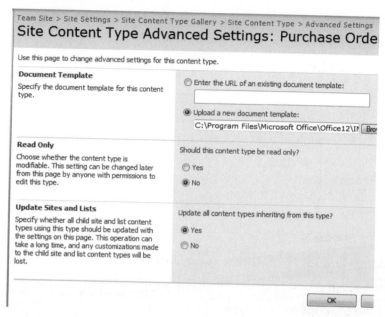

12. Click **OK**. The **Site Content Types: Purchase Orders** page appears.

13. Click the **Advanced Settings** link.

14. Select the **Upload a New Document Template** option.

15. Navigate to C:\Program Files\Microsoft Office\Office12\INFFORMS\1033 folder and select purchord.xsn template file. Note: Number 1033 in the path is a Locale ID (LCID) for English language. In this case, LCID is used as a folder name. If your Office installation is for language other than English , then the numbered folder name will be a LCID for the language used. For example, LCID for French is 1036, and LCID for Russian is 1049.

16. Click Open.

17. Click **OK**. You are taken to the **Site Content Type: Purchase Orders** page.

18. On the breadcrumb, click the **Team Site** link.

19. In the **Quick Launch** , click the **Purchase Orders** form library link.

20. From the **Settings** link, click **Form Library Settings**. The Customize Purchase Orders page will appear.

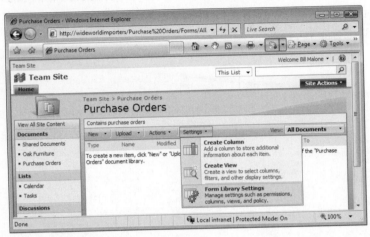

21. Click the **Advanced Settings** link. The Form Library Advanced Settings: Purchase Order page appears.

22. In the **Content Types** area, under **Allow Management of Content Types?**, select the **Yes** option.

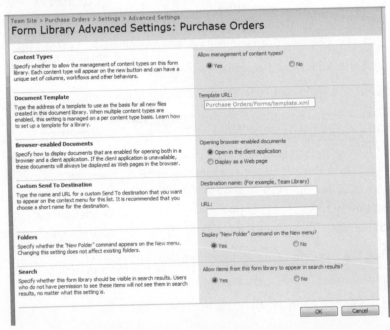

23. Leave the rest of the page at the default settings, and then click **OK**.

24. On the **Customize Purchase Orders** page, scroll down until you see the **Content Types** area. One content type, called Form, is associated with this form library.

25. Click the **Add From Existing Content Types** link. The Add Content Types: Purchase Order page appears.

26. From the **Available Site Content Types** list, click the **Purchase Order** content type.

27. Click the **Add** button, and then click **OK**.

28. Click the **Change New Button Order and Default Content Type** link.

29. On the **Position from Top** drop-down list, ensure that the **Purchase Order** content type is assigned the number one **(1)** and click **OK**.

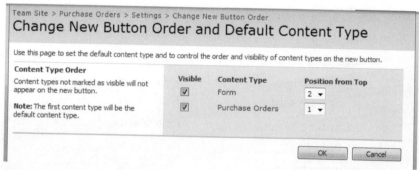

30. On the breadcrumb, click the **Purchase Orders** link and then click the **New** button.

This action invokes Office InfoPath 2007 (if it is installed on your computer), and the default Purchase Order form appears.

CLOSE the browser and InfoPath 2007.

Creating Picture Libraries

Picture libraries work in the same way as document libraries except that they are optimized for storing the picture file type. The picture library provides special views for looking at all of the pictures in the library as a slideshow. It also provides enhanced features for editing and downloading pictures by integrating with Microsoft Office Picture Manager.

In this exercise, you will open the SharePoint site and create a picture library for storing photographs of each employee.

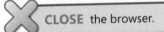

OPEN the SharePoint site in which you'd like to create a picture library. If prompted, type your user name and password, and then click OK.

BE SURE TO verify that you have sufficient rights to create a picture library. If in doubt, see the Appendix on page 435.

1. From the **Site Actions** menu, click **Create**. The Create Page page appears.

2. In the **Libraries** area, click **Picture Library**. The New Picture Library page appears.

3. In the **Name** box, type Employee Photos.

4. In the **Description** box, type Contains photographs of each employee.

   You have entered all of the necessary information to create a picture library.

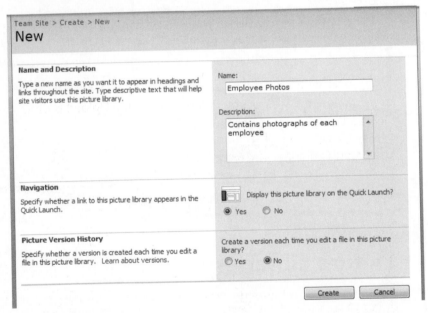

5. Click **Create**.

   The picture library is created, and you are taken to the Employee Photos picture library.

CLOSE the browser.

Adding Documents

After a library has been created, you can populate it with documents. Once documents are placed in the library, you can search for and filter them to make it easier to find what you are looking for, as well as collaborate with others to help develop the final version of the document. Document libraries give you the ability to keep track of new versions of a document as it is modified and revert to older versions if necessary. These topics will be covered in the next chapter. First, you need to ensure that your documents are uploaded and available in the SharePoint library.

In the following exercise, you will make two new furniture descriptions available to employees by uploading them to the Oak Furniture library.

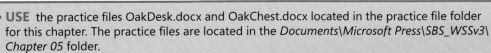

USE the practice files OakDesk.docx and OakChest.docx located in the practice file folder for this chapter. The practice files are located in the *Documents\Microsoft Press\SBS_WSSv3\ Chapter 05* folder.

OPEN the SharePoint site to which you'd like to upload a file to a document library. If prompted, type your user name and password, and then click OK.

1. In the **Quick Launch** pane, click the **Oak Furniture** document library link.

2. In the **Oak Furniture** document library, click the **Upload** button. The Oak Furniture: Upload Document page appears.

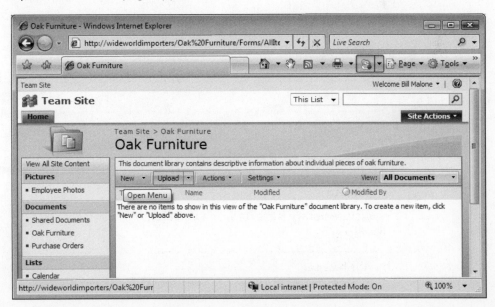

To upload a single document, click the Browse button. To upload multiple documents from the same location at the same time, click the Upload Multiple Files link. In this exercise, we'll upload a single document.

3. Click the **Browse** button.

4. In the **Choose File** dialog box, browse to the file you would like to upload, such as **OakDeck.docx**, and then click **Open**.

5. Click **Save** and **Close** to return to the Oak Furniture library.

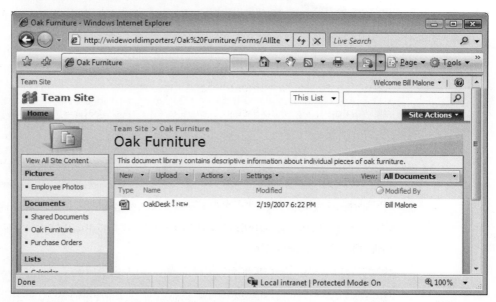

6. Repeat Steps 3–6 for the **OakChest.docx** file.

 **CLOSE** the browser.

> **Tip** You can also upload a document by copying and pasting from Windows Explorer and by using the Explorer view in Windows SharePoint Services, located on the left side of the document library page.

Adding Pictures

Adding pictures to a picture library is much like adding documents to a document library. In the following exercise, you will add an employee picture to the Employee Photos document library.

USE the practice file pjcov.jpg in the practice file folder for this chapter. The practice file is located in the *Documents\Microsoft Press\SBS_WSSv3\Chapter 05* folder.

OPEN the SharePoint site that you'd like to use to upload a picture to a picture library. If prompted, type your user name and password, and then click OK.

1. On the **Quick Launch**, click the **Employees Photos** picture library link. The Employee Photos document library appears.

2. Click **Upload.** The Add Pictures: Employee Photos page appears.

3. Click **Browse**.

4. In the **Choose File** dialog box, browse to the file you would like to upload, such as **pjcov.jpg**, and then click **Open**.

5. Click **OK**. The Employee Photos: pjcov page appears.

   This page is used to populate metadata on the picture, including name, date, description, and keywords.

6. Fill in the metadata if needed, and then click **OK**.

   The picture has been uploaded, and you are taken back to the Employee Photos picture library.

CLOSE the browser.

Creating a New Folder in a Library

When numerous documents exist in a library, you can create a new folder to help organize the documents in a more efficient way.

> **Tip** Windows SharePoint Services provides other mechanisms for organization, such as views and filters. However, people are often most familiar with folders and thus find it easier to create a folder structure.

In this exercise, you will create a folder for documents classified as In-Progress so that they can be differentiated from completed documents.

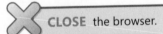

OPEN the SharePoint site that you'd like to use to add a folder to a document library. If prompted, type your user name and password, and then click OK.

BE SURE TO verify that you have sufficient permissions to create a folder in the document library. If in doubt, see the Appendix on page 435.

1. **In the Quick Launch pane, click Oak Furniture.** The Oak Furniture document library appears.

2. Click on the **New** drop-down list, and then click **New Folder**. The New Folder: Oak Furniture page appears.

3. In the **Name** box, type the name of the folder you would like to create, such as In Progress.

4. Click **OK**.

   The updated Oak Furniture page appears with the In Progress folder added to the page.

CLOSE the browser.

Checking Documents In and Out from the Document Library

One of the features provided by Windows SharePoint Services is basic document management. **Checking out** and **checking in** documents lets others know what documents you are working on so that they don't work on them at the same time. When using check-in, you can also enter comments about what you've changed that others can then view.

In the following exercise, you will change the comments in a document to reflect that this is the final version of the document.

USE the practice file Oakchest.docx in the practice file folder for this chapter. The practice file is located in the *Documents\Microsoft Press\SBS_WSSv3\Chapter 05* folder.

OPEN the SharePoint site from which you'd like to check in or check out a document. If prompted, type your user name and password, and then click OK.

BE SURE TO verify that you have sufficient permissions to modify the properties of a document in the document library. If in doubt, see the Appendix on page 435.

1. **On the Quick Launch, click Oak Furniture.** The Oak Furniture document library appears.

2. Move your mouse over the document you would like to check out, such as **OakChest.docx**.

3. An arrow appears to the right of the document name. Click the arrow.

A menu of options available for working with the document appears.

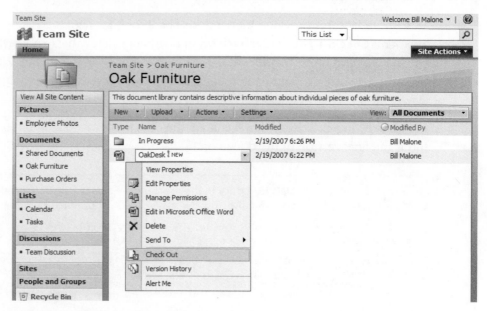

4. Click **Check Out**. A dialog box appears informing you that the document will be placed in the local drafts folder.

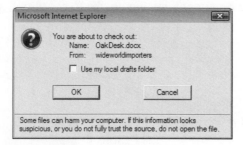

5. Click **OK**.

6. Move your mouse over **OakChest.docx**. When an arrow appears to the right of the file name, click the arrow.

7. Click **Check in**. The Check In page appears.

8. Click **Check In Document**.

9. In the **Check In** comments box, type *This is the final version of this document*

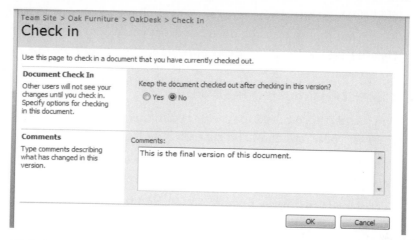

10. Click **OK** to return to the Oak Furniture document library.

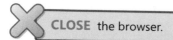

 CLOSE the browser.

Checking Documents In and Out from the 2007 Microsoft Office Suite

Checking documents in or out by using the browser is a nice feature, but not nearly as useful as checking documents in and out using the Microsoft Office System. The 2007 Microsoft Office suite has built-in SharePoint integration, and you can easily check documents in and out using any of the Microsoft Office suite applications.

In the following exercise, you will open and check out a document from a SharePoint library in Office Word. You will make minor modifications to the document, save it, and then check it back in to the document library.

USE the practice file Oakchest.docx in the practice file folder for this chapter. The practice file is located in the *Documents\Microsoft Press\SBS_WSSv3\Chapter 05* folder.
BE SURE TO verify that you have sufficient permissions to check out, modify, and check in a document in the document library. If in doubt, see the Appendix on page 435.
OPEN the SharePoint site from which you'd like to check in or check out a document. If prompted, type your user name and password, and then click OK.

1. From the **Quick Launch** click **Oak Furniture**. The Oak Furniture document library appears.

2. Move your mouse over the document that you would like to edit, such as **OakChest.docx**. When an arrow appears to the right of the document name, click the arrow.

3. Click **Edit in Microsoft Office Word**.

4. You might be prompted to re-enter your login credentials. If prompted to do this, re-enter your credentials and click **OK**. The file opens in Word.

5. You might be presented with a **User Name** dialog box to enter your name and initials. If so, enter your name and initials.

6. Click the **Office** button, point to **Server**, and then click **Check Out**.

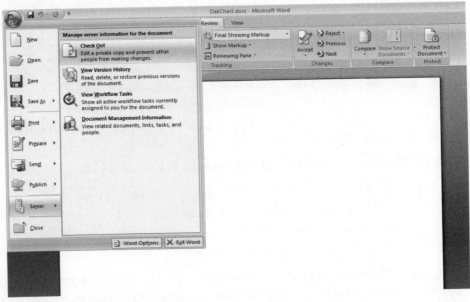

7. Make a change to the document, such as bolding some text.

8. Click **Office**, and then click **Save**.

9. Click **Office**, point to **Server**, and then click **Check In**.

10. In the **Check In Comments** dialog box, type This is the copy edited with Microsoft Office Word 2007.

11. Click **OK**, and then close Word.

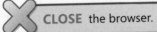 **CLOSE** the browser.

Working with Version History

When **versioning** is enabled, Windows SharePoint Services creates a separate copy of the document each time it is edited. Although this takes up extra space on the server, it also makes it easy to revert to an older version of the document if necessary. A more in-depth discussion of versioning will be covered in Chapter 6.

When you view a document's version history, you see a list of the occasions when this document was edited and saved as well as the author's comments on those changes.

In the following exercise, you will see what changes have been made to the OakChest. docx document and then revert back to the final copy of the document.

USE the practice file Oakchest.docx in the practice file folder for this chapter. The practice file is located in the *Documents\Microsoft Press\SBS_WSSv3\Chapter 05* folder.

BE SURE TO verify that you have sufficient permissions to check out, modify, and check in a document in the document library. If in doubt, see the Appendix on page 435.

OPEN the SharePoint site for which you'd like to see the version history for a document. If prompted, type your user name and password, and then click OK.

1. From the **Quick Launch**, click **Oak Furniture**. The Oak Furniture document library appears.

2. Move your mouse over the document for which you want to see the version history, such as **OakChest.docx**. When an arrow appears to the right of the document name, click the arrow.

    A drop-down menu appears.

3. Click **Version History**.

    You are taken to the versions saved for the OakChest.docx page. Each version of the saved document, the date and time that version was created, and any comments for the version appear.

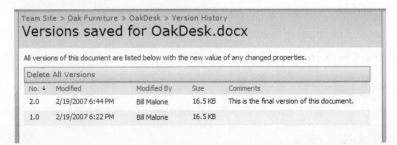

4. Move the mouse over an earlier version of the document and click the arrow that appears.

5. On the drop-down menu, click **Restore**.

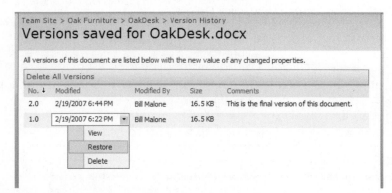

Team Site > Oak Furniture > OakDesk > Version History

Versions saved for OakDesk.docx

All versions of this document are listed below with the new value of any changed properties.

Delete All Versions

No. ↓	Modified	Modified By	Size	Comments
2.0	2/19/2007 6:44 PM	Bill Malone	16.5 KB	This is the final version of this document.
1.0	2/19/2007 6:22 PM ▼	Bill Malone	16.5 KB	

View
Restore
Delete

6. The dialog box that appears indicates that you are about to replace the current version with the selected version. Click **OK**.

There is now an additional, unpublished version. Windows SharePoint Services actually copies the version you want to restore and makes it the newest version. If you want to publish this version, you need to do so manually.

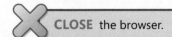 **CLOSE** the browser.

Deleting Documents

Documents accumulate over time, and you eventually need to delete those that are no longer needed. In this exercise, you will delete a document that is no longer in use.

 USE the practice file Oakchest.docx in the practice file folder for this chapter. The practice file is located in the *Documents\Microsoft Press\SBS_WSSv3\Chapter 05* folder.

BE SURE TO verify that you have sufficient permissions to check out, modify, and check in a document in the document library. If in doubt, see the Appendix on page 435.

OPEN the SharePoint site from which you'd like to delete a document. If prompted, type your user name and password, and then click OK.

1. From the **Quick Launch**, click **Oak Furniture**. The Oak Furniture document library appears.

2. Move your mouse over the document you would like to delete, such as **OakChest.docx**. When an arrow appears to the right of the document name, click the arrow.

3. On the drop-down menu, click **Delete**.

4. In the dialog box that asks whether you are sure you want to delete, click **OK**. The document is moved into your Recycle Bin.

5. To recover your document, on the **Quick Launch**, click the **Recycle Bin** link.

6. Select the check box next to the **OakChest.docx** document, and then click the **Restore Selection** link.

 CLOSE the browser.

Working with Workflows

You might want to route a document through an approval process before publishing it. You can create workflows within the document library without contacting your System Administrator.

There are several different ways to create workflows; you'll create a new workflow associated with the Oak Furniture document library. To create this workflow, you first need to specify at least three stages for the new workflow.

In the following exercise, you will add a site column to the Oak Furniture document library that gives you a choice for each workflow state.

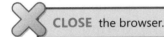 **USE** the practice file Oakchest.docx in the practice file folder for this chapter. The practice file is located in the *Documents\Microsoft Press\SBS_WSSv3\Chapter 05* folder.

BE SURE TO verify that you have sufficient permissions to create a workflow in the document in the document library. If in doubt, see the Appendix on page 435.

OPEN the SharePoint site from which you'd like to delete a document. If prompted, type your user name and password, and then click OK.

1. On the **Quick Launch** of the home page of **Team Site**, click the **Oak Furniture** library link.

2. Under the **Settings** menu options, click **Create Column**.

3. In the **Name** input box, type Workflow States.

4. Select the **Choice** option.

5. In the **Type Each Choice on a Separate Line:** input box, enter three choices: Submitted to Approver #1, Submitted to Approver #2 and Approved. Be sure to delete the three pre-defined generic choices first.

6. Click **OK**.

   Once the new column is created, you can create the new workflow.

7. From the **Settings** menu in the document library, click the **Document Library Settings** link.

8. Click the **Workflow Settings** link. The Add a Workflow: Oak Furniture page appears.

   By default, one workflow appears named Three-State Workflow.

9. Type a new name for this workflow, such as Approval Workflow.

10. On the drop-down list of the **Select a task** list, select **New Task List**.

11. In the **Start** options, leave the selections at their default settings and click Next.

12. In the **Workflow States** area, the column you added to the Oak Furniture document library automatically appears with the three choices that you entered for the three states of the workflow. If it does not appear, from the **Select a Choice** drop-down list, click **Workflow States**.

13. Enter the initial, middle, and final states on the drop-down list if you needed to select the workflow states as directed at the end of Step 13.

14. Clear both of the **Send E-mail Message** check boxes and then leave the rest of the workflow creation page as is and click **OK**.

   Now, when you click the drop-down list next to a document, a workflows selection appears from which you can choose the Approval workflow to route the document once it is ready to be approved.

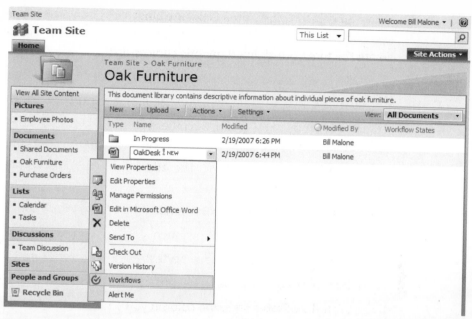

 CLOSE the browser.

Using Alerts

One of the most difficult obstacles encountered in the business world is knowing when information changes. Windows SharePoint Services can help with this problem by enabling you to subscribe to an **alert**. When a document changes to which you subscribe, you receive an e-mail message stating that the document has changed.

For example, you (Bill Malone in the example) may want to know when the OakChest.docx document is updated. In the following exercise, you will set up an alert for this document and then receive an alert that it has been changed.

USE the practice file Oakchest.docx in the practice file folder for this chapter. The practice file is located in the *Documents\Microsoft Press\SBS_WSSv3\Chapter 05* folder.

BE SURE TO verify that you have sufficient permissions to check out, modify, and check in a document in the document library, as well as create alerts in the site. If in doubt, see the Appendix on page 435.

OPEN the SharePoint site on which you'd like to set up an alert on a document. If prompted, type your user name and password, and then click OK.

1. From the **Quick Launch**, click **Oak Furniture**. The Oak Furniture document library appears.

2. Move your mouse over the document for which you would like an alert, such as **OakChest.docx**. When an arrow appears to the right of the document name, click the arrow.

3. Click **Alert Me**.

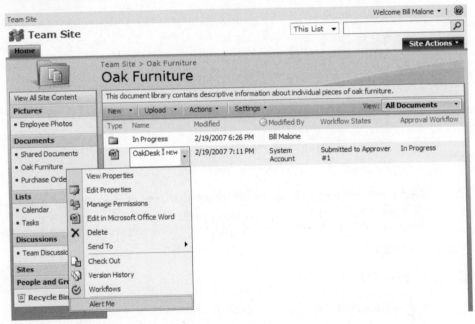

The New Alert: Oak Furniture: OakChest.docx page appears. You are given several options on the frequency of alerts as well as when to be alerted.

4. Retain the default values for this exercise and click **OK**.

> **Important** If your server is not configured to send an e-mail message, an Error page will appear. If this page appears, you cannot complete the rest of the steps in this section.

You are returned to the Oak Furniture document library.

5. Move your mouse over **OakChest.docx**. When an arrow appears to the right of the document name, click the arrow.

6. Click **Edit in Microsoft Office Word**.

7. When the dialog box appears that displays a warning, click **OK** to open the file. The file will open in Word.

8. Click **File**, and then click **Check Out**.

You now make a change to this document.

9. Click **File**, and then click **Save**.

10. Click **File,** and then click **Check In**.

11. In the **Check In Comments** dialog box, click **OK**.

12. Close **Word**.

After a few minutes, you should receive two e-mail messages. The first message indicates that an alert was successfully created. The second message indicates that OakChest.docx has been modified.

 CLOSE the browser.

Working with Offline Documents

There are two ways to work with offline documents in Windows SharePoint Services. The first method is to copy the documents to your Microsoft Office Outlook client. The second method is to synchronize your documents with a Microsoft Office Groove workspace.

 USE the practice file Oakchest.docx in the practice file folder for this chapter. The practice file is located in the *Documents\Microsoft Press\SBS_WSSv3\Chapter 05* folder.

BE SURE TO verify that you have sufficient permissions to check out, modify, and check in a document in the document library. If in doubt, see the Appendix on page 435.

OPEN the SharePoint site on which you'd like to copy documents offline. If prompted, type your user name and password, and then click OK.

To take documents offline by using Office Outlook, you can perform the following steps.

1. From the **Team Site** home page, click the **Oak Furniture** library link.

2. Click the **Actions** menu, and then choose **Connect to Outlook**.

A dialog box appears asking whether you trust this source and want to connect this document library to Outlook.

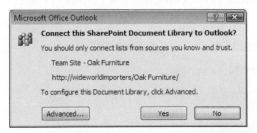

3. When you select **Yes**, a SharePoint list is automatically created in Outlook, and the documents in the library are automatically downloaded into Outlook as attachments to e-mails.

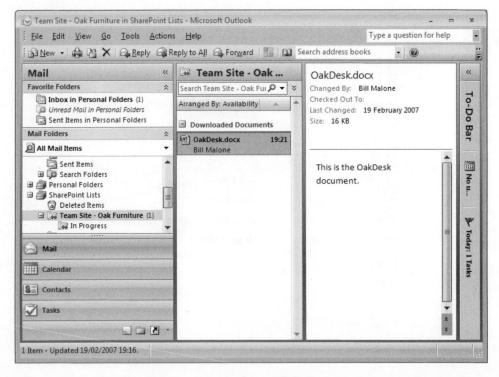

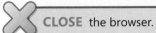 **CLOSE** the browser.

The other method to take documents offline is to synchronize them by using an Office Groove workspace. This method is a bit more complex, but its advantage is that you can synchronize various lists from different sites to the same Groove workspace. To synchronize documents to a Groove workspace, complete the following steps.

1. Open your **Groove** client. The shortcut can be found on the **All Programs** menu selection list inside the **2007 Microsoft Office suite** menu options.

2. In the **Groove** client, click **New Workspace**.

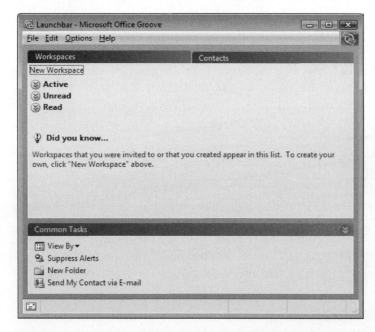

This invokes the Create New Workspace dialog box, where you can give the new workspace a name as well as specify the type of workspace you want to create.

3. Enter Oak Furniture Offline Documents as the name of the new workspace, and then click **OK**.

4. In the **Oak Furniture Offline Documents** workspace, under the **Common Tasks** list, click the **Add Tools** link.

5. In the **More Tools** dialog box, select the **SharePoint Files** check box and click **OK**.

6. Click the **Setup** button that automatically appears.

7. In the **Address**: input box, enter the URL of the SharePoint site with which you wish to connect, such as http://wideworldmporters, and click **Select**.

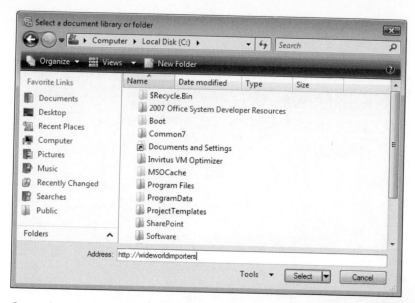

Once the Groove client connects to the SharePoint site, it delineates all of the lists and libraries in the site.

8. Choose the **Oak Furniture** document library by double-clicking the library.

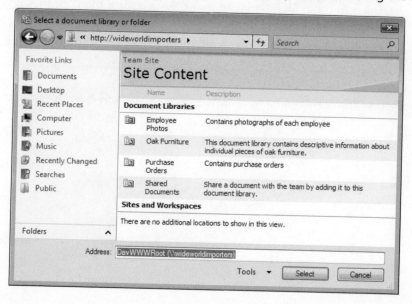

9. Click **Select**, which causes the Oak Furniture items to be synchronized to your local hard drive.

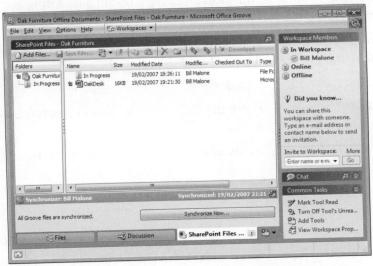

Note that both files and folders are synchronized to the Groove client, which holds copies of its documents on your local hard drive. You can repeat these steps to connect to other SharePoint sites and synchronize their libraries and lists into a common workspace. Of course, if you do this, give your workspace a more intuitive name than that shown in this exercise.

 CLOSE the browser and your Groove client.

Key Points

- Libraries provide a central location to store documents, forms, and pictures so they can be shared easily.

- You can create document libraries for specific topics and give them a descriptive name.

- Remember to check out a document before you edit it.

- You can check in and check out documents by using Microsoft Office suite applications.

- Set up alerts on documents when you want to know that a document has been changed.

Chapter at a Glance

Configure a document library, page 166

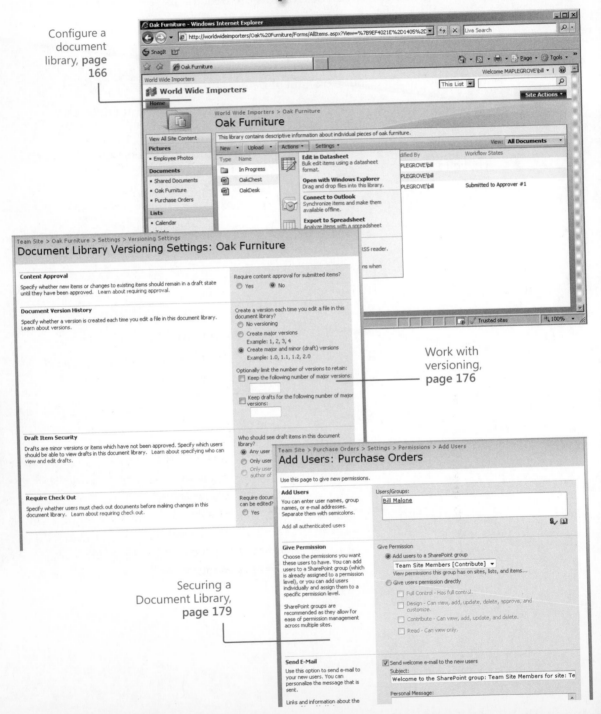

Work with versioning, page 176

Securing a Document Library, page 179

6 Working with Library Settings

In this chapter, you will learn to:

- ✔ Configure a document library.
- ✔ Create new columns.
- ✔ Work with content types.
- ✔ Add metadata to a document.
- ✔ Secure a document library.
- ✔ Delete a document library.

As we discussed in Chapter 5, "Creating and Managing Libraries," document libraries are one of the most powerful features of Microsoft Windows SharePoint Services. The additional features available in a Windows SharePoint Services library—such as versioning, approval, and navigation settings—are what make SharePoint document libraries more compelling than using networked shared folders. You can use SharePoint libraries to store multiple versions of your documents, require approval for documents to be published, and sort and filter content easily.

In this chapter, you will learn how to manage document libraries and enable additional library features. You will learn how to work with a library's columns, *content types*, and document metadata, including the Document Information Panel (DIP) in the 2007 Microsoft Office suite. You will also learn how to create a view of a document library, secure the library, use Web folders to access it, use the document discussions functionality, and delete a library. You will use the Oak Furniture document library and the Purchase Orders form library created in Chapter 5 to complete the exercises in this chapter.

Important Before you can use the practice files and sites provided for this chapter, you need to install them from the book's companion CD to their default locations. See "Using the Book's CD-ROM" on page xix for more information.

Important Remember to use your SharePoint site location in place of *http://wideworldimporters* in the following exercises.

Configuring a Library

Each document library contains settings that you can change from the library's Document Library settings page. You navigate to these settings by opening the document library and then clicking the Settings link. In addition, you can perform actions for the document library by using the Actions link within the document library.

By default, a document library opens in Standard view.

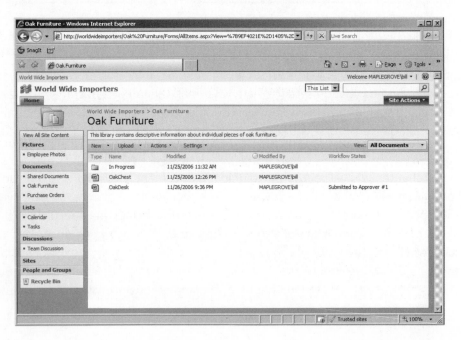

Sometimes, Standard view is not sufficient for what you need to do. For example, if you need to sort a list of documents quickly without creating a new view, you want to use Datasheet view. If you want to open the library by using Windows Explorer instead of your browser, you can do this from the Actions menu as well. In fact, from the Actions menu, you can perform the following actions.

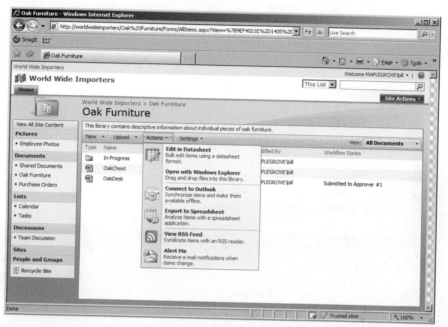

- Edit the library's contents from the Datasheet view. You can select this view when you wish to sort a library's contents quickly without going through the process of creating a new view based on sorted metadata.

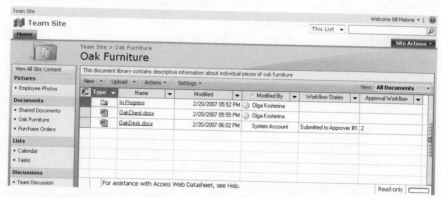

- Open the library using Windows Explorer. You can use this view to drag folders and files into the library.

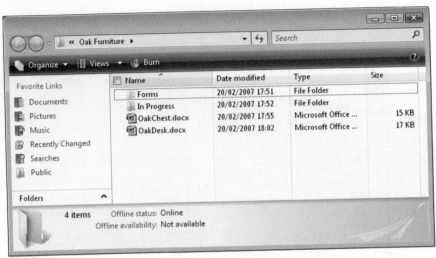

> **Important** Unless instructed by your System Administrator, you should not modify, add, or delete files in the Forms folder using the Windows Explorer view. This is mainly due to the fact that if you accidentally delete a template file in a forms folder, you can't copy another template file into that folder. In addition, modifying forms in the form folder is an advanced developer activity that non-technical personnel should avoid attempting.

- Connect the library to your Microsoft Office Outlook 2007 client to store files offline, which was discussed in Chapter 5.

- Export the content items in the library to a Microsoft Office Excel spreadsheet. You can do this if you have a large list of documents and need to modify metadata on the documents quickly and in bulk.

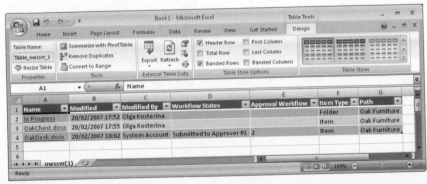

- View the document library via Really Simple Syndication (RSS). You can use this view if you want to aggregate a view of multiple document libraries in one location and then access those libraries from a single location (your RSS viewer).

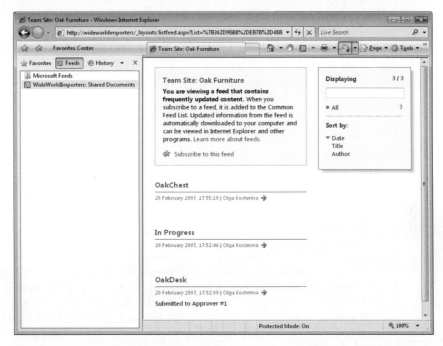

- Create alerts for the document library.

The Settings menu contains three basic options: Create Column, Create View, and Document Library Settings. Each option is discussed in the following text.

Creating New Columns and Working with Content Types

Like lists, library columns enable you to enter document *metadata* that can then be used by Document Library views to filter and sort documents. Metadata also makes it easier to find documents and determine what type of information a document contains without opening the document. You need to make sure that you have a sufficient number of columns to effectively describe the documents you are working with.

In the following exercise, you will add a column to the Oak Furniture document library for Document Number.

OPEN the SharePoint site in which you'd like to add columns to a document library. If prompted, type your user name and password, and then click OK.

BE SURE TO verify that you have sufficient rights to manage a document library. If in doubt, see the Appendix on page 435.

1. In the Oak Furniture library page, click **Settings**.

2. Click the **Create Column** link.

3. Enter a name for the column, such as Document Number.

4. Select the information type for the column. For this exercise, select the **Single line of text** option.

5. Configure the additional column settings and click **OK**.

Note that the Document Number column is added to the library. When you click to edit a document, an input field appears into which you can enter a document number for each individual document.

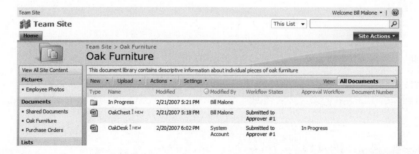

CLOSE the browser.

If you need to enter unique document numbers for various documents, you can use either Datasheet view or Office Excel to enter the metadata. When using Excel, you need to copy the metadata assignments back into the library.

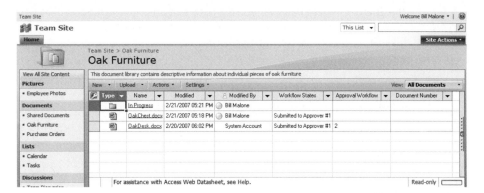

If you use the Windows Explorer view and either drag or upload documents into the library whose custom metadata field names match the column name in the document library, then the values are uploaded and added to the column automatically. Notice that the OakChairs.docx file already has a custom property named Document Number that is populated. When the document was uploaded, the number was automatically added to the Document Number column in the document library. In our illustration, the number was "12345."

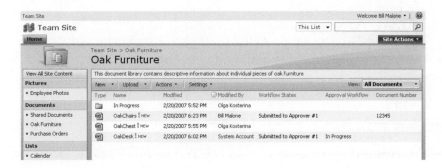

Using Content Types and Columns

A *content type* is simply a content item plus its metadata fields. We are combining the discussion of columns and content types because the way you assign metadata to a content item is by adding a column to the list and then populating that column for that data item.

Therefore, you can allow the library to manage content types. This means that you can allow multiple document templates in your library because different templates include a unique document (such as a Microsoft Office Word or Excel document) plus columns of metadata to populate. By doing this, users can then click on the New button in the library and select the document template they want to use when creating a new document. By default, each document library only has one template. If you need more than one document template in your site, select the Yes option in the Content Types area and choose the content types you wish to associate with your document library.

For example, you can have a Word document with one set of columns describing the Word documents, another set of columns describing Excel documents, and a third set of columns describing PowerPoint files—all within the same document library. Content types need not use the same columns, but they also are not restricted to using only unique columns. Different content types can both share columns with other content types as well as have their own unique columns. This flexible feature allows you to describe documents of different types in similar and/or different ways within the same document library.

> **Note** Consult your System Administrator if you need more information about content types, how they work, and how they are created.

Creating a New View

In the Create a View link from the Settings menu, you can create persistent views of the documents in the library. Five default views can be created.

1. Standard view
2. Datasheet view
3. Calendar view
4. Gantt view
5. Access view

Within each of these views, you have the ability to create views that incorporate sorting, grouping, ordering, and filtering, among other options.

In the following exercise, you will create a new view of a document library.

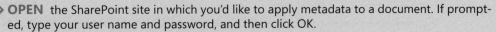

OPEN the SharePoint site in which you'd like to apply metadata to a document. If prompted, type your user name and password, and then click OK.

BE SURE TO complete the Adding Documents exercise in Chapter 5 and complete the previous exercise in this chapter on adding a column to a document library.

1. In the Oak Furniture document library page, from the **Settings** menu, click **Create View**.

2. Under the **Choose a view format**, click **Standard View**.

3. Enter a name for this view in the **View Name** input box, such as By Document Number.

4. Leave the default settings for **Audience** and **Columns**.

5. If you want to sort all documents based on their document number, in the **Sort** area, select the proper option to sort the documents in either ascending or descending order. If you want to filter the documents so that only certain documents appear in the By Document Number view, in the **Filter** area, choose the Document Number column, the type of operator used to filter the documents, and enter a value against which the filtering should be applied.

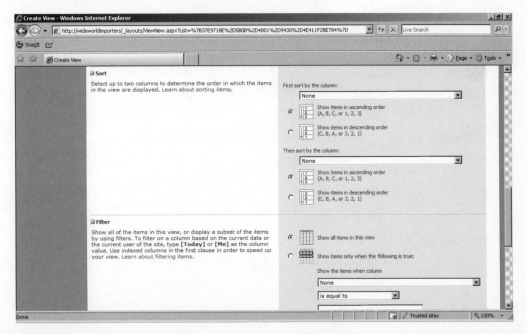

6. Click **OK**.

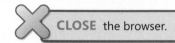 **CLOSE** the browser.

Using Document Library Settings

Document library settings are comprised of three sections: General Settings, Permissions and Management, and Communication. Each section is discussed in the text and exercises that follow.

The first option in the General Settings area is the Title, description, and navigation link, from which you can change the library's display name and description along with navigation, versioning, and approval settings.

In the following exercise, you will change the library's display name and description.

 OPEN the SharePoint site in which you'd like to change a library's display name and description. If prompted, type your user name and password, and then click OK.

BE SURE TO complete the Creating Document Libraries exercise in Chapter 5.

1. In the Oak Furniture document library page, from the **Settings** menu, choose **Document Library Settings**. The Customize Oak Furniture page appears.

2. Under **General Settings**, click the **Title, description, and navigation** link.

3. Enter the new display name for the library.

4. Enter a description for the library if needed.

5. Select an option in the **Display this document library on the Quick Launch** area.

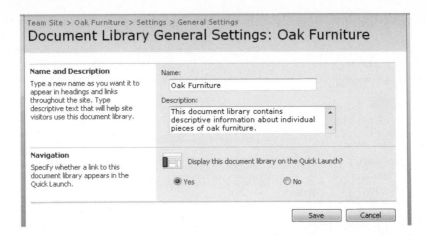

Team Site > Oak Furniture > Settings > General Settings
Document Library General Settings: Oak Furniture

Name and Description

Type a new name as you want it to appear in headings and links throughout the site. Type descriptive text that will help site visitors use this document library.

Name:

Oak Furniture

Description:

This document library contains descriptive information about individual pieces of oak furniture.

Navigation

Specify whether a link to this document library appears in the Quick Launch.

Display this document library on the Quick Launch?

⦿ Yes   ◯ No

[Save]   [Cancel]

CLOSE the browser.

In the following exercise, you will make changes to the settings of the Oak Furniture library. Your employees have mentioned that they find it difficult to locate the specifications for Oak Furniture on the site, so you want the link to the library to show up in the Quick Launch on the home page of the site.

OPEN the SharePoint site in which you'd like to edit library settings. If prompted, type your user name and password, and then click OK.

BE SURE TO verify that you have sufficient rights to configure a library. If in doubt, see the Appendix on page 435.

1. In the **Document** area on the **Quick Launch**, click **Oak Furniture.** The Oak Furniture library page appears.

2. Under **Settings,** click **Document Library Settings**. The Customize Oak Furniture page appears.

3. In the **General Settings** area, click the **Title, description, and navigation** link.

4. In the **Navigation** area, choose **Yes** to the question: **Display this document library on the Quick Launch?**

5. Click **Save.**

6. On the top link bar, click **Home**. Oak Furniture is now displayed on the Quick Launch.

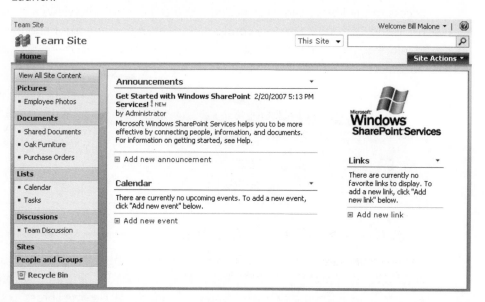

CLOSE the browser.

Libraries that are not displayed on the Quick Launch can be accessed by using the Documents link at the top of the Documents area on the Quick Launch. However, placing document libraries on the Quick Launch makes it easier to find specific libraries.

By using Document Versions settings, you can turn on or turn off the versioning of documents stored in the library. Each time a document is changed when versioning is turned on, Windows SharePoint Services saves a copy of the edited version of the document. This provides you with multiple versions of the same document so that you can easily see what the document contained before the modifications and revert to any previous version if necessary.

When versioning is turned on, you can select between two types of versioning: major versions only or major and minor versions. Major versions store a full-text copy of each document version. The latest version is always published, meaning that those with access to the document library can view the most recent version of the document.

Major and minor versioning allows you to publish major versions of a document while creating modified, minor versions of the same document that only a subset of users with access to the library can view and edit. You can control who views a minor version by using the Draft Item Security configuration setting. When major and minor versioning is selected, you can control how many versions of each document are retained in the document library. You can think of this as "version pruning."

Finally, you can also enforce the check-out of a document before a user can edit it by selecting the Require Check Out feature. The default selection, as illustrated, is set to "No," meaning that users are not required to check out a document before it can be edited.

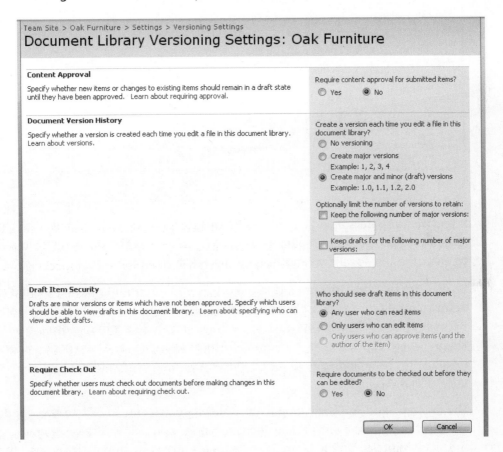

In the Advanced Settings area, a plethora of library configuration values are available to consider.

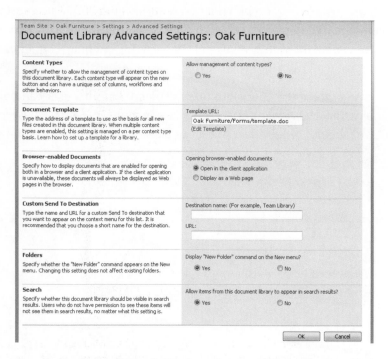

If you want to retain a single document template for your library but want to change the document that is used as the template for the library, use the Document Template area to enter the URL for the location of your new document template.

If you want to display documents in the browser as opposed to having them display in their native application, select the Display As A Web Page option in the Opening Browser-Enabled Documents area. You will most likely select this if you're in a Form Library where you want the InfoPath 2007 form to appear as a web page rather than an InfoPath document so that users can use their browser to enter information into the InfoPath form.

The Custom Send To Destination feature allows you to enter a URL to another document library other than the Official File Repository that your Administrators might have set at the SharePoint Server 2007 farm level, to which users can automatically send their documents once they are finished and ready for a wider audience's consumption. This is a handy feature if you want to ensure that all documents under development are written in one document library while those available for public consumption are hosted in a different document library (with different permissions) in the same site. You can also ensure that the contents in this library are not included in the search results by removing them from the indexing feature in Microsoft Office SharePoint Server 2007.

Using the Document Information Panel

The *Document Information Panel* (DIP) is a new feature in the 2007 Microsoft Office suite that exposes the metadata for a content type in an area above the document when working with that document in its native application.

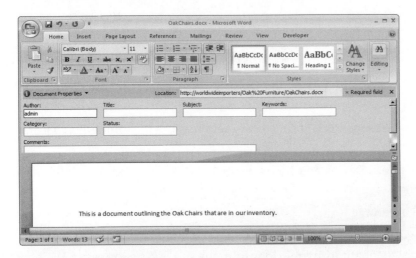

Troubleshooting If you don't immediately see the DIP when Microsoft Office Word 2007 opens, you can invoke it by clicking the Office icon, pointing to Prepare, and then choosing Properties.

The information that you enter into the metadata fields are down-stepped into the document library for that document.

Securing a Library

After creating a library, you might want to grant more privileges to certain people or restrict their privileges. More often than not, you might want to give some people more access rights to a particular library. For example, Olga Kosterina might have given Reader permission to the overall site to Bill Malone when it was created. However, she might decide later that she wants him to create purchase orders in the Purchase Orders library. Mike currently has only Reader access to this library because that is his overall permissions level on the site. Olga Kosterina can give Bill additional access to the Purchase Orders library so that Bill can add new documents. However, Bill isn't required to create documents on the rest of the site, but only to read documents.

In this exercise, you will open the SharePoint site, navigate to the Purchase Orders form library, and grant a user, such as Bill, access to add and modify purchase orders.

> **OPEN** the SharePoint site in which you'd like to secure a document library. If prompted, type your user name and password, and then click OK.
>
> **BE SURE TO** verify that you have completed the Creating Form Libraries exercises from Chapter 5 and that you have sufficient rights to change document library security. If in doubt, see the Appendix on page 435.

1. In the **Document** area on the **Quick Launch**, click **Purchase Orders**. The Purchase Orders document library appears.

2. Under **Settings**, click **Form Library** settings. The Customize Purchase Orders page appears.

3. Under **Permissions and Management**, click **Permissions for this Form Library**. The Change Permissions: Purchase Orders page appears.

4. Click **Actions**.

5. On the **Actions** menu, choose **Manage Permissions of Parent** if you want this form library to inherit its permissions from the site permission settings. Choose **Edit Permissions** if you want to block permission inheritance and assign a unique set of permissions to the form library. In this exercise, choose **Edit Permissions**.

6. From the **New** Menu, choose **Add Users**.

7. In the **Users/Groups:** box, type the user name or e-mail address of the user to whom you'd like to grant permissions, such as bmallone.

8. Under **Give Permissions**, click **Team Site Members [Contribute]**.

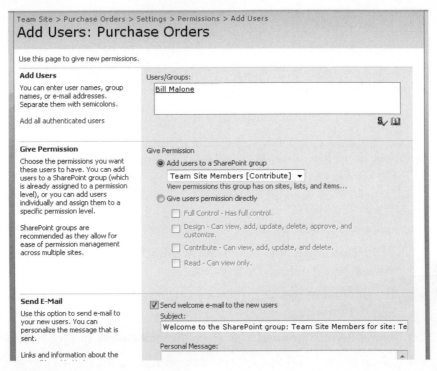

9. Click **OK**.

Bill is now added as a user and can create and modify purchase orders. Windows SharePoint Services also sends an e-mail message to Bill to inform him that he has been granted these permissions.

CLOSE the browser.

Deleting a Library

Over time, libraries can accumulate that are no longer needed. You might want to delete them because they consume space or because corporate policy dictates that communications be kept for only a set period of time.

In the following exercise, you will delete a library that is no longer in use.

OPEN the SharePoint site in which you'd like to delete a library. If prompted, type your user name and password, and then click OK.

BE SURE TO verify that you have sufficient rights to delete a library. If in doubt, see the Appendix on page 435.

1. In the **Document** area on the **Quick Launch**, click the library you would like to delete, such as **Purchase Orders**. The Purchase Orders form library appears.

2. Under **Actions**, click **Form Library Settings**. The Customize Purchase Orders page appears.

3. Under **Permissions and Management**, click **Delete this form library**.

4. When the warning box appears stating that the library will be permanently deleted, click **OK**.

   You are returned to the All Site Content page.

CLOSE the browser.

Key Points

- You can use General Settings to make libraries appear on the Quick Launch.

- You can configure a library to save all versions of a document when changes are made.

- You can require approval before documents in the library appear to other users by using an approval workflow process.

- Views use document metadata to sort, filter, or group information, so make sure you have the right columns on your library to sort, filter, and group effectively.

- You can secure a document library by either granting additional permissions or restricting permissions to others.

Chapter at a Glance

Create a
Document
Workspace,
page 186

Work with the 2007
Microsoft Office suite
Shared Workspace task
pane, **page 194**

Delete a
Document
Workspace,
page 199

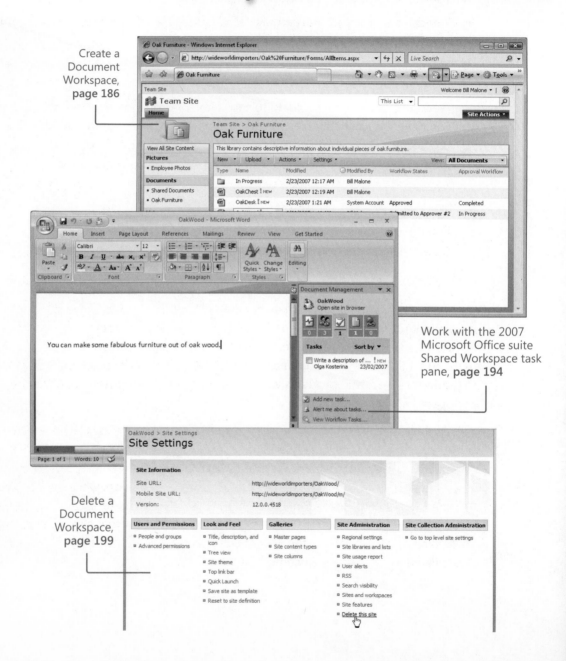

7 Working with Document Workspaces

In this chapter, you will learn to:

✔ Create a Document Workspace.

✔ Create a Document Workspace within the 2007 Microsoft Office suite.

✔ Access an existing Document Workspace.

✔ Work with the 2007 Microsoft Office Shared Workspace task pane.

✔ Publish a document back to a document library.

✔ Delete a Document Workspace.

Document Workspaces contain many features that enable you to work on a particular document more easily. You can collaborate with others on a single document in a convenient environment where you can create or store a document as well as associate links with that document. Additionally, the 2007 Microsoft Office suite maintains tight integration between the products within the Microsoft Office System and Document Workspaces.

You can think of a *Document Workspace* as a temporary SharePoint site. It is a collaborative environment for discussing, editing, and writing a single document, and it enhances content creation. The Document Workspace typically has a short life—several months at most—because its main purpose is to help with content creation. Once the document is finished, it should be stored in a document library for others to access and read, as discussed in previous chapters. The Document Workspace for that specific document can then be deleted. Because the life cycle of a Document Workspace is short, you can expect to create and delete Document Workspaces fairly often.

In this chapter, you will learn how to efficiently work with Document Workspaces by both creating them and accessing existing workspaces. You will also learn how to work with the 2007 Microsoft Office Shared Workspace task pane, publish a document back to a document library, and delete a Document Workspace.

> **Important** Before you can use the practice sites provided for this chapter, you need to install them from the book's companion CD to their default locations. See "Using the Book's CD" on page xix for more information.

> **Important** Remember to use your SharePoint site location in place of *http://wideworldmporters* in the following exercises.

Creating a Document Workspace

There are two ways to create a document library. The first method is to create it through the SharePoint Web interface, and the second method is to create it using a 2007 Microsoft Office suite application. Both methods are covered in this chapter. When using either method, the resulting Document Workspace is the same, and only the procedure you use to create it differs.

A Document Workspace centers around one particular document. It is important to stress this fact. You want only one document per Document Workspace because Document Workspaces are linked back to the original document when they are created from an existing document in an existing library. This enables you to easily copy the document from the Document Workspace back to its original source location. This unique feature of Document Workspaces is not found in any other type of SharePoint site. In this way, you and your team members can work on the document without interfering with the main site or allowing others to read the document before it is complete.

In the following exercise, you will create a Document Workspace from an existing document by using the SharePoint Web interface.

OPEN the SharePoint site in which you'd like to create a Document Workspace. If prompted, type your user name and password, and then click OK.

BE SURE TO complete the Adding Documents exercise in Chapter 5, "Creating and Managing Libraries."

1. On the **Quick Launch**, click **Oak Furniture**. You are taken to the Oak Furniture document library.

2. Move your mouse over **OakWood.docx**. When an arrow appears to the right of the document name, click the arrow.

3. Point to **Send To**, and then click **Create Document Workspace**. The Create Document Workspace page appears.

4. Click **OK**.

A new Document Workspace is created for you and populates with information from the OakWood.docx document.

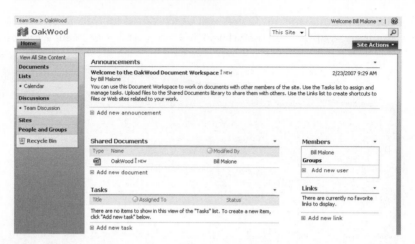

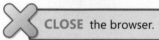 **CLOSE** the browser.

Tip You can also create a Document Workspace manually by using the Create link on the home page of the site. However, this method does not provide the same integration with an existing document as does the process outlined in the previous exercise. To obtain the full benefits of a Document Workspace, you should create it from an existing document or from a 2007 Microsoft Office suite application, which is explained in the next section.

Creating a Document Workspace Within the 2007 Microsoft Office Suite

The 2007 Microsoft Office suite provides tools that enable you to work with a Document Workspace through a task pane. Many of the administration tasks in a document workspace are exposed through the task pane in Microsoft Office Word 2007 so that you can perform basic site administration from within the same interface (Word) that you're using to edit the document.

In this section, you will use the 2007 Microsoft Office suite task pane to create a Document Workspace. The Document Workspace created by using a task pane is the same as the one you created in the last exercise. The only difference is that the Document Workspace is created from within a 2007 Microsoft Office suite application.

In this exercise, you will create a new document and then use Office Word 2007 to generate a new Document Workspace for the document.

OPEN the SharePoint site in which you'd like to create a Document Workspace for a document in Word 2007. If prompted, type your user name and password, and then click OK.

BE SURE TO verify that you have sufficient permissions to create a Document Workspace. If in doubt, see the Appendix on page 435.

1. On the **Quick Launch**, click **Oak Furniture**. The Oak Furniture document library appears.

2. Click **New Document**. A new document is opened in Word 2007.

3. Type some information into the document, such as This is the OakTable Document.

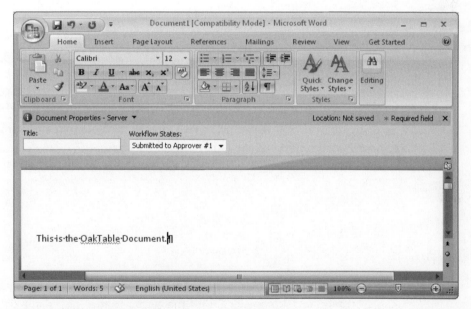

4. If the Create Document Workspace command is not displayed by default in the Quick Access Toolbar in Word 2007, then perform Steps 5-9. If it does appear, then you can skip to Step 10. You can customize the Quick Access toolbar display to invoke this command.

5. To customize the Quick Access Toolbar, click the **Customize Quick Access Toolbar** drop-down arrow.

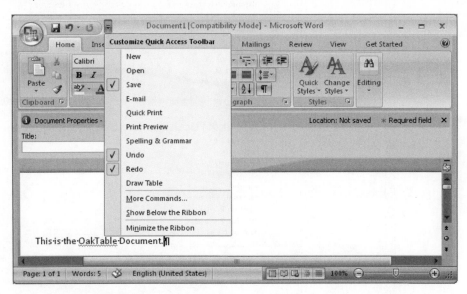

6. Click **More Commands**.

7. On the **Commands to Choose from** drop-down list, choose **All Commands**.

8. Scroll down until you find the **Create Document Workspace** command. Click **Add** to add this command to the Quick Access Toolbar.

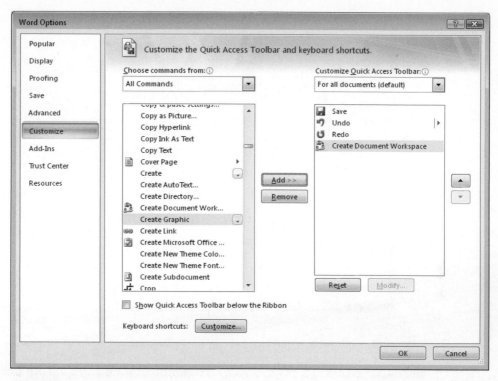

9. Click **OK**.

10. From the **Quick Access Toolbar**, click the **Create a Document Workspace** button. The Document Workspace pane appears to the right of the document.

11. Enter a name for the workspace and the URL where you'll want the workspace created. In this exercise, we'll enter OakTable Workspace for the name and http://wideworldimporters for the URL location.

    Do not enter the name of the workspace in the URL location input box. If you do this, the save action will fail.

12. Click **Create**. If you receive a pop-up box asking you to save the file, click **Yes** and save the file to your local hard drive to continue this process.

The site should now be created.

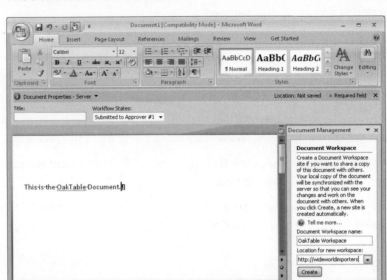

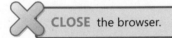 **CLOSE** the browser.

Accessing an Existing Document Workspace

After creating a Document Workspace, you must access it to work on the document. Unless you know specifically where to look, it can be difficult to locate the Document Workspace after you first create it, especially if you created the workspace several days or weeks ago and now don't remember exactly where the workspace is located. Moreover, if you create a large number of workspaces, it can then become problematic to remember the URL for each workspace.

Having a built-in method for finding workspaces is very helpful when you need to return to them quickly and easily. Word 2007 provides this capability to you.

In this exercise, you will browse to the Document Workspace for OakTable.docx, which you created in the previous exercise.

 OPEN the SharePoint site from which you'd like to access an existing Document Workspace. If prompted, type your user name and password, and then click OK.

BE SURE TO verify that you have sufficient permissions to access this workspace. If in doubt, see the Appendix on page 435. Also be sure to complete the exercise earlier in this chapter on creating a Document Workspace.

1. On the **Quick Launch**, click the **Sites** link. The **All Site Content** page is displayed in the **Sites and Workspaces** view.

2. On the **All Site Content** page, click the link of the Document Workspace that you would like to open, such as **OakTable Workspace**.

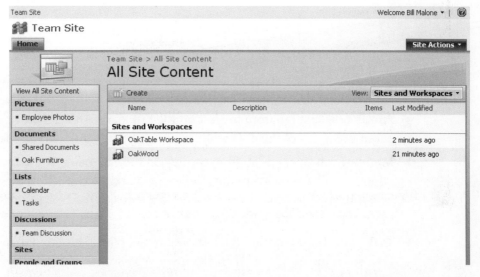

The OakTable Document Workspace appears. You can work with this site as you would any other SharePoint site.

 **CLOSE** the browser.

Working with the 2007 Microsoft Office Suite Document Management Task Pane

The 2007 Microsoft Office suite Shared Workspace task pane contains tabs from which you can access various information. Refer to the following figure as you read through a description of each tab.

- **Status tab** First tab from the left on the task pane. This tab provides information about the status of the document, such as who has checked out the document.
- **Member tab** Second tab from the left on the task pane. This tab displays a list of people who have access to the Document Workspace. It also allows you to view who is online if you have a presence client installed, such as Microsoft Windows Messenger.
- **Tasks tab** Third tab from the left on the task pane. This tab displays the list of tasks from the Task list of the Document Workspace.
- **Documents tab** Fourth tab from the left on the task pane. This tab displays a list of documents in the SharePoint site.
- **Links tab** Fifth tab from the left on the task pane. This tab displays links from the Links list of the Document Workspace.

In the following exercise, you will work with some of the features of the Document Management task pane in Word 2007. You will add a task and a user to the Document Workspace from within the Word 2007 program, as well as check document information,.

> **OPEN** the SharePoint site in which you'd like to work with a document in a Document Workspace. If prompted, type your user name and password, and then click OK.
>
> **BE SURE TO** use the 2007 Microsoft Office suite to perform this exercise. Also be sure you have completed the first exercise in this chapter.

1. On the **Quick Launch**, click **Sites**.

2. On the **All Sites** page, click **OakChairs**. The OakWood Document Workspace appears.

3. Move your mouse over **OakWood.docx**. When an arrow appears to the right of the document name, click the arrow.

4. **In Word 2007**, click **Edit in Microsoft Office Word**. The document is opened in Word 2007.

   The Document Management task pane appears to the right of the document. If it does not appear, you can manually make the task pane appear by clicking the Office button, pointing to Server, and then clicking Document Management Information.

5. Click the **Members** tab.

   Your name (Bill Malone in this exercise) is listed as the only member of this Document Workspace.

6. Toward the bottom of the task pane, click the **Add New Members** link. The Add New Members dialog box displays.

7. In the **Enter e-mail addresses or user names, separated by semicolons** input box of the **Add New Members Wizard**, type the e-mail address or user name of a user you want to add to the Document Workspace, such as Olga.

8. Click **Next**.

   The next page of the Add New Members Wizard appears, which allows you to enter the e-mail address of the user you wish to add to your workspace. If you are connected to the network and the user's account has an e-mail address, that user's e-mail address appears in this page automatically.

9. Click **Finish**.

   If you do not enter an e-mail address for the user or if one is not available, you are then prompted by a pop-up box that asks whether you want to send an e-mail invitation to the new member.

10. Make your selection, and then click **OK**. If you choose to send an invitation to the new user, select the checkbox and then click **OK** on the next screen to send the e-mail invitation.

The user is listed as one of the members of the Shared Workspace and now has permissions to edit the document.

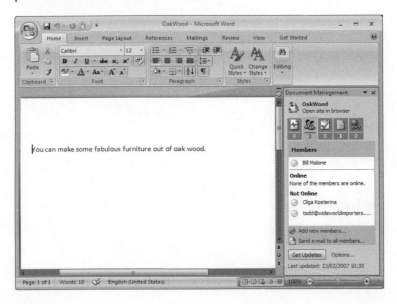

11. Click the **Tasks** tab. In the bottom section of the pane, click the **Add New Task** link. The Task dialog box appears.

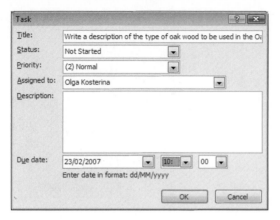

12. In the **Title** box, type a name for the task, such as Write a description of the type of oak wood to be used in the OakWood document.

13. Leave the **Status** and **Priority** boxes set to their default settings.

14. In the **Assigned To** box, select a user to whom to assign the task, such as **Olga**.

15. In the **Description** box, type a description for the task, if needed

16. In the **Due Date** box, select the due date for the task and click **OK**.

The new task you just entered appears in the task pane.

17. Click the **Documents** tab.

The date and time that the document was modified, as well as the user who created the document and the user who most recently modified it, are displayed.

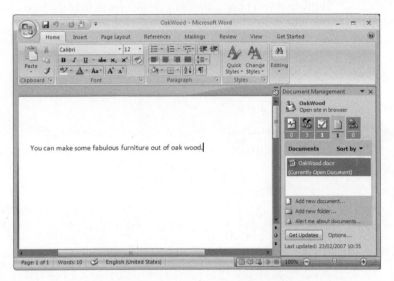

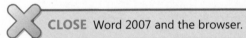 **CLOSE** Word 2007 and the browser.

Publishing a Document Back to a Document Library

The ability to publish a document back to its original source document library is one of the unique features of Document Workspaces. If the Document Workspace was created from an existing document in a document library, then the Publish To Source Location feature will be available. This feature will not be available if the Document Workspace was not created from an existing document in a document library. Document Workspaces are used because you can keep the source document free of changes while editing and updating the document in the workspace.

The Publish To Source Location feature essentially copies the updated document from the Document Workspace back into the source library, thereby replacing the existing parent copy. It prevents you from having to recall the original location of the document while still keeping the source document up to date.

In the following exercise, you will publish a document from the Document Workspace back to the document library.

OPEN the SharePoint site in which you'd like to publish a document from a document library back to the main site. If prompted, type your user name and password, and then click OK.

BE SURE TO verify that you have sufficient permissions to publish the document back to its parent site after modifying the document. If in doubt, see the Appendix on page 435.

1. On the **Quick Launch**, click **Sites**.

2. On the **All Site Content** page, click **Oak Wood**. The Oak Wood Document Workspace is displayed.

3. Move your mouse over **OakWood.docx**. When an arrow appears to the right of the document name, click the arrow, point to **Send to**, and then click **Publish to Source Location**.

   The Publish to Source Location page appears.

4. Click **OK**. The Operation Completed Successfully page appears.

5. Click **OK**. You are returned to the home page of the Document Workspace.

   This action copies the latest version of OakWood.docx from the Document Workspace back to the document's original document library (in this case, Oak Furniture). Confirmation that the operation has completed successfully appears.

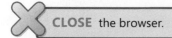 **CLOSE** the browser.

Deleting a Document Workspace

When you are finished with a Document Workspace, you want to delete the workspace so as to save space on your SharePoint server and also reduce the clutter that numerous workspaces can cause when people are trying to locate other Document Workspaces.

In this exercise, you will delete the OakWood.docx Document Workspace.

> **OPEN** the SharePoint site from which you'd like to delete a Document Workspace. If prompted, type your user name and password, and then click OK.
>
> **BE SURE TO** verify that you have sufficient permissions to delete the document workspace. If in doubt, see the Appendix on page 435.

1. On the **Quick Launch** bar, click **Sites**.

2. On the **All Site Content** page, click the document workspace that you wish to delete. In this exercise, click the **Oak Wood** Document Workspace.

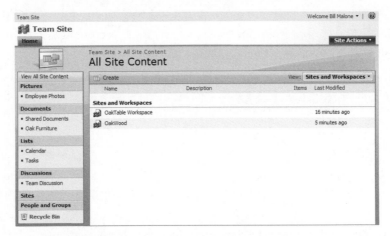

3. From the **Site Actions** menu, click **Site Settings**.

4. From the **Site Administration** column, choose **Delete this site**.

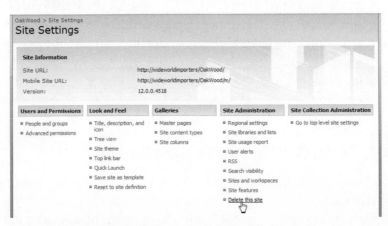

The Delete This Site confirmation page appears, informing you that everything in the site will be deleted.

5. Click **Delete**.

6. Click **OK** in the warning box that appears. Your Document Workspace is now deleted.

CLOSE the browser.

Key Points

- You can create Document Workspaces for documents that are in progress.

- By using Document Workspaces, you can more easily communicate and collaborate with others about a particular document.

- When using the 2007 Microsoft Office suite Shared Workspace task pane, you have access to information directly from a SharePoint site and are able to update that information directly within the 2007 Microsoft Office suite.

- You can create a document library from an existing document in a document library so that you can use the Publish To Source Location feature to update the original document with the latest version.

Chapter at a Glance

Creating Meeting
Workspaces, **page 204**

Managing Recurring
Meetings, **page 210**

Use the Standard
and Advanced Web
Part Galleries, **page
216**

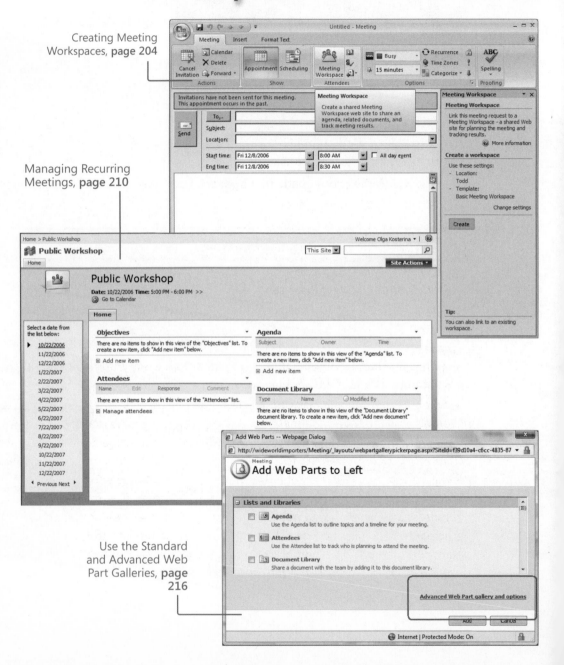

8 Working with Meeting Workspaces

In this chapter, you will learn to:

✔ Create a Meeting Workspace by using a template.

✔ Create a Meeting Workspace for a calendar event.

✔ Understand the home page of a Meeting Workspace.

✔ Add an objective to a Meeting Workspace.

✔ Add an agenda to a Meeting Workspace.

✔ Add an attendee to a Meeting Workspace.

✔ Add a Things To Bring list.

✔ Add a Web Part to a Page tab.

Every company holds meetings. These meetings often have a specific agenda; if they don't, the company would benefit if they did. Sometimes participants need to prepare for a meeting by completing a task or two prior to the meeting. The task may be simply reviewing a document, assembling a list of questions, or perhaps creating a prototype of something to bring to the meeting. A meeting can become inefficient or even ineffective because the preparation tasks that participants are expected to complete are not communicated effectively. All too frequently when participants do make preparations, they use an outdated version of a document or complete the wrong tasks because they are confused by the barrage of tasks sent through numerous e-mails. In addition, after the meeting is over, meeting notes or follow-up steps may need to be provided to the participants. Wouldn't it be nice if all of the notes, documents, tasks, and other meeting details could be kept in a centralized location that was easy to find? A bonus would be if all of the content in this centralized store could be searched.

Microsoft Windows SharePoint Services provides a site template called a *Meeting Workspace* that helps improve communication before and after a meeting by supplying a common place to store information that is relevant to the meeting. By providing a single point of communication, Meeting Workspaces can help make meetings more efficient—something every organization, both large and small, can use.

In this chapter, you will learn to create a Meeting Workspace by using a site template. After the Meeting Workspace is created, you will learn how to add items such as objectives, agendas, and attendees to the workspace. You will also learn how to customize the Meeting Workspace by adding a *Web Part* and then adding items to the list represented by that Web Part.

Chapter 11, "Using Windows SharePoint Services with Outlook 2007," contains a section that focuses on creating Meeting Workspaces from a Microsoft Office Outlook 2007 calendar appointment displayed on the ribbon when inviting others to join the meeting. Therefore, the current chapter focuses only on the browser interface.

> **Important** Before you can use the practice sites provided for this chapter, you need to install them from the book's companion CD to their default locations. See "Using the Book's CD" on page xix for more information.

> **Important** Remember to use your SharePoint site location in place of *http://wideworldimporters* in the exercises in this chapter.

Creating a Meeting Workspace by Using a Template

There are two different ways to create a Meeting Workspace in the browser:

1. Create a new SharePoint site by using one of the five Meeting Workspace templates installed by Windows SharePoint Services. This new SharePoint site has all of the functionality of a Meeting Workspace, but is not tied directly to any event.

2. Use a calendar event to generate the Meeting Workspace associated with this event. The new site will forever be associated with the event that was its genesis.

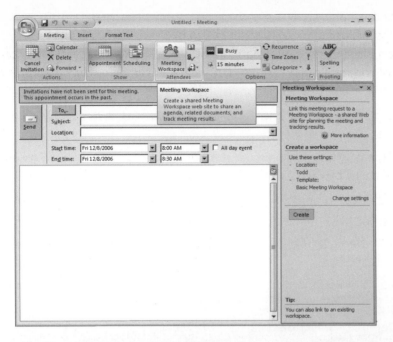

Creating and accessing a Meeting Workspace from Office Outlook 2007 is covered in Chapter 11.

When you create a Meeting Workspace by using the *Basic Meeting Workspace* template, three default lists are automatically added: Objectives, Agenda, and Attendees. A document library is also created to house meeting documents. These lists and the library function just like any list or library described in previous chapters. Each list has a Web Part on the front page of the Meeting Workspace, making it easy to interact with the information within any of them. Additionally, the Attendees list displays the name of the user who created the Meeting Workspace as the meeting organizer.

In the following exercise, you will create a Meeting Workspace by using the Basic Meeting Workspace template to store notes from the weekly status meeting.

OPEN a top-level SharePoint site. The exercise will use the *http://wideworldimporters* site, but you can use whatever site you wish. If prompted, type your user name and password, and click OK.

BE SURE TO verify that you have sufficient rights to create a site. If in doubt, see the Appendix on page 435.

1. From the **Site Actions** menu at the top right of the page, choose **Create** to display the Create page.

> **Tip** Oddly, if your parent site is a Meeting Workspace, it won't have a Create option in the Site Actions menu. Therefore, you must click the list name in one of the Web Parts on the home page, click View All Site Content at the top of the Quick Launch, and then click Create on the toolbar.

2. In the **Web Pages** group, click **Sites and Workspaces** to display the New SharePoint Site page.

3. In the **Title** box, type the name of the workspace you would like to create, such as Weekly Status Meeting.

4. In the **Description** box, type a description for the Meeting Workspace, such as This site contains the latest information regarding the weekly status meeting.

5. In the **URL Name** box, type the URL for the Meeting Workspace, such as weeklystatus.

See the Naming a URL sidebar in Chapter 3, "Creating and Managing Sites," for details about good naming conventions for the URL Name field.

6. In the **Template Selection** area, click the **Meetings** tab and select **Basic Meeting Workspace**.

7. Leave the default settings for the three remaining sections. They are described in detail in Chapter 3.

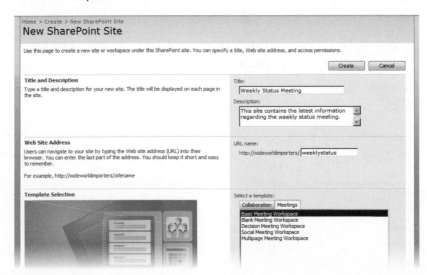

8. Click **Create** and a new site is created at *http://wideworldimporters/weeklystatus*. You are taken to the newly created Weekly Status Meeting page.

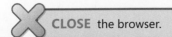

CLOSE the browser.

Creating a Meeting Workspace for a Calendar Event

You might want to create a Meeting Workspace for an event that is already in a SharePoint calendar list. This type of workspace is even easier to create because Windows SharePoint Services performs most of the work on your behalf.

In the following exercise, you will create a Meeting Workspace for the recurring Public Workshops event created in Chapter 4, "Working with Lists." Many people are involved with the Public Workshops, and having details in a Meeting Workspace on a SharePoint site makes it easier to communicate information, including changes, to everyone involved. You will be adding information to this workspace in the next several sections.

OPEN the SharePoint site where the calendar event is located. The exercise will use the Calendar list on the *http://wideworldimporters* site, but you can use whatever list and site you wish. If prompted, type your user name and password, and click OK.

BE SURE TO verify that you have sufficient rights to create a site. If in doubt, see the Appendix on page 435.

BE SURE TO complete the steps to create recurring Public Workshops events in the Adding, Editing, and Deleting List Items exercise in Chapter 4. Alternatively, you can create a practice site for this chapter based on the Chapter 8 Starter.stp site template in the practice file folder for this chapter on the CD-ROM. See "Using the Book's CD" on page xix for instructions on how to create a practice site. The Calendar list is already created for you on the practice site.

1. In the **List** area of the **Quick Launch**, click **Calendar** to display the Calendar list's Calendar list view for the current month.

2. In the top right corner from the **View** drop-down menu, choose **All Events** to display the event list items in a standard basic table format.

3. From the smart menu of the **Public Workshop** list item, choose **Edit Item**.

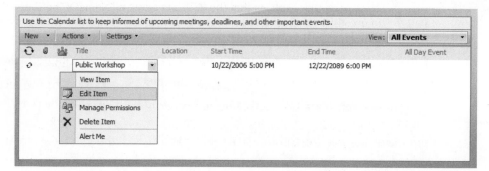

4. In the **Workspace** area at the bottom of the page, select the **Use a Meeting Workspace to organize attendees, agendas, documents, minutes, and other details for this event** check box and click **OK**.

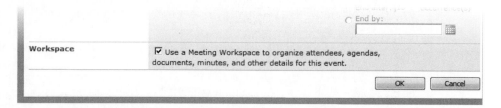

5. Click **OK** again to confirm that recurrence pattern losses are not a concern.

   Because a Meeting Workspace has never been created for this event, you are taken to the New Meeting Workspace page to create one. All of the information is already filled out for you. You might want to remove the spaces from the URL name field or change the permission to be unique, but neither are required.

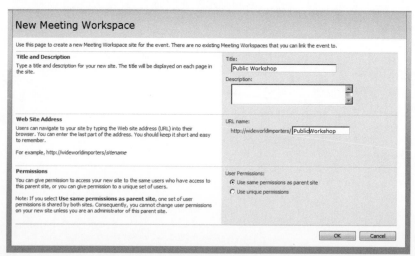

Back

> **Tip** If the chosen URL name already exists in this scope, SharePoint takes you to an
> error page that explains that the Web site address "NameOfTheChosenSite" is already
> in use. Click the Back button in the browser to choose another URL name.

6. Click **OK**. From the **Template Selection** area of the **New SharePoint Site** page,
   SharePoint will subsequently show the Meeting Workspace templates.

7. In the **Template** box, select **Basic Meeting Workspace**.

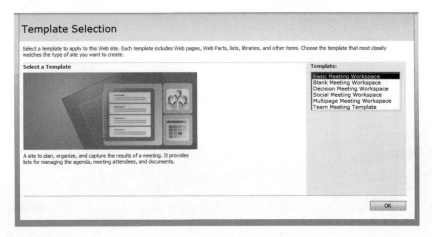

8. Click **OK**.

You are taken to the newly created Public Workshops site. In the left pane, notice the links for each recurrence of the event. There is typically only one site for each meeting date; however, with a recurring meeting, there is a virtual instance for each meeting date.

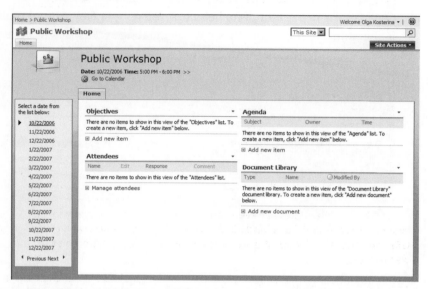

9. Directly below the date and time near the top of the page, click the **Go To Calendar** link to return to the calendar.

Go To Calendar

10. Locate the original recurring meeting and click its name to view it.

Notice the link next to the Workspace attribute near the bottom of the page. Clicking this link returns you to the associated Meeting Workspace. It's a shame that Document Workspaces don't have the same feature.

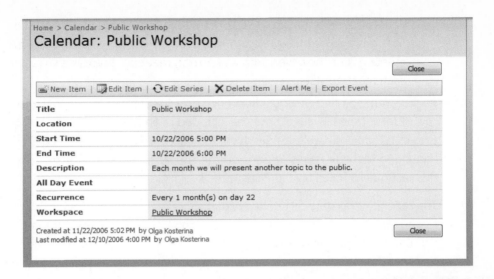

Important If the Calendar event is subsequently deleted, the associated Meeting Workspace is orphaned. It, and all of its data, can still be accessed directly from the original URL, but one of the following warnings is displayed (depending on how the Calendar event was deleted).

● This meeting is no longer associated with a meeting in your calendar or scheduling program. Either this meeting date was canceled, or the link to the workspace was removed from the scheduled meeting.

● This meeting series was canceled from your calendar and scheduling program.

Of course, the orphaned site can be deleted from the Site Settings page accessed through the Site Actions menu.

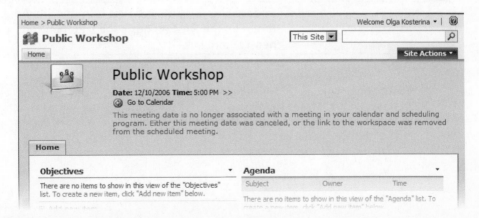

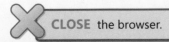 **CLOSE** the browser.

Understanding the Home Page of a Meeting Workspace

Once you have created a Meeting Workspace, you can familiarize yourself with the home page layout. The first obvious difference on a Meeting Workspace is the use of a second row of tabs, called *Pages*. These are included in addition to the top link bar found on all sites in Windows SharePoint Services. You can manipulate these Pages by using the Add Pages and Manage Pages options on the Site Actions menu. The exercise at the end of this section will focus on the Page tabs.

The second noticeable difference is that there isn't a *Quick Launch*, which also means that the common functionality found on the Quick Launch must be found elsewhere. The Create option is also missing from the Site Actions menu. The following table should help you find links on a Meeting Workspace that are exposed by using the Quick Launch and Site Actions menu on the home page of a typical *Team Site*.

Common Link	Meeting Workspace Location
View All Site Contents	Choose Site Libraries and Lists from the Site Administration group on the Site Settings page.
People and Groups	Choose People and groups from the Users and Permission group on the Site Settings page.
Recycle Bin	Unfortunately, the Meeting Workspace doesn't have a user interface option on the home page to access the Recycle Bin (see the note following the table for another option). So, you must replace the default.aspx in the address bar with _layouts/recyclebin.aspx to undo an errant delete.
Create	Choose Site Libraries and Lists from the Site Administration group on the Site Settings page and then choose the Create new content link.

> **Tip** Clicking the name of any default Web Part (Objectives, Agenda, Attendees, or Document Library) takes you to that list's default list view. From any list view, you can find the familiar View All Site Content and Recycle Bin links in the left nav. You can use these instead of the links in the above table.

The home page of a basic Meeting Workspace also contains four Web Parts.

1. One that displays the details in the Objectives list,

2. One for the Attendees list

3. One for the Agenda list

4. One for a document library

These four items apply to every meeting. A meeting should typically have at least one *objective* as well as an *agenda* to inform people about the meeting. The Meeting Workspace is organized in a way that makes it easy for the organizer to communicate their reason for holding the meeting. Also, there should typically be a list of meeting attendees. The document library does not necessarily need to be used, but it is a convenient place to store documents such as information that attendees might need to read before the meeting, meeting minutes after the meeting concludes, or Microsoft Office PowerPoint presentations used during the meeting. At the top of the page, the date and time of the meeting as well as the location (if specified) is found, which can be useful information.

If you create a Meeting Workspace from a *recurring event* (as in the following exercise), additional information is provided on the Meeting Workspace page. On the left side of the page is located a list of dates that represents each instance of the recurring meeting. Each dates has its own virtual Meeting Workspace page associated with it, enabling you to establish different objectives, agendas, attendees, and documents for each specific instance of the meeting. For example, the Public Workshops meeting presents a different topic each month, so it is sensible to post different objectives, agendas, attendees, and documents for every monthly event.

In this exercise, you will add another Page to the Meeting Workspace for use later in this chapter.

> **OPEN** the SharePoint Meeting Workspace created in the first exercise: *http://wideworldimporters/PublicWorkshops* site. If prompted, type your user name and password, and click OK.
>
> **BE SURE TO** verify that you have sufficient rights to manage the site. If in doubt, see the Appendix on page 435.

1. On the **Site Actions** menu, choose **Add Pages** to open the Add Pages tool pane.

2. In the **Page Name** textbox, enter the word More.

3. Leave the **Appears for all meetings** default option selected.

Choosing the Appears for this meeting only option generates the new Page for the current meeting only.

4. Click **Add** to create the new Page.

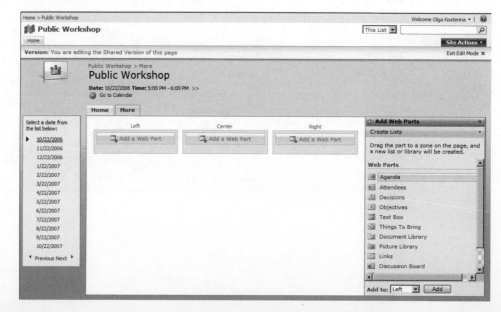

You can then toggle between the Home and More Page tabs. Each Page represents a place where you can put Web Parts.

> **Tip** In addition to the Left and Right Web Part Zones that you typically find on a Team Site, you might notice that there is also a third Web Part Zone called Center. This Zone simply gives you another column in which to put Web Parts when using this site template.

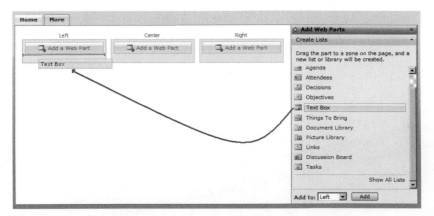

5. On the right side of the page is the Add Web Parts tool pane from the previous release. Drag the **Text Box** option to the **Left Web Part Zone**.

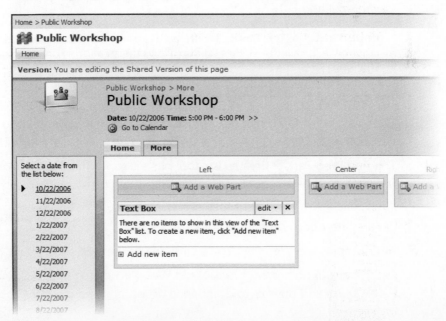

Not only does this action put a Web Part into the Web Part Zone, but it also creates the list that will hold the information presented by the Web Part. This response to a drag and drop is different than any other SharePoint site.

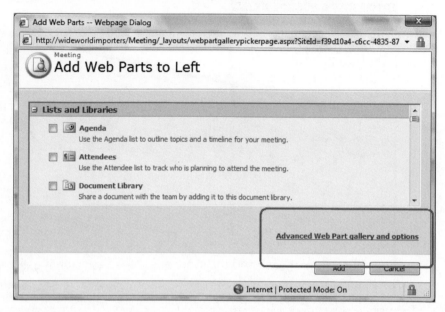

6. At the bottom of the **Text Box** Web Part, click **Add new item** to enter notes for this meeting.

> **Important** The Text Box list is different than all other lists. It contains only one required field called Text. This list also allows the creation of only a single list item. Therefore, once the first text is entered, the Add New Item option is replaced with an Edit Item option.

This Web Part is typically used to take notes during the meeting, so you can click Cancel to exit this screen without saving any changes.

The Add Web Parts – Create Lists tool pane is somewhat hidden in the user inter-face. If you close the tool pane, you must either create another Page to open it again or use the following steps.

7. On the **Site Actions** menu, choose **Edit Page**.

8. At the top of any **Web Part Zone**, click one of the **Add a Web Part** buttons.

Add a Web Part

9. In the bottom right corner of the **Add Web Part** dialog box, click **Advanced Web Part gallery** and options to dismiss the dialog box and open the tool pane.

10. From the drop-down smart menu to the right of the **Browse** setting near the top of the tool pane, choose **Create Lists**.

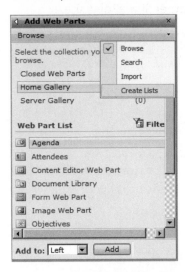

The page will post back and the tool pane will refresh with the elusive Create Lists tool pane that appears when a new Page tab is created.

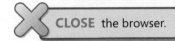 **CLOSE** the browser.

Adding an Objective to a Meeting Workspace

To get the most use from a Meeting Workspace, you must add information and relevant details to it so people are motivated to visit the workspace. In the next three sections, you will add information to each of the default lists in the Public Workshops Meeting Workspace.

The topic for the next Public Workshop focuses on selling imported items. Olga Kosterina wants to communicate this focus to anyone who visits the Meeting Workspace page.

In the following exercise, you will add this topic as an objective to the Meeting Workspace.

OPEN the SharePoint Meeting Workspace created in the first exercise: *http://wideworldimporters/PublicWorkshops* site. If prompted, type your user name and password, and click OK. You can also access the Meeting Workspace by opening the top-level SharePoint site (*http://wideworldimporters*), clicking one of the Public Workshops under the Events Web Part, and then clicking the Workspace link.

BE SURE TO verify that you have sufficient rights to contribute to the site. If in doubt, see the Appendix on page 435.

1. On the left side of the page under **Select a date from the list below:**, click the date of the next meeting (**10/22/2006** in this exercise; your date will vary based on the date you perform this exercise.)

   If you didn't use a repeating event, there won't be a list of dates from which to choose from. Simply use the default instance.

2. Under the **Objectives** Web Part, click **Add new item**. You are taken to the Objectives: New Item page.

3. In the **Objective** box, type the meeting objective, such as How to efficiently sell imported items.

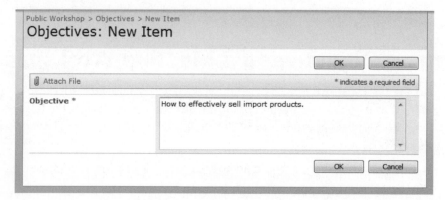

4. Click **OK** to save the object and return to the home page of the Meeting Workspace. The new objective appears in the Objectives Web Part.

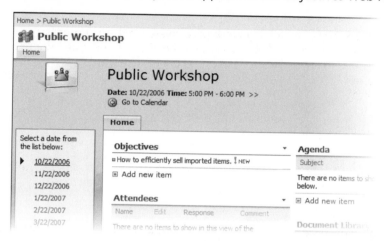

Since objectives are simply list items, you are not limited to only one objective.

 LEAVE the browser open for the following exercise.

Adding an Agenda to a Meeting Workspace

Next, Olga Kosterina wants to communicate the agenda for the next Public Workshop. This action includes assigning an owner to each agenda item and scheduling a time for the Public Workshop. Olga decides that Todd Rowe will present both the Introduction and the Establishing an International Vendor sessions. She will present the pros and cons of Buying in Bulk, and she will also answer questions. Each session will last for 15 minutes.

In this exercise, you will create an agenda for the Meeting Workspace based on the aforementioned scenario.

 OPEN the SharePoint Meeting Workspace created in the first exercise in this chapter: *http://wideworldimporters/PublicWorkshops* site. If prompted, type your user name and password, and click OK.

BE SURE TO verify that you have sufficient rights to contribute to the site. If in doubt, see the Appendix on page 435.

1. Under the **Agenda** Web Part, click **Add new item**. The Agenda: New Item page appears.

2. In the **Subject** box, type a subject for the agenda, such as Introduction.

3. In the **Owner** box, type the name of a person who is responsible for this agenda item, such as Todd Rowe.

> **Tip** Oddly, the person listed as the Owner does not have to be listed as an Attendee. The Owner field is simply a free-form text field.

4. In the **Time** box, type the time for this agenda item, such as 5:00-5:15 PM.

5. Optionally, enter some **Notes** (not illustrated in this exercise).

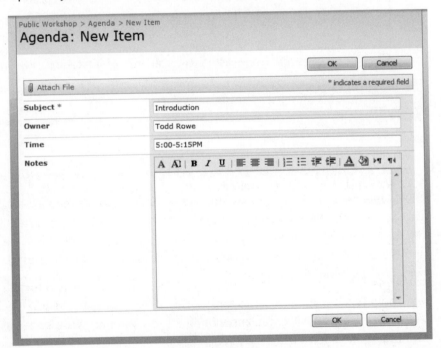

6. Click **OK** to save the agenda item for this Public Workshop. You are taken back to the home page of the Meeting Workspace.

   The new agenda appears in the Agenda Web Part.

7. Using Steps 1–6 as a guide, create another three items for the workshop agenda. The information for each agenda item is provided in the following table.

Subject	Owner	Time
Establishing an International Vendor	Todd Rowe	5:15-5:30 PM
Buying in Bulk	Olga Kosterina	5:30-5:45 PM
Questions and Answers	Olga Kosterina	5:45-6:00 PM

After you have created the final agenda item for this Public Workshop, the home page of the Meeting Workspace reflects the overall agenda.

> **Tip** Oddly, SharePoint doesn't automatically order the agenda items by time, but rather organizes them in the order in which each item is entered into the list.

Agenda

Subject	Owner	Time
Introduction ! NEW	Todd Rowe	5:00-5:15PM
Establishing an International Vendor ! NEW	Todd Rowe	5:15-5:30PM
Buying in Bulk ! NEW	Olga Kosterina	5:30-5:45PM
Questions and Answers ! NEW	Olga Kosterina	5:45-6:00PM

⊞ Add new item

 LEAVE the browser open for the following exercise.

Adding an Attendee to a Meeting Workspace

Finally, since you specified that Todd Rowe will be presenting two topics in the meeting, you should probably add him to the Attendees list. Listing Todd as an attendee ensures that visitors to the workspace know he is attending the meeting so that they can contact him by e-mail if necessary.

In this exercise, you will add a user, Todd Rowe, to the Attendees list.

 OPEN the SharePoint Meeting Workspace created in the first exercise in this chapter: *http://wideworldimporters/PublicWorkshops* site. If prompted, type your user name and password, and click OK.

BE SURE TO verify that you have sufficient rights to contribute to the site. If in doubt, see the Appendix on page 435.

1. Under the **Attendees** Web Part, click Manage attendees. The Attendees page appears.

2. In the toolbar, click **New**. You are taken to the Attendees: New Item page.

3. In the **Name** box, type the e-mail address or user name of the attendee, such as ToddR.

Check Names

4. Click the person icon with the check mark on it, or press Ctrl + K to invoke the Check Names routine.

   This action verifies that the typed name is valid. SharePoint automatically adds a domain name, such as wideworldimporters\, to properly prefix the name. If an incomplete name is provided, SharePoint prompts with the message No exact match was found.

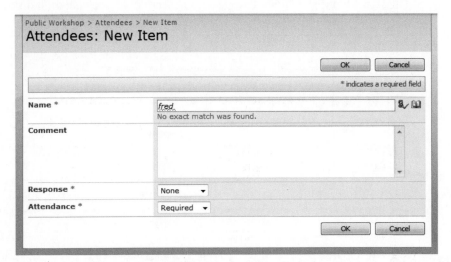

5. Click the errant name, and a menu appears that attempts to aid in choosing a correct name.

   Failing that, there is an option to open the Select Names dialog box to continue to search for the person by choosing More Names... Of course, you can also remove the name.

> **Important** All attendees are required to have an e-mail address in the Active Directory.

Select Names
icon

6. If you are unsure of the correct name, you can manually invoke the **Select Names** dialog box by clicking on the rightmost icon.

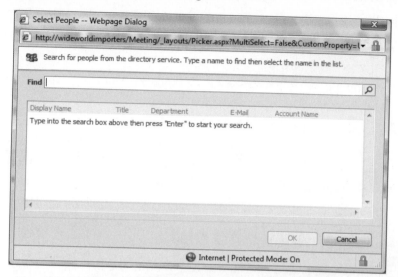

7. In the required **Response** drop-down list, select **Accepted**.

8. In the required **Attendance** drop-down list, leave the default set to **Required**.

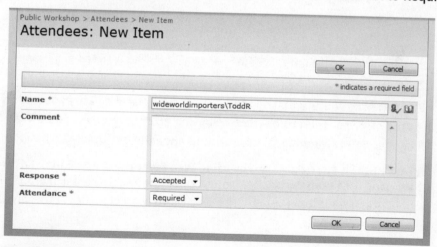

9. Click **OK**.

Todd is added as an attendee for this Public Workshop, and you are returned to the Attendees list. You can add additional attendees if desired by using the same procedure.

10. In the breadcrumb, click **Public Workshop** or, in the top nav, click **Home** to return to the home page of the Meeting Workspace.

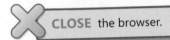 **CLOSE** the browser.

Adding a Things To Bring List

Now that you have added all of the information to the default Meeting Workspace, you might want to add more information for the attendees. You can accomplish this by creating new lists and libraries and by adding Web Parts that display their contents to the Page tabs.

> **Tip** If you add a Web Part to any page in a Meeting Workspace that contains multiple dates listed on the left side of the page, the Web Part is added to all pages.

Olga wants to ensure that all attendees know what they are expected to bring with them to the meeting. Therefore, in the following exercise, you will add a Web Part on the More Page tab in the Meeting Workspace to a new Things To Bring list.

Customizing a SharePoint site by using Web Parts is discussed in detail in Chapter 15, "Working with Web Parts."

OPEN the SharePoint Meeting Workspace created in the first exercise in this chapter: *http://wideworldimporters/PublicWorkshops* site. If prompted, type your user name and password, and click OK.

BE SURE TO verify that you have sufficient rights to create lists and add Web Parts. If in doubt, see the Appendix on page 435.

1. On the **Site Actions** menu on the right side near the top of the page, choose **Site Settings**.

2. From the **Site Administration** group on the **Site Settings** page, click **Site Libraries and Lists**.

3. Click the **Create new content** link to display the Create page.

4. In the **Custom Lists** group on the far right side of the page, click **Things To Bring**.

5. Enter a **Name**, such as Homework.

6. Enter a **Description**, such as This list represents the items that you need to prepare in advance to be ready to attend the meeting.

7. Leave the default option selected for **Change items into series items** set to **No**.

   Changing this value to Yes indicates that these items are things that should be presented on every meeting in the series. Since the items to be added only apply to this meeting, you do not want this to be a series list.

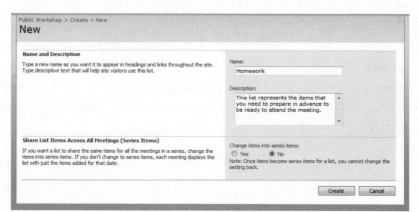

8. Click **Create**. The default list view of the new list is displayed.

    Olga wants people to bring their international vendor list to this meeting.

9. On the toolbar, click **New** to add an item to the list.

10. In the **Item** textbox, enter a value such as International Vendor List.

11. You can leave the **Comment** and **Owner** fields blank.

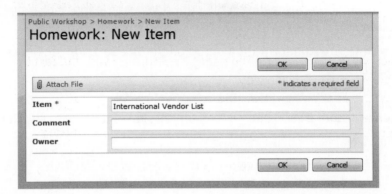

12. Click **OK** to save the new list item and return to the default list view.

 LEAVE the browser open for the following exercise.

Adding a Web Part to the More Page Tab

Now that a Things To Bring list called Homework has been created, you should probably make this list visible to all of the people who will be attending the meeting. In our scenario, Olga Kosterina wants to ensure that attendees bring their international vendor lists to the Public Workshop.

In this exercise, you will add a Web Part that displays the contents of the Homework list on the More Page tab.

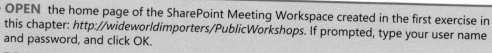

OPEN the home page of the SharePoint Meeting Workspace created in the first exercise in this chapter: *http://wideworldimporters/PublicWorkshops*. If prompted, type your user name and password, and click OK.

BE SURE TO verify that you have sufficient rights to add Web Parts. If in doubt, see the Appendix on page 435.

1. Click the **More** Page tab. The page should display with the Text Box Web Part from a previous exercise showing.

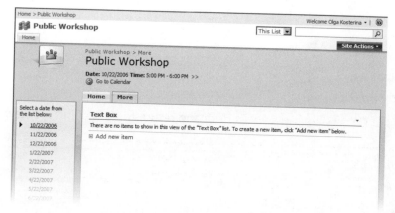

2. On the **Site Actions** menu, choose **Edit Page**.

3. In the **Left Web Part Zone**, click **Add a Web Part**.

4. In the **Add Web Parts – Web Page Dialog**, choose the check box to the left of the **Homework** list and click **Add**.

5. In the top right corner of the page, click **Exit Edit Mode**. The item from the Homework list displays directly above the Text Box Web Part on the More Page tab.

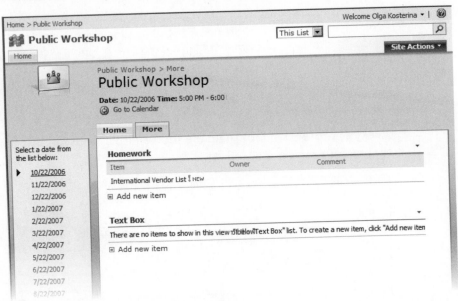

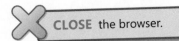 **CLOSE** the browser.

Key Points

- Meeting Workspaces communicate key information about a meeting.
- You can create a Meeting Workspace from recurring events if you want to present different information each time the meeting occurs.
- After the Meeting Workspace is created, add relevant information to the Objectives, Agenda, and Attendees Web Parts.
- Use the document library in a Meeting Workspace to store presentations, documents, pictures, meeting minutes, or other material relevant to the meeting.
- You can customize a Meeting Workspace by adding new Page tabs, lists, and Web Parts.

Chapter at a Glance

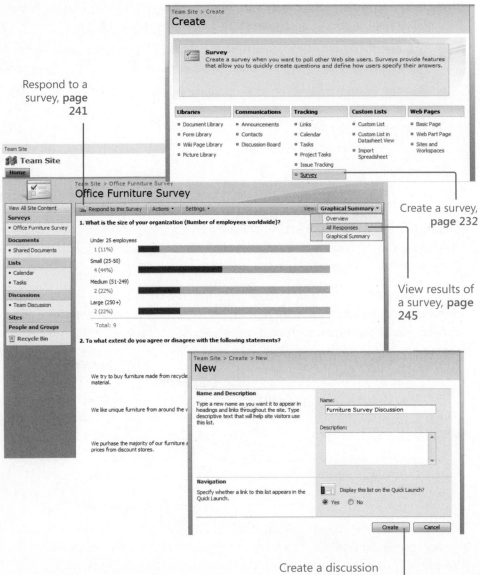

Respond to a survey, **page 241**

Create a survey, **page 232**

View results of a survey, **page 245**

Create a discussion board, **page 250**

9 Working with Surveys and Discussion Boards

In this chapter, you will learn to:

✔ Create a survey.

✔ Respond to a survey.

✔ View the results of a survey.

✔ Use a discussion board.

Chapter 4, "Working with Lists," introduced you to lists in Microsoft Windows SharePoint Services. By using two specialized SharePoint lists, surveys and discussion boards, you can gather feedback and information from users of your site.

By creating a *survey*, you can determine the format of the user's feedback and configure whether respondents' names appear in the survey results. If names are configured to appear, you can see how each user responded; if names are configured not to appear, the survey is anonymous. Windows SharePoint Services tallies the results and compiles a graphical summary of the responses.

By creating a *discussion board*, you can allow users to determine the type of response they give. A discussion board invites users to discuss issues with one another by initiating topics and posting replies.

> **Tip** Discussion boards are also known as message boards or, on the Internet, as Internet forums.

In this chapter, you will learn how to create and respond to a survey and then view the survey results. You will also learn how to create and use a discussion board, including viewing a discussion board from within Microsoft Office Outlook 2007.

> **Important** Before you can use the practice sites provided for this chapter, you need to install them from the book's companion CD to their default locations. See "Using the Book's CD" on page xix for more information.

> **Important** Remember to use your SharePoint site location in place of *http://wideworldimporters* in the following exercises.

Creating a Survey

Surveys are created for a number of reasons. For example, you might need to create a survey to ask a user's opinions or to collect factual information for marketing purposes. No matter what their purpose, all surveys involve the creation of a survey "container," followed by the creation and administration of questions.

These questions can be formatted as one of two basic types.

- *Open-ended* These questions have no definite answer. Open-ended questions give users the opportunity to answer in their own words rather than simply checking one of a limited list of alternatives. An example of an open-ended question is, "Are there any other comments you would like to add about the services or products supplied by Wide World Importers?" The advantage of open-ended questions is that responses can be very useful, often yielding quotable material and an insight into the issues that are of most concern to the respondents of the survey. The disadvantage is that the responses are more difficult to catalog and interpret.

- *Closed-ended* These questions have a finite set of answers from which the user must choose. One of the choices may be "Other" or "N/A" to allow users to specify that their answer is not one of those supplied or that the question is not applicable to them. The advantages of closed-ended questions are that data can be gathered from them easily and they lend themselves to statistical analysis. The disadvantage is that they are more difficult to write than open-ended questions because the choices must include all of the possible answers a user could offer for each question.

Users can respond to a survey in a number of ways such as by typing text, selecting items from a menu, clicking yes or no, or entering a numeric or currency value. When you use Windows SharePoint Services to create a question, you can specify the type of answer, as summarized in the following table.

Answer	Question Type	Description
Single line of text	Open	Use this answer type when you want users to enter only a few words. You can specify the maximum number of characters that a user can type.
Multiple lines of text	Open	Use this answer type when you want users to type one or more sentences. You can specify the maximum number of lines that a user can type and the type of text in which a user can format responses. The three formatting options are: ● plain text ● rich text, whereby users can change font or text color and alignment ● enhanced text, whereby users can add pictures, tables, and hyperlinks
Choice	Open, Closed	Use this answer type when you want users to choose from a set of selections that you provide. You can create a multiple choice question in which users pick the best answer or answers from among the possible choices, represented as a drop-down list, set of option buttons, or set of check boxes. You can make the question open-ended by allowing users to type their own choice.
Rating Scale	Closed	This answer type is often called a *Likert scale*. Use this answer type when you want users to choose their preference on a numeric scale. Questions with this type of answer are often used to obtain feedback on provided services. Users indicate how closely their feelings match the question or statement by using a rating scale. The number at one end of the scale represents most agreement, or "Strongly Agree," and the number at the other end of the scale represents least agreement, or "Strongly Disagree."
Number	Open	Use this answer type when you want users to enter a numeric value. You can specify a lower and upper limit for the value as well as the number of decimal places that users can enter.
Currency	Open	Use this answer type when you want users to enter a monetary value. You can select the currency format based on a geographic region, a lower and upper limit for the value, and the number of decimal places that users can enter.
Date and Time	Open	Use this answer type when you want users to enter a date or a date and time.
Lookup	Closed	This answer type is very similar to the Choice answer type in that responses are predetermined. Use this answer type to point users to an existing list on your site that contains the available choices.

Yes/No	Closed	This answer type presents the user with a check box and can be used when you want users to respond with Yes or No (True or False). Questions that require this answer type are sometimes known as *categorical* questions.
Person or Group	Closed	This answer type is very similar to the Choice answer type in that responses are predetermined. Use this answer type to choose a user or SharePoint Group who have access to the SharePoint site as the response.
Page Separator	Not applicable	Use this answer type when you want your survey to span multiple pages.
Business Data	Closed	If your Web site is created on a Microsoft Office SharePoint Server 2007 installation, you are presented with this data type. This answer type is very similar to the Choice answer type in that responses are predetermined. Use this answer type to point users to a data source outside Windows SharePoint Services that contains the available choices.

When using each of these answer types, you can specify whether an answer is required or optional and provide a default answer for each question. A new feature to Windows SharePoint Services 3.0 is that you can define branching in the survey, whereby you can skip to a specific question based on the user response. A page break is automatically inserted after a branch-enabled question.

In the following exercise, you will create a survey on a SharePoint Web site.

OPEN the SharePoint site in which you would like to create your survey. The exercise will use the *http://wideworldimporters* site, but you can use whatever site you wish. If prompted, type your user name and password, and click OK.

BE SURE TO verify that you have sufficient rights to create a list. If in doubt, see the Appendix on page 435.

1. In the left navigation panel, click **View All Site Content**. The All Site Content Page is displayed.

2. Click the **Create** button. The Create page is displayed.

Create

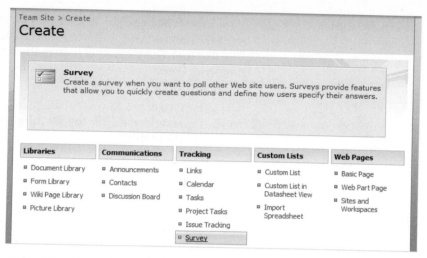

3. Under **Tracking**, click **Survey**. The New form is displayed.

4. In the **Name** box, type Office Furniture Survey.

5. In the **Navigation** area, leave the **Yes** option selected.

6. In the **Survey Options** area, for the **Show user names in survey results?** and **Allow multiple responses?** options, select **Yes**.

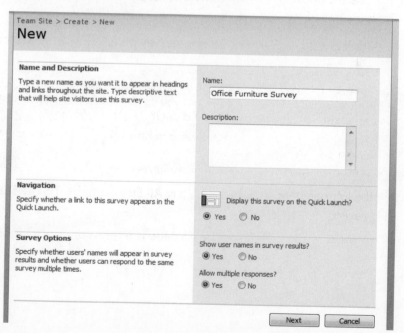

Next

7. At the bottom of the page, click the **Next** button. The New Question: Office Furniture Survey page is displayed.

8. In the **Question and Type** area, in the **Question** box, type What is the size of your organization (Number of employees worldwide)?, and then select the **Choice (menu to choose from)** option.

9. In the **Optional settings for your question** area, for the **Require a response to this question** option, select **Yes**.

10. In the **Type each choice on a separate line** box, type the following three lines:

    Under 25 employees
    Small (25-50)
    Medium (51-249)
    Large (250+)

11. Under **Display choices using**, make sure the **Radio Buttons** option is selected. This is the default setting.

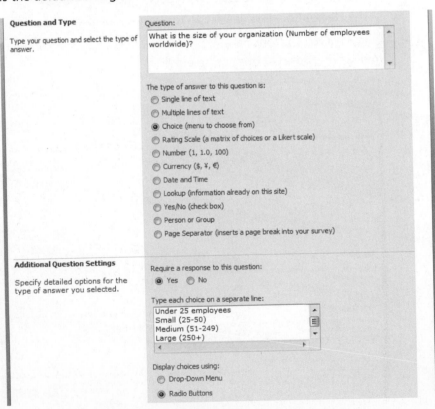

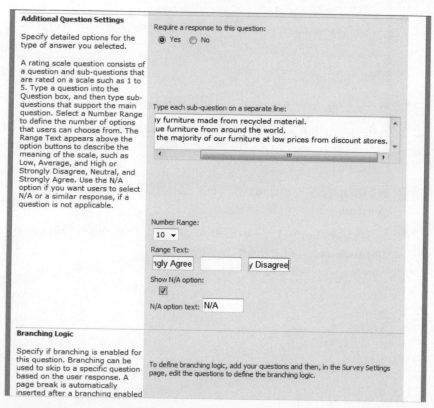

Next Question
Next Question

12. At the bottom of the page, click the **Next Question** button.

13. In the **Question and Type** area, in the **Question** box, type To what extent do you agree or disagree with the following statements?, and then select the **Rating Scale (a matrix of choices or a Likert scale)** option.

14. In the **Optional settings for your question** area, for the **Require a response to this question** option, select **Yes**.

15. In the **Type each choice on a separate line** area, replace the existing text with the following three lines:

We try to buy furniture made from recycled material.
We like unique furniture from around the world.
We purchase the majority of our furniture at low prices from discount stores.

16. Click the down arrow to the right of the **Number Range** box, and click **10**.

17. In the first **Range Text** box, type Strongly Agree. Delete the text in the middle box with a space, and in the last box, type Strongly Disagree.

18. At the bottom of the Web page, click **Next Question**.

19. In the **Question and Type** area, in the **Question** box, type Would you like us to contact you?, and then select the **Yes/No (checkbox)** option.

20. In the **Additional Question Settings** area, select **Yes**. This is the default setting.

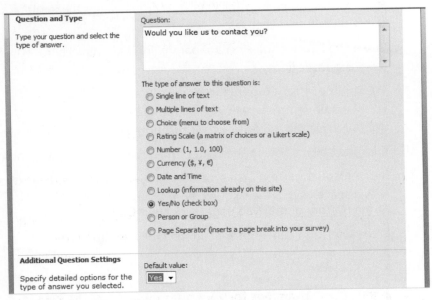

21. At the bottom of the Web page, click **Next Question**.

22. In the **Question and Type** area, in the **Question** box, type Please enter your name, address and any queries you may have:, and then select the **Multiple lines of text** option.

23. In the **Optional settings for your question** area, for the **Require a response to this question** option, select **Yes**.

24. In the **Specify the type of text to allow** option, select **Enhanced rich text (Rich text with pictures, tables, and hyperlinks)**.

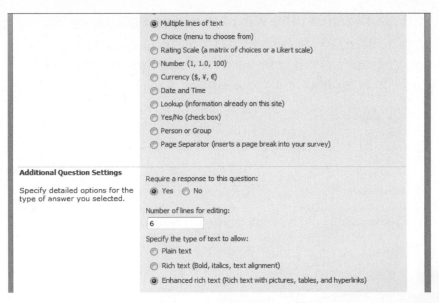

25. At the bottom of the Web page, click **Next Question**.

26. In the **Question and Type** area, in the **Question** box, type How much money, in total, did you spend on furniture over the last year?, and then select the **Currency** ($, ¥, £) option.

27. In the **Optional settings for your question** area, for the **Require a response to this question** option, select **Yes**.

28. To the right of the **Number of decimal places** box, click the down arrow, and then click **2**.

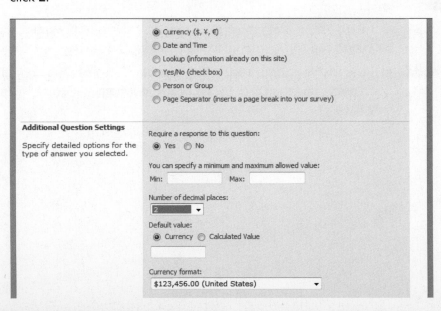

Finish

29. At the bottom of the Web page, click the **Finish** button. The Customize Office Furniture Survey page is displayed.

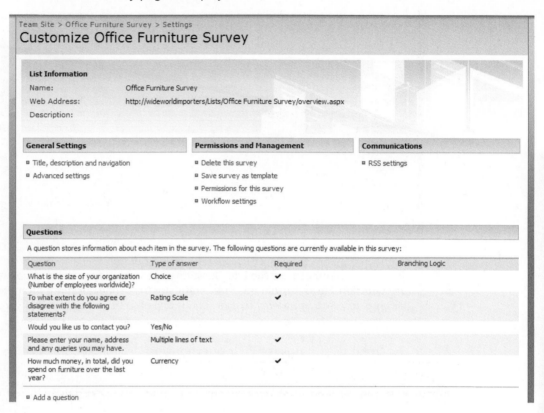

Team Site > Office Furniture Survey > Settings

Customize Office Furniture Survey

List Information

Name: Office Furniture Survey

Web Address: http://wideworldimporters/Lists/Office Furniture Survey/overview.aspx

Description:

General Settings	Permissions and Management	Communications
▫ Title, description and navigation	▫ Delete this survey	▫ RSS settings
▫ Advanced settings	▫ Save survey as template	
	▫ Permissions for this survey	
	▫ Workflow settings	

Questions

A question stores information about each item in the survey. The following questions are currently available in this survey:

Question	Type of answer	Required	Branching Logic
What is the size of your organization (Number of employees worldwide)?	Choice	✔	
To what extent do you agree or disagree with the following statements?	Rating Scale	✔	
Would you like us to contact you?	Yes/No		
Please enter your name, address and any queries you may have.	Multiple lines of text	✔	
How much money, in total, did you spend on furniture over the last year?	Currency	✔	

▫ Add a question

30. In the **Questions** area, under the **Question** column, click **Would you like us to contact you?**. The Edit Question: Office Furniture Survey page is displayed.

31. In the **Branching Logic** area, under **Possible Choices** to the right of **Yes**, click the down arrow, and then click **Please enter your name, address and any queries you may have.**

32. To the right of **No**, click the down arrow, and then click **How much money, in total, did you spend on furniture over the last year?**

33. Click **OK**. The Customize Office Furniture Survey page is displayed.

> **Important** You can use the Edit Question page to modify or delete an existing survey question. However, you must be careful not to change questions after you have allowed access to the survey to users and received some responses. Changing a survey question might cause you to lose data that you have already collected.

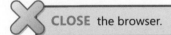 **CLOSE** the browser.

Responding to a Survey

As surveys are created on a SharePoint Web site, you might find that you need to respond to them. Surveys are created to gather information, and it is important that you know how to respond to surveys. As a survey creator, users must respond to your survey so you can analyze their responses. Once you have created a survey, it is good practice that you view the survey from a user's perspective by completing at least one test response.

In this exercise, you will respond to a survey.

OPEN the SharePoint site in which the survey is located. If prompted, type your user name and password, and click OK. The exercise uses the Office Furniture Survey created in the previous exercise, but you can use whatever survey you wish.

BE SURE TO verify that you have sufficient rights to contribute to the list. If in doubt, see the Appendix on page 435.

1. On the **Quick Launch**, under **Surveys**, click **Office Furniture Survey**. The Office Furniture Survey is displayed.

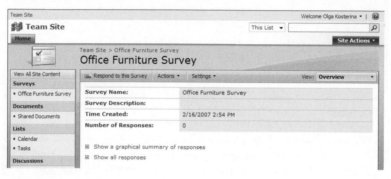

Respond to this
Survey

2. Click the **Respond to this Survey** button. The Office Furniture Survey page is displayed.

3. Select the **Under 25 employees** option. For the ranking questions options, select **1**, **2**, and **8** to the ranking questions, and leave the check box selected for the **Would you like us to contact you?** question.

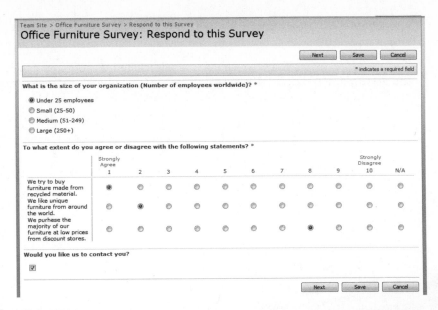

4. Click **Next**.

Save

Save

Important When you add a page separator to a survey, a Save button is added to all but the final page of the survey. You must answer all required responses on a survey page before you can successfully click Save. If you click Save, the survey responses are saved and categorized as not completed. You are not prompted for responses to questions on subsequent pages, even if the responses were set as required. For those questions in which you have enabled branching, survey questions automatically insert a page separator after the branch-enabled question.

5. In the text box, type Peter Connelly, peter@contoso.msft. For the money question, type 200.

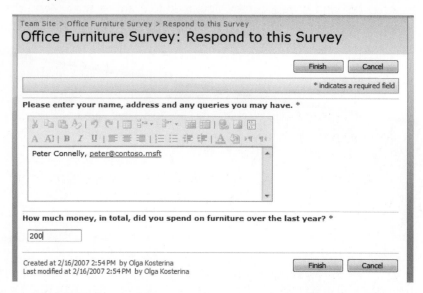

6. Click **Finish**. The Office Furniture Survey page is displayed.

7. Repeat Steps 2 through 6 several times, entering different responses each time.

   Notice that when you clear the check box for the Would you like us to contact you? question, you are not presented with a text box.

CLOSE the browser.

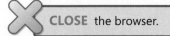

Settings

Troubleshooting If you do not allow multiple responses when you create a survey and you try to test the survey more than once, an Error page is displayed stating that you are not allowed to respond to the survey again. To correct this problem, display the Office Furniture Survey page, click the Settings button, and then click Survey Settings. On the Customize Office Furniture Survey page, under the General Settings area, click Title, Description And Navigation. On the Survey General Settings: Office Furniture Survey page, in the Survey Options area, select Yes as the Allow Multiple Responses option, and then click Save. Click the Office Furniture Survey breadcrumb to enter additional responses.

Viewing the Results of a Survey

After users respond to your survey, you need to examine and analyze the results. Windows SharePoint Services provides three ways to display a quick summary of the survey data.

1. **Overview** This view displays the survey's name, description, date, and time of creation as well as the number of responses.

2. **Graphical Summary** This view displays the response data for each survey question in a graphical form. The number of responses is displayed as a value and as a percentage of the total number of responses received.

3. **All Responses** This view displays a list of each survey response, the date and time the response was last modified, whether the user completed the survey, and the name of the user who created it, if applicable. In this view, responses can be modified or deleted.

> **Important** Surveys are created with item-level permissions so that all responses can be read by all users, but users can only edit their own responses. If you want to prevent users from changing their responses, display the survey, click Settings, and then click Survey Settings. On the Customize Office Furniture Survey page, under the General Settings area, click Advanced Settings. On the Survey Advanced Settings: page, in the Item-Level Permissions area, under the Edit Access: Specify Which Responses Users Can Edit list, click None.
>
> Setting survey permissions is similar to setting document library permissions. You can also set whether the survey should be visible in the search results on this page.

For more information about setting document library permissions, see Chapter 5, "Creating and Managing Libraries."

You can also export survey result data to a spreadsheet, where you can use the data analysis features available in Microsoft Office Excel 2007.

In the following exercise, you will view the survey responses. After editing one of your responses to the survey, you will export the results of the survey to Microsoft Office Excel and then find the average amount spent on office furniture by users who responded to your survey.

OPEN the SharePoint site in which the survey is located. If prompted, type your user name and password, and click OK. The exercise will use the Garden Survey used in the previous two exercises, but you can use whatever survey you wish.

BE SURE TO verify that you have sufficient rights to the list. If in doubt, see the Appendix on page 435.

Overview

1. On the **Quick Launch**, under **Surveys**, click **Office Furniture Survey**. The Office Furniture Survey page is displayed in Overview view.

View: Graphical
Summary

2. To the right of the page, next to **View**, click **Overview** and then click **Graphical Summary**. The Office Furniture Survey page is displayed in Graphical Summary view.

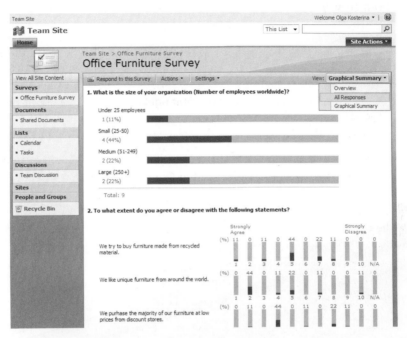

3. To the right of the page, next to **View**, click **Graphical Summary** and then click **All Responses**. The Office Furniture Survey page is displayed in All Responses view.

4. Point to the **View Response #1** survey item, and click the down arrow. On the drop-down list, click **Edit Response**.

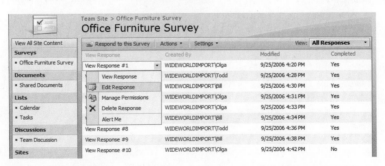

5. Select the **Medium (51-249)** option, and then click **Save**.

Actions

Open

Open

6. Click the **Actions** button, and then click **Export to Spreadsheet**.

7. If the File Download dialog box appears with a warning that some files can harm your computer, click the **Open** button. In the **Microsoft Office Excel Security Notice** dialog box, click **Enable**.

8. If an Office Excel dialog box appears with a warning, click **OK**.

The survey responses are displayed within Excel, with AutoFilter enabled in the header row of every column. The Excel workbook contains a column for each question, and a column for created by, item type and path to the list.

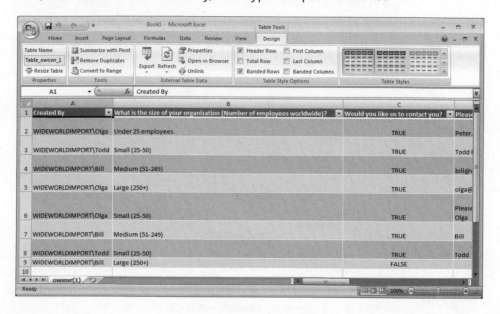

> **Important** Unlike the previous version of Windows SharePoint Services, the Rating Scale survey questions are exported into the spreadsheet.

9. In column E, click the first blank cell outside the Excel list, and then click the **Formulas** tab.

10. Click the down arrow to the right of **AutoSum** and click **AVERAGE**.

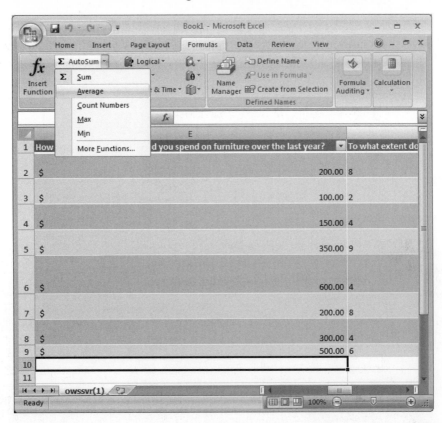

Excel displays the average amount that survey respondents spent on their office furniture in the last year.

11. On the ribbon, click **Save**. The Save As dialog box appears.

12. In the **File name** box, type OfficeFurnitureSurvey.xlsx, and click **Save**.

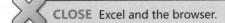 **CLOSE** Excel and the browser.

For more information about how to use Excel with Windows SharePoint Services, see Chapter 12, "Using Windows SharePoint Services with Excel 2007."

Creating and Using a Discussion Board

Discussion boards provide a forum on which visitors to your site can converse about topics of interest. SharePoint sites created with the Team, Document Workspace, or Social Meeting site templates include a discussion board. You can display the discussion board by using the Quick Launch for the Team and Document Workspace sites or the Discussion tab on Social Meeting workspaces.

You can use a discussion board to initiate new discussions as well as sort and filter existing discussions. You can also change the design of the discussion board and create alerts that notify you of changes to the discussion board.

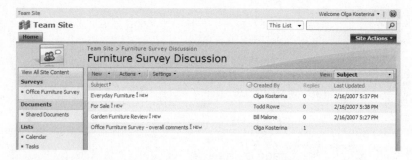

Discussion boards are usually displayed in one of three views.

1. **Subject view** This view enables you to view a list of discussions.

2. **Threaded view** This view enables you to view comments grouped by discussion, or thread. All messages that are a part of the same thread appear together in the order in which they were created.

3. **Flat view** This view lists replies in chronological order in the order in which they were created.

You can post replies to the Team Discussion discussion board, or you can create new discussion boards. You can configure discussion board security settings so that users can participate in one discussion board but not another.

> **Important** Discussion boards are created with the same item-level permissions as surveys; that is, all discussions and replies can be read by all users, but users can edit only their own discussions and replies.

In this exercise, you will create a new discussion board, add a new topic, delete a topic, and then remove the discussion board.

OPEN the SharePoint site in which you would like to create a discussion board. If prompted, type your user name and password, and click OK.

BE SURE TO verify that you have sufficient rights to create a list. If in doubt, see the Appendix on page 435.

1. On the **Quick Launch**, click **Discussions**. The All Site Content page is displayed.

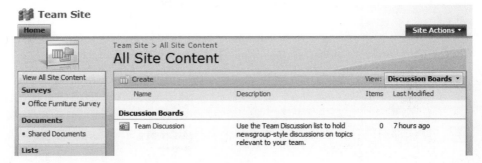

2. Click **Create**. The Create page is displayed.

3. Under the **Communications** area, click **Discussion Board**. The New form is displayed.

4. In the **Name** box, type Furniture Survey Discussion.

> **Tip** The Name field is the Subject of the discussion, as well as the URL for the discussion board.

5. In the **Navigation** area, make sure that the **Yes** option is selected. This is the default setting.

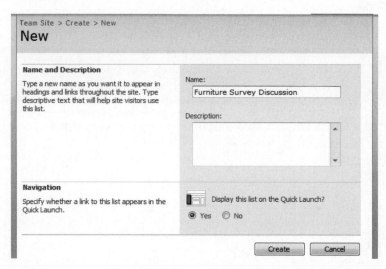

6. At the bottom of the Web page, click **Create**. The Furniture Survey Discussion page is displayed.

> **Important** Because surveys and discussion boards are both lists, the name of the list needs to be unique within the site. Therefore, you cannot call the discussion board in this exercise Furniture *Survey* because this name would conflict with the Furniture Survey survey you created in the first exercise.

New

7. Click the **New** button.

8. In the **Subject** box, type Office Furniture Survey – overall comments.

9. In the **Text** box, type What did you think of the range of questions on the Office Furniture Survey?

10. Click **OK**.

View: Flat

View Properties
View Properties

Reply
Reply

11. Click **Office Furniture Survey – overall comments**.

The Furniture Survey Discussion page is displayed in Flat view, where each reply has a title bar that displays the date and time the reply was created, a View Properties button, and a Reply button.

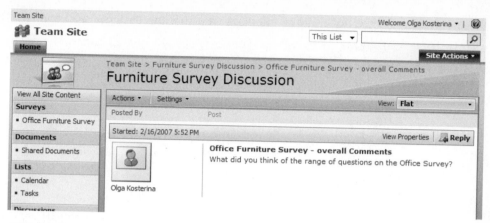

12. Click **Reply**.

13. In the **Body** textbox, type We could add an additional question that asks users whether they subscribe to Wide World Importer's monthly newsletter. The answer type would be Yes/No.

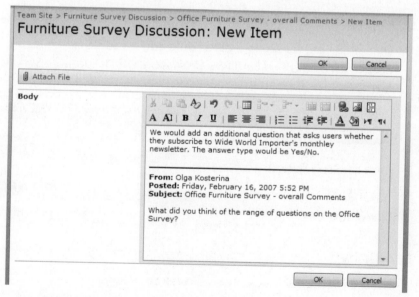

14. Click **OK**. The Furniture Survey Discussion discussion board is displayed in Flat view.

15. On the right side of the page next to **View**, click **Flat** and then click **Threaded**.

All replies to the Office Furniture Survey – overall comments discussion are displayed in Threaded view.

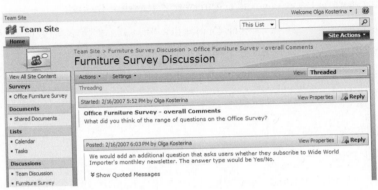

> **Tip** To return to Subject view, click Furniture Survey Discussion on the bread crumb or, in the Quick Launch, under Discussions, click Furniture Survey Discussion.

16. On the title bar for the reply **We could add an additional question**, click **View Properties**. The Office Furniture Discussion: Office Furniture Survey – overall comments page is displayed.

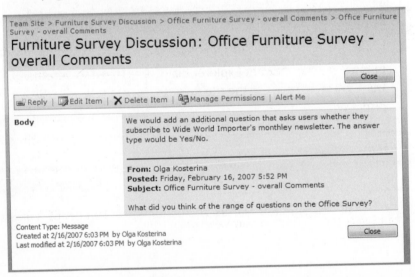

17. Click the **Delete Item** button.

18. In the Windows Internet Explorer dialog box that asks whether you are sure you want to send this item to the site Recycle Bin, click **OK**.

The Office Furniture Discussion page is displayed in Threaded view for the Office Furniture Survey – overall comments discussion thread.

19. On the **Settings menu** click **Discussion Board Settings**. The Customize Furniture Survey Discussion page is displayed.

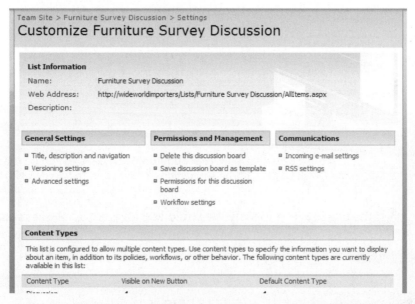

Team Site > Furniture Survey Discussion > Settings

Customize Furniture Survey Discussion

List Information

Name: Furniture Survey Discussion
Web Address: http://wideworldimporters/Lists/Furniture Survey Discussion/AllItems.aspx
Description:

General Settings	**Permissions and Management**	**Communications**
▫ Title, description and navigation	▫ Delete this discussion board	▫ Incoming e-mail settings
▫ Versioning settings	▫ Save discussion board as template	▫ RSS settings
▫ Advanced settings	▫ Permissions for this discussion board	
	▫ Workflow settings	

Content Types

This list is configured to allow multiple content types. Use content types to specify the information you want to display about an item, in addition to its policies, workflows, or other behavior. The following content types are currently available in this list:

Content Type	Visible on New Button	Default Content Type

20. Under the **Permissions and Management** area, click **Delete this discussion board**.

21. In the Windows Internet Explorer dialog box that asks whether you are sure you want to send this list to the site Recycle Bin, click **OK**. The All Site Content page is displayed.

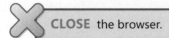

CLOSE the browser.

Tip From the Customize Web page, you can enable content approval, create columns other than Subject and Text, or display views other than Threaded and Flat.

Enabling Discussion Board for E-Mail

As detailed in Chapter 4, Windows SharePoint Services allows list managers to assign an e-mail address to discussion boards. Before this e-mail feature can be used, the Windows SharePoint Services farm administrator must configure the Web application for outgoing e-mail. You should contact this person in your organization if you wish to use this e-mail feature. If the e-mail feature is enabled, then the Incoming E-Mail area is visible on the Create page.

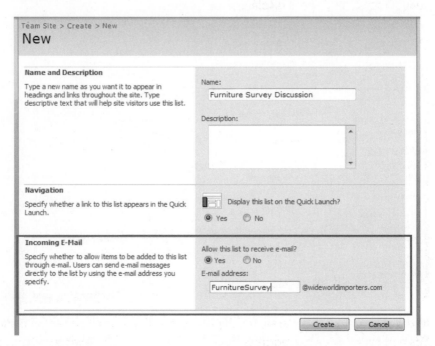

If the e-mail feature is configured by the Windows SharePoint Services farm administrator after the discussion board is created or if you decided not to enable the e-mail feature when you created the discussion board, then you can allow the list to subsequently receive e-mails. In the following exercise, you will enable an existing discussion board so that users can e-mail their discussions.

OPEN the SharePoint site in which the discussion board is located. If prompted, type your user name and password, and click OK. The exercise uses the Team Discussion created as part of a Team site, but you can use whatever discussion board you wish.

BE SURE TO verify that you have sufficient rights to create a list. If in doubt, see the Appendix on page 435.

1. On the **Quick Launch**, under **Discussions, click Team Discussion**. The Team Discussion is displayed.

2. On the **Settings** menu, click **Discussion Board Settings**. The Customize Team Discussion page is displayed.

3. Under the **Communications** area, click **Incoming e-mail settings**. If this option is not available, a Windows SharePoint Services farm administrator will need to configure the Web application for incoming e-mails. The Incoming E-Mail Settings: Team Discussion page is displayed.

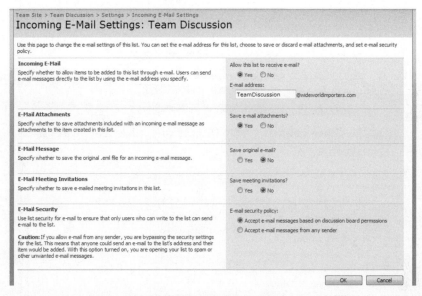

4. In the **Incoming E-Mail** area, for the **Allow this list to receive e-mail** option, select **Yes** and enter an e-mail address, such as **TeamDiscussion@wideworldimporters. com**. You need only provide the part of the e-mail address that precedes the "at" sign ("@").

5. At the bottom of the page, click the **Next** button. The Team Discussion page is displayed.

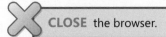

CLOSE the browser.

> **Tip** Further details concerning the e-mail feature are found in Chapter 4.

Viewing a Discussion Board in Outlook 2007

Windows SharePoint Services 3.0 allows you to contribute and search discussion boards from within Outlook 2007. Discussion questions and replies can be made available even when you are offline. Chapter 11, "Using Windows SharePoint Services with Outlook 2007," provides more details on the integration of Outlook 2007 and Windows SharePoint Services.

In the following exercise, you will view a discussion board from within Outlook 2007.

OPEN the SharePoint site in which the discussion board is located. If prompted, type your user name and password, and click OK. The exercise uses the Team Discussion created in a Team Site, but you can use whatever discussion board you wish.

BE SURE TO verify that you have sufficient rights to create a list. If in doubt, see the Appendix on page 435.

1. On the **Quick Launch**, under **Discussions, click Team Discussion**. The Team Discussion is displayed.

2. Click **Actions**, and then select **Connect to Outlook**.

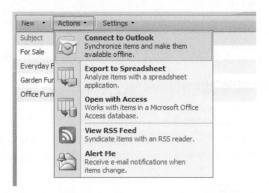

3. If the Internet Explorer Security warning dialog box appears stating that a website wants to open web content using outlook on your computer, click **Allow**.

Outlook opens and might ask you to supply your user name and password.

A Microsoft Office Outlook dialog box appears, stating you should only connect lists from sources you know and trust.

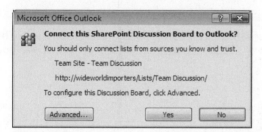

4. Click the **Advanced** button. A SharePoint List Options dialog box appears.

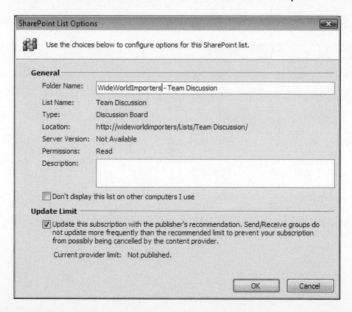

5. In the **Folder Name** textbox, type WideWorldImporters – Furniture Survey Discussion, and click **OK**. In the **Microsoft Office Outlook** dialog box, click **Yes**. Outlook displays the WideWorldImporters – Furniture Discussion area under the Outlook SharePoint Lists folder.

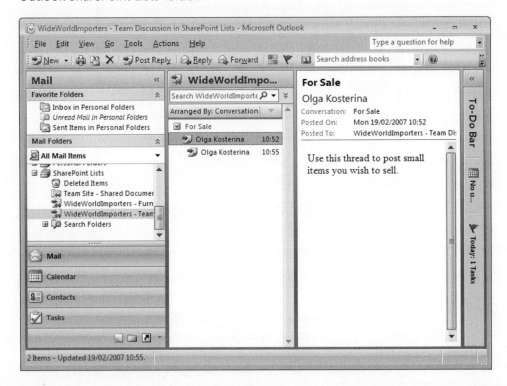

CLOSE Outlook and any browser windows that you might have open.

Key Points

- A survey allows you to create questions and control the response format.

- In a survey, you can create both open-ended and closed-ended questions.

- Windows SharePoint Services provides three views in which to summarize survey responses: Overview, Graphical Summary, and All Responses. You can export survey responses to a spreadsheet to perform more complex data analysis.

- A discussion board allows users to create and reply to discussion subjects.

- You can view discussions in either Subject, Flat, or Threaded view.

- You can enable a discussion board to receive incoming e-mail.

- You can connect any discussion board to Outlook. These appear under the SharePoint Lists folder.

- Surveys and discussion boards are specialized lists. Their permissions can be controlled independently of both the site and of other lists. You can apply item-level permissions to prevent users from editing their survey responses or discussion messages.

Chapter at a Glance

Create a new wiki page gallery, **page 264**

Create a new Wiki page, **page 269**

Create a blog site, **page 275**

Create a blog post, **page 278**

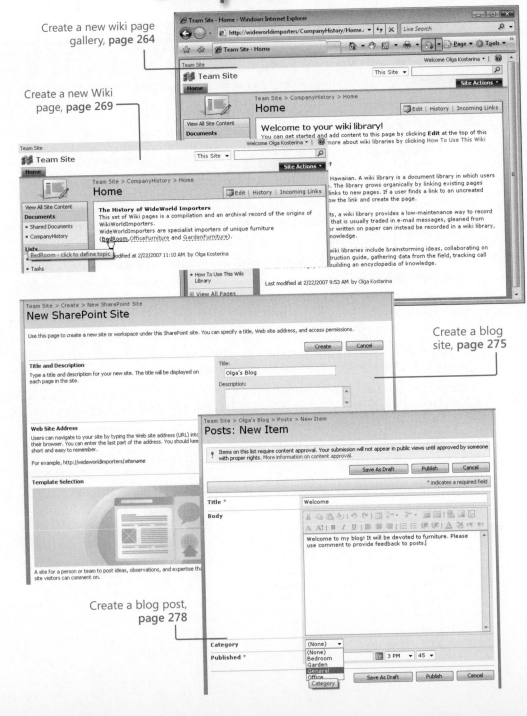

10 Working with Wikis and Blogs

In this chapter, you will learn to:

✔ Understand Wikis.

✔ Create a new wiki page library.

✔ Create a new Wiki page.

✔ Understand blogs.

✔ Create a blog Site.

✔ Create a blog post.

✔ Add a blog comment.

✔ Use RSS feeds.

Wikis and *blogs* are methods that enable anyone, including nontechnical users, to write Web pages and publish them on Internet, extranet, and intranet Web sites for other users to see. Both allow users a freedom to publish content for broad consumption. Blogs are personal journals or observations, whereas anyone can contribute to content on a wiki Web site. The onus is on wiki Web site users to manage changes and ensure accuracy and relevance. Most wikis and blogs can use Really Simple Syndication (RSS) feeds to notify users when site content changes. Microsoft Windows SharePoint Services offers both wikis and blogs.

In this chapter, you will learn how to use wikis and blogs as well as how to enable an RSS feed on a blog.

Important Before you can use the practice sites provided for this chapter, you need to install them from the book's companion CD to their default locations. See "Using the Book's CD" on page xix for more information.

> **Important** Remember to use your SharePoint site location in place of
> *http://wideworldimporters* in the exercises.

Understanding Wikis

The very first wiki (pronounced wee-kee) site, WikiWikiWeb, was created for the Portland Pattern Repository in 1995 by Ward Cunningham, who devised a system that created Web pages quickly and allowed users to freely create and edit Web page content by using a Web browser. Wiki is the Hawaiian word for quick, and as Hawaiian words are doubled for emphasis, wikiwiki means very quick. WikiWikiWeb is the proper name of the concept, of which wiki or wikis are abbreviations.

A wiki Web site allows you to change any wiki page or create new pages, which is known as "open editing." If a page is found to be incomplete or poorly organized, any user can edit it as they see fit. Therefore, as users share their information, knowledge, experience, ideas, and views, the content evolves. All users control and check the content because wikis rely on the assumption that most readers have good intentions. A wiki, therefore, provides collaborative and democratic use of Web sites. Wikis are purportedly more often used within companies than on the Internet, and common uses included intranets, project communication, and documentation.. A wiki enables users to work together to change or update information without the need to send e-mails or attend meetings or conference calls. One wiki implementation is Wikipedia from Wikimedia Foundation Inc. (http://www.wikipedia.org), which is an encyclopedia-like Web site that has inherited many of the nonencyclopedic properties of a wiki site.

Creating a New Wiki Page Library

Although you can create a site on Windows SharePoint Services based on the wiki Web site template, the use of wikis is not limited to those sites. Wikis can be used within any team site by making use of the wiki page library. A wiki page library allows you to create an interconnected collection of Wiki pages.

In the following exercise, you will create a wiki page library and edit the home page.

OPEN the SharePoint site in which you would like to create a wiki page library. The exercise will use the *http://wideworldimporters* site, but you can use whatever site you want. If prompted, type your user name and password, and then click OK.

BE SURE TO verify that you have sufficient rights to create a wiki page library. If in doubt, see the Appendix on page 435.

1. Click **Site Actions**. From the drop-down list, click **Create**. The Create page appears.

2. Under **Libraries**, click **Wiki Page Library**. The New page appears.

3. In the **Name** text box, type CompanyHistory.

> **Important** The Name field is used for both the title and Web address of the wiki page library. Any Web address (URL) in SharePoint is limited to 260 characters and must not contain the characters /\ : * ? " < > |# { } % & or ~. Tab characters and multiple periods should also not be used. Spaces in URLs should be avoided because they are replaced by the characters %20 and therefore take up three characters. A Wiki page name should not exceed 128 characters, so you should therefore choose a terse but meaningful name.

4. In the **Description** text box, type This wiki page library contains a set of Wiki pages that describe the history of our company.

5. Leave the default setting set at **Display this document library on the Quick Launch**.

Create

6. Click the **Create** button. The home page appears with the title Welcome to your wiki library.

The CompanyHistory wiki page library is listed on the Quick Launch under Documents.

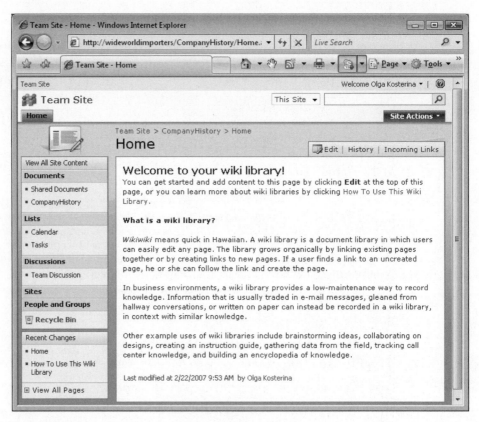

7. In the breadcrumb, click **CompanyHistory**. The AllPages view of the CompanyHistory library is displayed.

8. Click **Settings**, and then click **Document Library Settings**. The Customize CompanyHistory page is displayed.

9. Under **General Settings**, click **Title, description and navigation**. The Document Library General Settings: Company History page is displayed.

10. In the **Name** textbox, type WideWorldImporters History and then click **Save**. The Customize WideWorldImporters History page is displayed.

    The title of the wiki page library is now WideWorldImporters History; however, the Web address is unchanged and remains as http://wideworldimporters/companyhistory.

11. In the breadcrumb, click **WideWorldImporters History** and then click **Home**. The home page appears with the title Welcome to your wiki library.

The WideWorldImporters History wiki page library is listed on the Quick Launch under Documents.

12. Under **Recent Changes**, click **How To Use This Wiki Library**. The How To Use This Wiki Library page is displayed.

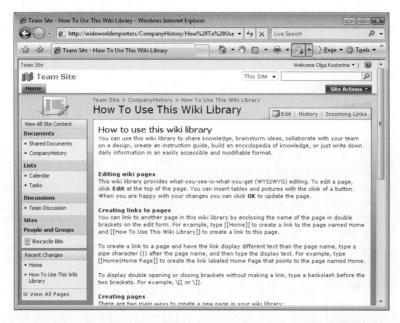

13. Under **Recent Changes**, click **Home**. The home page appears.

Edit

14. At the top of the page, click the **Edit** button.

The edit form for the WideWorldImporters History: Home page is displayed with a formatting toolbar placed above the Wiki Content area.

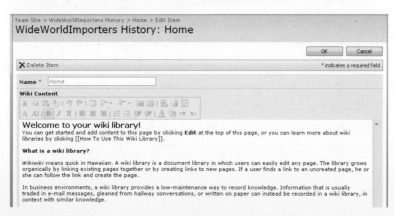

15. Place the cursor in the Wiki Content area to the left of the **Welcome** title. Press Ctrl + A to select all of the content, and then press Del.

    The contents of the Wiki page are deleted.

    > **Tip** Other keyboard shortcuts can be found by hovering the cursor above the buttons on the formatting toolbar.

16. In the **Wiki Content** area, type The History of WideWorld Importers, and then press Enter to move the cursor to a new line.

17. Select the sentence you just typed, and press Ctrl + B.

18. On a new line, type This set of Wiki pages is a compilation and an archival record of the origins of WideWorldImporters.

    > **Tip** Start a Wiki page with an introduction that states its purpose. The first page in the wiki page library is labeled Home and should contain the context or any assumptions that will apply to all Wiki pages stored in that library. If you edit an existing wiki page, you should not place new content before the introduction, nor should the content necessarily be added to the bottom of the page. You should emphasize the flow of ideas, be concise, write factual information, and stay on topic for the page. Check for spelling and grammar errors that can detract from the wiki content. You might consider entering the text in Microsoft Office Word first, check it for spelling and grammar, and then paste it into the Wiki Content area.

19. Click **OK**. The home page is displayed, together with a last-modified date and time, plus the name of the person who modified it.

> **Tip** You can add Web Parts to a Wiki page by selecting Edit Page from the Site Actions menu. A Wiki page contains one Web Part Zone, labeled Bottom, where Web Parts can be added. See Chapter 15, "Working with Web Parts," for more information.

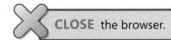 **CLOSE** the browser.

Creating a New Wiki Page

A Wiki page is a chunk of factual content or concrete advice that is typically limited to no more than two or three screens of information in an easily accessible and modifiable format. Two methods are used to create a new page in a wiki page library.

1. Create a forward link and then click on it to create a page. This is the recommended method because it is easier for people to find a page when another page is linked to it.

2. Create a page that is not linked to another page by using the All Pages view of the wiki page library.

In this exercise, you will create a Wiki page by using these two methods.

OPEN the SharePoint site in which the wiki page library exists. This exercise will use the *http://wideworldimporters* site and the WideWorldImporters History wiki page library, but you can use whatever site and wiki page library you want. If prompted, type your user name and password, and then click OK.

BE SURE TO complete the first exercise in this chapter before beginning this exercise.

1. On the **Quick Launch**, under **Documents**, click **WideWorldImporters History**. The home page of the WideWorldImporters History wiki page library appears.

2. Click **Edit**. The edit form for the home page is displayed.

3. Place the cursor on a new line and type WideWorldImporters are specialist importers of unique furniture ([[BedRoom]], [[OfficeFurniture]] and [[GardenFurniture]]).

4. Click **OK**.

The home page is displayed with the words BedRoom, OfficeFurniture, and GardenFurniture shown as hyperlinks and underlined with a dotted line. By using double brackets on the edit form, you create three forward-linked pages. Linked pages do not have to exist, and such nonexistent pages are denoted by a dotted underline, as is the case with BedRoom, OfficeFurniture, and GardenFurniture.

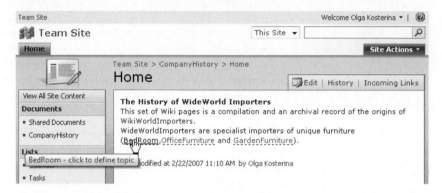

> **Tip** The naming convention for Wiki pages, known as *WikiWords* or *WikiNames*, is to concatenate two or more words. Each word is composed of two or more letters, with no spaces between words. The first letter of each word is capitalized and the remaining letters are lowercase. This formatting is known as *Camel case*. The Wiki page name is used to form part of the URL.

5. Click **BedRoom**. The New Wiki Page page is displayed, with the Name textbox containing the word BedRoom.

6. In the **Wiki Content** area, type **WideWorldImporters Bed Room Furniture** and then click **Create**.

   The BedRoom page is displayed, and BedRoom appears in the list of Recent Changes in the left navigation pane.

7. In the **Recent Changes** area, click **View All Pages**. The WideWorldImporters History wiki page library is displayed in the All Pages view.

New

8. Click the **New** button. The New Wiki Page page is displayed.

9. In the **Name** textbox, type Seating.

10. In the **Wiki Content** area, type WideWorldImporters Seating and then click **Create**.

The Seating page is displayed, and Seating appears in the list of Recent Changes in the left navigation pane.

CLOSE the browser.

Linking

Within a wiki, you can only link to an entire page and not to part of a page. Because a Wiki page contains information about a specific topic, it is easier for users to find information on that topic by providing a forward link to a Wiki page.

In the previous section, you created a forward link to a Wiki page yet to be created by enclosing the name of the page in double square brackets on the edit form. In the following exercise, you will create a link to a page and have the link display text that is different than the page name. You will then use Incoming Links to identify those pages that link to a Wiki page before you delete the page.

> **Tip** When you add content to a Wiki page and pose a question that other contributors to the Wiki page may know the answer to, try to enter text on the Wiki page in the form of a forward link; that is, place text between double square brackets. Other contributors to the Wiki page can answer your question by clicking the forward link and creating new Wiki pages.

OPEN the SharePoint site in which the wiki page library exists. The exercise will use the *http://wideworldimporters* site and the WideWorldImporters History wiki page library, but you can use whatever site and wiki page library you want. If prompted, type your user name and password, and then click OK.

BE SURE TO complete the previous exercises in this chapter before beginning this exercise.

1. On the **Quick Launch**, under **Documents**, click **WideWorldImporters History**. The home page of the WideWorldImporters History wiki page library appears.

2. Click **Edit**. The edit form for the home page is displayed.

3. Place the cursor on a new line and type [[Seating|Seating Furniture]] and then click **OK**. The home page is displayed.

> **Tip** To display double open or closed square brackets without making a link, type a backslash before the two brackets, such as \[[or \]].

The words Seating Furniture are not underlined with dashes; therefore, this forward link points to the existing Seating Wiki page that you created in the previous exercise.

4. Click **Seating Furniture**. The Seating Wiki page is displayed.

Incoming Links

5. Click the **Incoming Links** button. The Wiki pages that link to the Seating Wiki page are listed; the home page is the only one listed here.

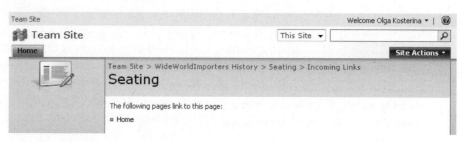

6. Click **Home**, and then click **Edit**.

7. In the **Wiki Content** area, select **[[Seating|Seating Furniture]]**, press ⌦, and then click **OK**.

8. Under **Recent Changes**, click **Seating**, and then click **Edit**.

> **Important** If the Seating Wiki page is not listed under Recent Changes, click View All Pages. In the All Pages view of the WideWorldImporters History library, click Seating.

✗ Delete Item
Delete Item

9. Click the **Delete Item** button. A Windows Internet Explorer window appears.

10. Click **OK** to send the Wiki page to the Recycle Bin.

> **Important** If you do not delete the forward links to a Wiki page before you delete the Wiki page, the forward links are displayed with a dashed underline, identifying them as forward links to a nonexistent Wiki page; that is, a Wiki page that has yet to be created.

 CLOSE the browser.

Versioning

A wiki in Windows SharePoint Services is implemented as a document library and therefore has all of the features of a document library, such as history and version management. Therefore, no amendments are lost. Major versioning is turned on by default when you create a wiki page library. You can also make use of content approval and workflow, as well as restrict the rights as to who can publish and edit Wiki pages. One useful capability of wikis in Windows SharePoint Services is to add metadata columns to the wiki page library. The metadata appears at the bottom of the Wiki page and can be used for page classification.

In the following exercise, you will view the history of a Wiki page, observe the changes to the Wiki page, and then revert back to the previous copy of the Wiki page.

 OPEN the SharePoint site in which the wiki page library exists. The exercise will use the *http://wideworldimporters* site and the WideWorldImporters History wiki page library, but you can use whatever site and wiki page library you want. If prompted, type your user name and password, and then click OK.

BE SURE TO complete the exercises in this chapter before beginning this exercise.

1. On the **Quick Launch**, under **Documents**, click **WideWorldImporters History**. The home page of the WideWorldImporters History wiki page library appears.

2. Click the **History** button.

| History

History

You are taken to the History page of the Wiki home page. In the Wiki Content area, deletions have a blue background with a strikethrough font, and additions have a light orange background color. In the left navigation pane, each version of the Wiki page is listed with the date and time that the version was created.

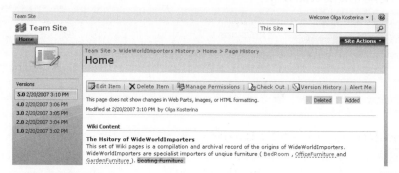

3. In the left navigation pane, under **Versions**, click **4.0**. The fourth version of the Wiki page is displayed.

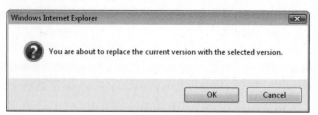

Restore This
Version

4. Click the **Restore this version** button. A Windows Internet Explorer window appears.

5. Click **OK** to replace the current version of the Wiki page with the selected version. The Wiki home page is displayed.

The words Seating Furniture are dashed and underlined and therefore point to a nonexistent Wiki page.

CLOSE the browser.

Understanding Blogs

A Web log, known as a blog, is a personal journal or commentary shared on a Web site. *Blogging* is the term that refers to a person, called a *blogger*, who publishes their thoughts on the blog Web site. The thoughts shared on the blog Web site are called *posts* or articles. Each posting or article is displayed in reverse chronological order, with the most recent additions featured most prominently and older blogs grouped in archives by the month in which they were created.

Blog posts can be categorized to help users find past conversations. Also, blogs are indexed so that a visitor can search through old blogs and learn from past conversations. Most bloggers write blogs frequently, often on a daily basis. Some allow visitors to comment on the blog, provide feedback, and ask questions.

Creating a Blog Site

Strictly speaking, creating a blog site is not a new feature to Windows SharePoint Services 3.0. Using Windows SharePoint Services 2.0, it was possible to create a blog site from Microsoft Office FrontPage 2003. However, blog sites can be created from the browser in Windows SharePoint Services 3.0. When using Microsoft Office SharePoint Server 2007, the logical location for a blog site is a user's personal site, or My Site, where a link exists with which to create a blog.

In this exercise, you will create a blog site and then establish categories for your blog posts.

OPEN the SharePoint site in which you would like to create a blog site. The exercise will use the *http://wideworldimporters* site, but you can use whatever site you want. If prompted, type your user name and password, and then click OK.

BE SURE TO verify that you have sufficient rights to create a blog site. If in doubt, see the Appendix on page 435.

1. From the **Site Actions** menu. select **Create**. The Create page appears.
2. Under **Web Pages**, click **Sites and Workspaces**.
3. In the **Title and Description** section, in the **Title** textbox, type Olga's Blog.
4. In the **Web Site Address** section, in the **URL name** textbox, type OlgaBlog.
5. In the **Template Selection** section, on the **Collaboration** tab, select **Blog**.

6. Click **Create**. The Operation in Progress page is displayed, which is then replaced by the home page of the Olga's Blog Web site.

   The home page of a blog site consists of two Web Parts, Posts and Admin Links. Three areas can be found on the Quick Launch .

   1. Categories Area where three sample categories are listed: Category 1, Category 2, and Category 3.

   2. Other Blogs Area containing a link list where you can add link items to point to other user's blogs.

   3. Links Area containing another link list with three link items.

   ● Photos Redirects users to the Photos picture library on the Olga's Blog Web site.

   ● Archive Redirects users to the Archive view for the Posts list. This view displays only those posts that are approved.

   ● Calendar Redirects users to the Calendar view for the Posts list.

7. On the **Quick Launch**, click **Categories**. The All Categories view of the Categories list is displayed.

8. Move the mouse over the **Category 1** list item, and then click the down arrow that appears.

9. On the drop-down menu, click **Edit Item** to display the Categories: Category 1 page.

10. In the **Title** textbox, delete **Category 1** and type Office.

11. Click **OK**.

12. Repeat Steps 8 to 11 to replace **Category 2** with Bedroom and **Category 3** with Garden.

13. Click the **Olga's Blog** tab to display the home page of the blog site.

    Under the Categories area are listed Office, Bedroom, and Garden.

14. Under **Categories**, click **Add new category**. The Categories: New Item page is displayed.

15. In the **Title** textbox, type General and then click **OK**.

    Under the Categories area are listed Office, Bedroom, Garden, and General.

16. On the blog site's home page, in the **Admin Links** Web Part, click **Manage posts**. The Posts list is displayed using the All Posts view.

17. Move the mouse over the **Welcome to your Blog** list item, and then click the down arrow that appears.

18. On the drop-down menu, click **Delete Item**. A Windows Internet Explorer dialog box appears.

19. Click **OK** to send the list item to the Recycle Bin.

   The Posts list is redisplayed. The Welcome to your Blog list item is not listed.

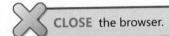 **CLOSE** the browser.

Creating a Blog Post

A blog post is the method by which you share your opinions and knowledge. You must remember that, as a blogger, you are responsible for the commentary you post and can be held personally liable if your posting is considered defamatory, obscene, proprietary, or libelous. Similar to posting information on a wiki, you should practice good manners and understatement.

You can create a blog post by using many tools including Microsoft Office Word 2007, Microsoft Office OneNote 2007, Microsoft Office Live Writer, and the browser. To quickly launch Office Word 2007 to create a blog post, on the blog Web site in the Admin Links Web Part, click the link Launch blog program to post. Word 2007 opens, and the New SharePoint Blog Account dialog box appears. The Web address of the blog site is listed in the Blog URL textbox.

Once a blog post is opened in Word 2007, the Blog Post tab is active. The Blog group provides easy access to the home page of your blog site where you can assign a category to the blog post, open an existing blog, manage accounts, and publish the blog. Any pictures that you insert into the post by using Word 2007 are automatically copied to the Photos picture library when the blog post is published or published as draft.

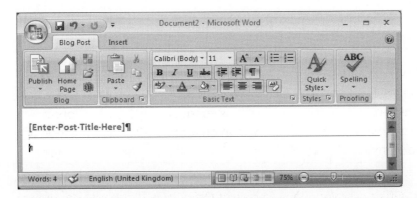

In the following exercise, you will create a blog post by using the browser and sort the post into multiple categories.

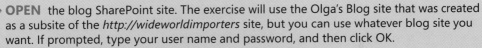

OPEN the blog SharePoint site. The exercise will use the Olga's Blog site that was created as a subsite of the *http://wideworldimporters* site, but you can use whatever blog site you want. If prompted, type your user name and password, and then click OK.

BE SURE TO complete the first exercise in this chapter before beginning this exercise.

1. On the blog site's home page, in the **Admins Links** Web Part, click **Create a post**. The Posts: New Item page is displayed.

   Notice that the Posts list has content approval enabled.

2. In the **Title** textbox, type Welcome.

3. In the **Body** textbox, type Welcome to my blog! It will be devoted to furniture. Please use comments to provide feedback to posts.

4. On the **Category** dropdown list, select **General**.

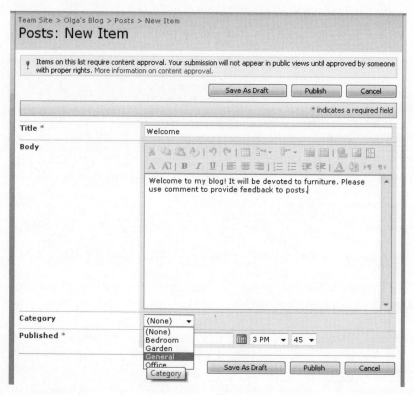

5. Click **Publish**.

The blog site's home page is displayed with the Welcome posting as the first posting on the page. The last line of the post states the time that the post was published, together with its category. Clicking the category link on this line displays a page where all similarly categorized posts are listed. This behavior is the same as clicking the category under the Categories area on the Quick Launch.

Tip If you include pictures on any of your posts, upload them into the Photos picture library on your blog Web site.

6. In the **Admin Links** Web Part, click **Manage posts**. The Posts list is displayed using the All Posts view.

7. Click **Settings**, and then click **List Settings**. The Customize Posts page is displayed.

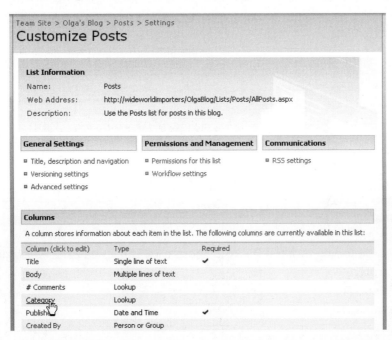

8. In the **Columns** section, click the **Category** column. The Change Column: Posts page is displayed.

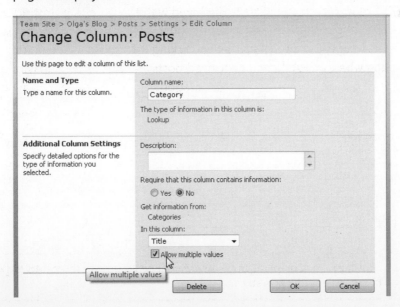

9. At the bottom of the **Additional Column Settings** section, select the **Allow multiple values** check box, and then click **OK**.

10. In the breadcrumb, click **Olga's Blog**. The blog site's home page is displayed.

11. On the last line of the Welcome blog, which starts with the words Posted at, click **Permalink**. The Welcome post is displayed.

12. At the top right of the Welcome post, click **Edit**. The Posts: Welcome page is displayed.

Team Site > Olga's Blog > Posts > Welcome > Edit Item
Posts: Welcome

13. Scroll to the bottom of the page. In the **Category** section, click **Bedroom** and then click **Add**.

> **Tip** Similar to other Microsoft programs, it is possible to add multiple categories by holding down the Shift key while selecting the categories between the first click and the second click. Holding down the Ctrl key selects or deselects categories.

14. Click **Publish**. The blog site's home page is displayed.

Two categories are listed for the Welcome post: General and Bedroom.

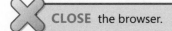 **CLOSE** the browser.

Adding a Blog Comment

To interact with a blogger, you can leave comments on a blog post. As a blogger, you must review comments left on your posts, not only to respond to comments, but also to delete comments that are either off topic or are used to advertise Web sites or spam. If the aim of a blog post is to start a discussion and you receive virtually no responses, then you could use a comment to post a question to your own blog post.

In this exercise, you will add a blog and delete a comment to a blog post.

OPEN the blog SharePoint site. The exercise will use the Olga's Blog site that was created as a subsite of the *http://wideworldimporters* site, but you can use whatever blog site you want. If prompted, type your user name and password, and then click OK.

BE SURE TO complete the blog-related exercises in this chapter before beginning this exercise.

1. On the blog site's home page, in the last line of a post, click **Comments(0)**. The post is displayed with a Comments form.

2. In the **Title** textbox, type Re: Welcome to your blog. In the **Body** textbox, type Welcome Olga!

3. Click the **Submit Comment** button.

The post is redisplayed with both a Comments and an Add Comment area. The last line of the post displays Comments(1).

4. To the right of the **Re: Welcome to your blog comment**, click **Edit**. The Comments: Re: Welcome to your blog page is displayed.

5. Click **Delete Item**. A Windows Internet Explorer dialog box appears.

6. Click **OK** to send the comment item to the Recycle Bin.

The post page is displayed with no comments, and the last line of the post displays Comments(0).

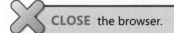

CLOSE the browser.

Using Really Simple Syndication Feeds

RSS feeds is a data format that provides users with a means of keeping up to date with content that is added to a Web site. Originally, the data format was known as RDF (Resource Description Framework) Site Summary, and then it became known as Rich Site Summary. Today RSS is known as Really Simple Syndication. By using Windows SharePoint Services, you can decide to syndicate content. This means that you can create an RSS feed for any list or library, thereby allowing users to subscribe to it by using an RSS feed aggregator such as Microsoft Office Outlook 2007 and Internet Explorer 7.0. The blog site, blog post list, and wiki page library are RSS support enabled by default.

In the following exercise, you will view the RSS field for the blog posts in your browser and disable RSS support for a blog.

> **OPEN** the blog SharePoint site. The exercise will use the Olga's Blog site that was created as a subsite of the *http://wideworldimporters* site, but you can use whatever blog site you want. If prompted, type your user name and password, and then click OK.
>
> **BE SURE TO** complete the exercise that creates a blog site in this chapter before beginning this exercise.

1. On the **Quick Launch**, under Links, click **RSS Feed**. The RSS feed for the blog posts is displayed.

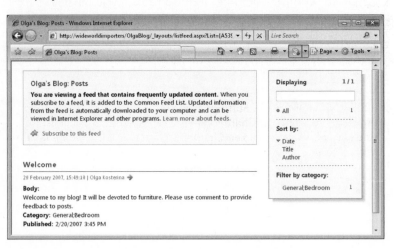

Back

2. On Internet Explorer, click the **Back** button. The home page of Olga's Blog site is displayed.

3. In the **Admin Links** Web Part, click **Manage posts**. The Posts list is displayed using the All Posts view.

4. Click **Settings**, and then click **List Settings**. The Customize Posts page is displayed.

5. Under **Communications**, click **RSS settings**. The Modify List RSS Settings: Posts page is displayed.

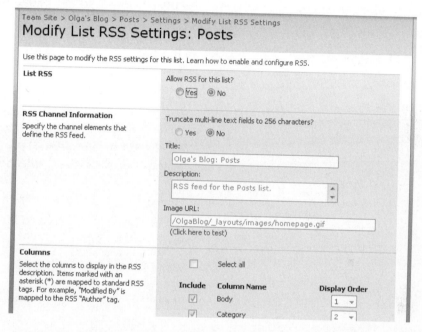

> **Important** If the RSS Settings link is not available, then RSS support is not enabled in either the Windows SharePoint Services 3.0 Central Administration Web site or the site collection level. See Chapter 3, "Creating and Managing Sites," for more information.

6. In the **List RSS** section, under **Allow RSS for this list**, click the **No** option.

7. Scroll to the bottom of the page and click **OK**. The Customize Posts page is displayed.

8. Click the **Olga's Blog** tab to redisplay the blog site's home page. The RSS Feed link under Links is no longer displayed.

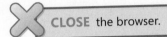 **CLOSE** the browser.

Key Points

- A wiki allows you to create Web pages quickly, and also allows users to freely create and edit Web page content by using a Web browser.

- A Wiki page is a chunk of factual content or concrete advice that is typically limited to no more than two or three screens of information.

- Create forward links to pages by using the double square brackets around a WikiWord. For example, type [[BedRoom]] to create a link to the page named BedRoom. The page does not have to exist when the forward link is created.

- The easiest way to create a new Wiki page is to create a forward link to a nonexistent page.

- Major versions is enabled on wiki page libraries, and therefore no amendments are lost.

- Blogs are personal journals or observations that are usually maintained by one person.

- Blog posts can be categorized to help users find past conversations.

- To interact with a blogger, you can leave comments to a blog post.

- Bloggers should moderate comments to their posts.

- The wiki page library and Blog Posts list are RSS support enabled, thereby allowing users to syndicate content.

Chapter at a Glance

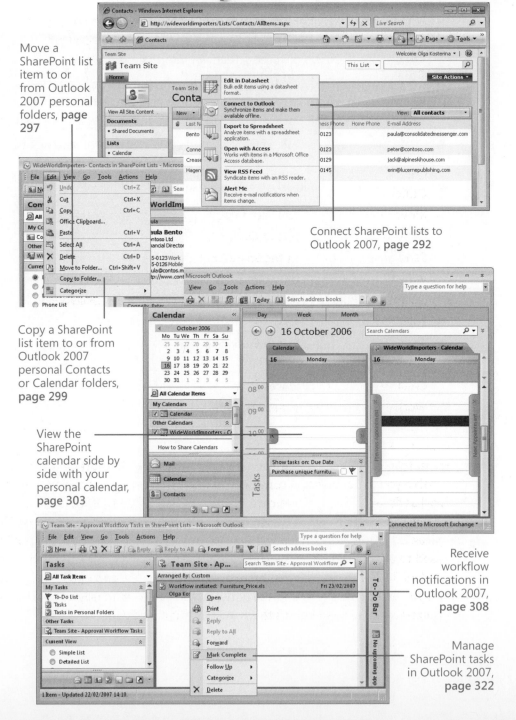

Move a SharePoint list item to or from Outlook 2007 personal folders, **page 297**

Connect SharePoint lists to Outlook 2007, **page 292**

Copy a SharePoint list item to or from Outlook 2007 personal Contacts or Calendar folders, **page 299**

View the SharePoint calendar side by side with your personal calendar, **page 303**

Receive workflow notifications in Outlook 2007, **page 308**

Manage SharePoint tasks in Outlook 2007, **page 322**

11 Using Windows SharePoint Services with Outlook 2007

In this chapter, you will learn to:

✔ Connect a Microsoft Windows SharePoint Services Contacts list to Microsoft Office Outlook 2007.

✔ Move Office Outlook 2007 contacts to SharePoint Contacts lists.

✔ Copy SharePoint contacts to Outlook 2007.

✔ Send an e-mail by using the SharePoint Contacts list.

✔ View SharePoint calendars side by side with personal calendars.

✔ Download SharePoint Tasks list content and make it available offline.

✔ Edit tasks offline.

✔ Manage SharePoint alerts in Outlook 2007.

✔ Configure an RSS feed.

✔ Create Meeting Workspaces from Outlook 2007.

✔ Work with workflow in Outlook 2007.

Microsoft Windows SharePoint Services integrates with Microsoft Office Outlook 2007 to enable you to keep a local copy of your team's Calendars, Tasks, and Contacts lists, as well as libraries. Similar to Microsoft Office Outlook 2003, Office Outlook 2007 allows read-only access to Contacts, Calendar, and Tasks lists in Microsoft Windows SharePoint Services 2.0 Web sites. In Windows SharePoint Services 3.0 Web sites, the capability is increased to allow information synchronization in two directions for items in Contacts lists, calendars, Tasks lists, and discussion boards. These local copies of data are then available when you are not connected to the network and can be manually or automatically synchronized with the SharePoint site when you next connect.

When dealing with documents, Outlook 2007 provides a method of taking libraries or folders offline. Documents held with SharePoint libraries or folders can also be synchronized with their offline copies using the other 2007 Microsoft Office suite applications. Other types of standard lists—such as Issues, Link lists, Custom lists, or properties, such as views and metadata—are not supported in Outlook 2007. Microsoft Office Access 2007 should be used to synchronize these SharePoint resources with their offline copies.

Outlook 2007 supports *Really Simple Syndication (RSS)* feeds so that you can subscribe to and stay up to date with the latest news sites and blogs. You can manage your *RSS feeds* in Outlook 2007 just like your other mail by flagging them for follow-up, assigning them a specific color, or automating any process by using Rules.

By using other integration features, you can manage all of your SharePoint *alerts* from one Outlook 2007 dialog box. By using Outlook 2007 *meeting requests*, you can create Meeting Workspace sites.

In this chapter, you will learn how to copy and move Outlook 2007 contacts to and from a SharePoint Contacts list. You will also learn how to connect SharePoint Calendar lists to Outlook 2007, view SharePoint calendars side by side with personal calendars, edit SharePoint task items offline, subscribe to a SharePoint list's RSS feed, manage SharePoint alerts in Outlook 2007, create Meeting Workspaces from Outlook 2007, and work with workflows in Outlook 2007.

> **Important** Remember to use your SharePoint site location in place of *http://wideworldimporters* in the following exercises.

> **Important** Before you can use the practice sites provided for this chapter, you need to install them from the book's companion CD to their default locations. See "Using the Book's CD" on page xix for more information.

Connecting a SharePoint Contacts List to Outlook 2007

To initiate the integration between SharePoint lists and libraries and Outlook 2007, you need to connect the list or library. You can connect most SharePoint lists as well as all SharePoint library types to Outlook 2007. The following list and library types are not supported for connection to Outlook 2007.

- Survey
- Issue tracking
- Announcements
- Links
- Custom
- Site template
- List template
- Web Part galleries

Connecting to a SharePoint list in Office Outlook 2003 was called linking, and you were only allowed to link to SharePoint Contacts and Calendar lists. Although you could see the contents of these SharePoint lists within Outlook 2003, both online and offline, the information presented was read-only. To edit the contents of these lists, you had to use the browser.

Outlook 2007 provides greater integration with Windows SharePoint Services. Once a list is connected to Outlook 2007, you can modify that list within Outlook 2007 at any time whether you are online or offline. You can also share the connection with others through a Sharing Message.

> **Important** SharePoint permissions carry over when using SharePoint resources in Outlook 2007. For example, if you have permission to edit a document or list on the SharePoint site, you can also edit the document or list within Outlook 2007.

In the following exercise, you will connect to Outlook 2007 from a Contacts list on a SharePoint site. You can also use the same technique to connect to other SharePoint lists or libraries.

OPEN the SharePoint site from which you would like to import the contact information. The exercise will use the *http://wideworldimporters* site, but you can use whatever site you want. If prompted, type your user name and password, and then click OK.

BE SURE TO install and activate the 2007 Microsoft Office suite before beginning any of the exercises in this chapter.

BE SURE TO have a Contacts list. If you do not have a Contacts list, complete the exercise in Chapter 4, "Working with Lists," that explains how to create a list. Alternatively, you can create a practice site for this chapter based on the site template Chapter 11 Starter.stp in the practice file folder for this chapter. The practice file is located in the *Documents\Microsoft Press\SBS_WSSv3\Chapter 11* folder.

See **"Using the Book's CD" on page xix for instructions on how to create a practice site.**

> **Tip** This exercise works when using Outlook 2003 as well as Outlook 2007.

1. On the **Quick Launch**, under the **Lists** section, click **Contacts**.

2. Click **Actions**, and then select **Connect to Outlook**.

3. An Internet Explorer Security warning dialog box might appear stating: A website wants to open web content using this program on your computer. If so, click **Allow**.

Outlook 2007 opens, and you might be asked to supply your user name and password.

A Microsoft Office Outlook dialog box appears stating: You should only connect lists from sources you know and trust.

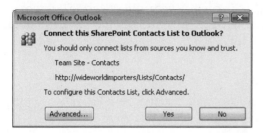

Advanced

4. Click the **Advanced** button. A SharePoint List Options dialog box appears.

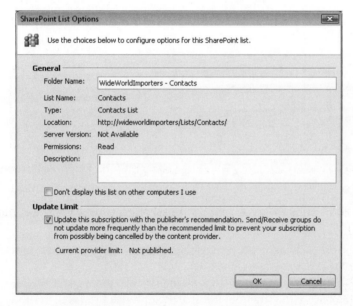

5. In the **Folder Name** textbox, type WideWorldImporters – Contacts and click **OK**.

6. In the **Microsoft Office Outlook** dialog box, click **Yes**. Outlook 2007 displays the WideWorldImporters Contacts list.

When you connect a list or library to Outlook 2007, the list or library appears in the respective areas of the Outlook 2007 navigation pane. Calendars appear in the Calendar pane under Other Calendars, tasks appear in the Tasks pane under Other Tasks, and Contacts lists appear in the Contacts pane under Other Contacts. Discussion lists and libraries appear in a folder in the Mail pane under SharePoint Lists.

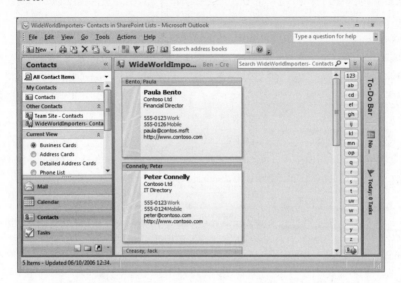

Tip To remove a connected SharePoint list or library from Outlook 2007, right-click the name of the folder in the navigation pane and then select Delete (*folder name)* from the drop-down menu. Removing connected lists or libraries from Outlook 2007 helps you to focus on current projects.

Deleting a connected SharePoint list folder from Outlook 2007 does not delete the SharePoint list or its data from the SharePoint server; however, the data in that list is no longer available offline from within Outlook 2007. An alternative method of managing connected SharePoint lists or libraries is to click Tools on the standard toolbar, select Account Settings, and then click the SharePoint Lists tab.

 CLOSE Outlook 2007 and any open browser.

Moving an Outlook 2007 Contact to a SharePoint Contact List

By connecting a SharePoint Contacts list to Outlook 2007, you are creating an Outlook 2007 Contacts folder. You can then copy the contact information in your Outlook 2007 Contacts folder back into a SharePoint Contacts list. The new contacts within the Contacts folder are added to the SharePoint Contacts list the next time Outlook 2007 synchronizes with SharePoint, and you can then share the contact information with users who visit your SharePoint site. Any other users who also have connected the SharePoint Contacts list to their copy of Outlook 2007 will observe the new contacts within their Outlook contacts folder, when they next synchronize with SharePoint.

In this exercise, you will move contact information from your Outlook 2007 Address Book, to a Contacts list on a SharePoint site. Use the same technique to move calendar items from a SharePoint Calendar list to your Calendar folder, as well as to move task and event items into their respective Outlook 2007 folders.

Office

Troubleshooting You cannot move a recurring series of events by using the steps detailed in this exercise. Instead, open the recurring series or the individual occurrence from a recurring series within Outlook 2007. Click the Office button, select Move, and then click either Other Folder or Copy To Folder.

 OPEN Outlook 2007 before you begin this exercise.

BE SURE TO have a connected Contacts list within Outlook 2007. If you do not, complete the first exercise in this chapter on how to connect a SharePoint Contacts list with Outlook 2007.

1. In the Outlook 2007 navigation pane, under **My Contacts**, select **Contacts**.

2. Select the two or more users you wish to move by holding down the [Ctrl] or [Shift] key and then right-click one of the users you have selected.

    Tip Press Ctrl + A to select all contacts.

3. From the drop-down menu, select **Move to Folder**. The Move Items dialog box appears.

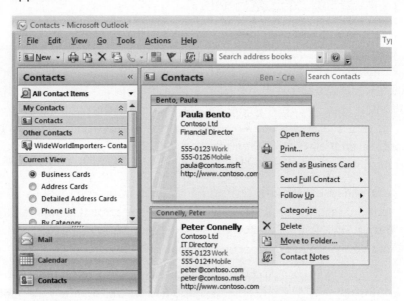

4. Scroll to the bottom of the dialog box. To the left of **SharePoint Lists**, click the + sign and then select **WideWorldImporters – Contacts**.

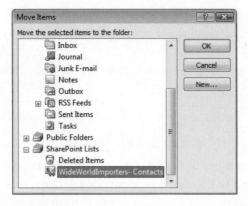

5. Click **OK**.

A Microsoft Office Outlook dialog box appears stating that any incompatible content will be removed during the next synchronization and that the original version of each affected item will be preserved in the "Local Failures" folder.

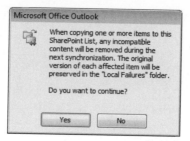

6. Click **Yes**. The Contacts folder is displayed.

> **Troubleshooting** If the name or e-mail address of the contact already exists in your Outlook 2007 Contacts folder, the Duplicate Contact Detected dialog box is displayed so that you can resolve the conflict.

The contacts that you selected to move are no longer found in the Contacts folder.

> **Tip** To move a single contact, select the contact and press Ctrl + Shift + V to activate the Move Items dialog box. Alternatively, while holding down the mouse button, drag the contact to WideWorldImporters – Contacts in the Outlook 2007 navigation page. You can also use these techniques to move more than one contact.

 CLOSE Outlook 2007.

Copying SharePoint Contacts into Outlook 2007

You can copy any single contact or event item from a SharePoint list to Outlook 2007. Once the contact item is copied into the Contacts folder, the contacts item in the Contacts folder and the contacts item on the SharePoint Contacts list are independent of each other—that is, there is no link between the two items. Therefore, amendments made to the contact in the Outlook 2007 Contacts folder are not reflected on the SharePoint Contacts list. To ensure that your contact information does not become out of date, you should assign a definitive location for a specific contact by maintaining it as a contacts item on either a SharePoint Contacts list or in your Outlook 2007 Contacts folder. If contact information is to be shared between a team, then a SharePoint Contacts list should be the preferred location.

Office

Copy To My
Calendar

> **Troubleshooting** You cannot copy a recurring series of events by using the steps de-
> tailed in the following exercise. Instead, copy a recurring series or an individual occurrence
> from a recurring series by opening it within Outlook 2007. Click the Office button, select
> Move, and then click Copy to Folder. If you are copying from a connected Calendar or
> Events list to the Outlook 2007 Calendar list, then click the Copy To My Calendar button in
> the Actions group.

In the following exercise, you will copy contacts from a Contacts list in a SharePoint site
into Outlook 2007. You can also copy a calendar, event, or task item by using the same
technique.

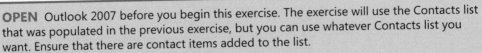

> **OPEN** Outlook 2007 before you begin this exercise. The exercise will use the Contacts list
> that was populated in the previous exercise, but you can use whatever Contacts list you
> want. Ensure that there are contact items added to the list.
>
> **BE SURE TO** verify that you have sufficient rights to read the contents of a Contacts list. If
> in doubt, see the Appendix on page 435.

1. In the Outlook 2007 navigation pane, under **Other Contacts**, select
   WideWorldImporters – Contacts.

2. Select the one or more users you wish to move by holding down the `Ctrl` or `Shift`
   key when selecting the users.

   > **Tip** Press Ctrl + A to select all contacts.

3. On the standard toolbar, click **Edit**, and then select **Copy to Folder**. The Copy Items
   dialog box appears.

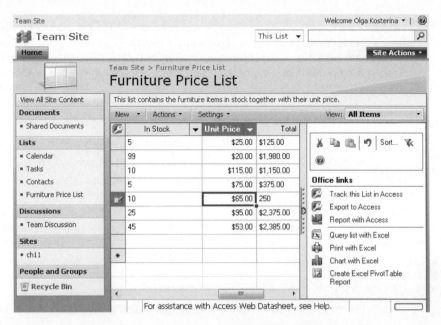

4. Scroll to the top of the dialog box and select **Contacts**.

5. Click **OK**. The contact is added to your Outlook 2007 Contacts folder.

> **Troubleshooting** If the name or e-mail address of the contact already exists in your Outlook 2007 Contacts folder, the Duplicate Contact Detected dialog box is displayed so that you can resolve the conflict.

> **Tip** An alternative method to copy contacts is to select one or more contacts and, while holding down the Ctrl key and the mouse button, drag the contacts to the Contacts folder in the Outlook 2007 navigation pane.

 CLOSE Outlook 2007.

Sending E-Mail by Using a SharePoint Contacts List

You might occasionally move and copy contacts to a SharePoint Contacts list. However, you might frequently use a Contacts list to look up specific contact details, such as a telephone number, or send the contact an e-mail.

In this exercise, you will send an e-mail by using a SharePoint Contacts list.

OPEN Outlook 2007 before you begin this exercise. The exercise will use the Contacts list that was populated in the second exercise in this chapter, but you can use whatever Contacts list you want. Ensure that there are contact items added to the list and that you have connected the Contacts list to Outlook 2007.

BE SURE TO verify that you have sufficient rights to read the contents of a Contacts list. If in doubt, see the Appendix on page 435.

New

1. In the Outlook 2007 navigation pane, select **Mail**.

2. Click the **New** button on the standard toolbar. The New Message window appears.

To

3. Click the **To** button. The Select Names Global Address List dialog box appears.

4. On the **Address Book** drop-down list, select **WideWorldImporters – Contacts**.

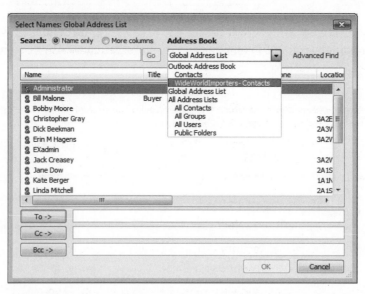

5. Double-click the name of the contact to whom you wish to send a new e-mail message and then click **OK**.

6. Enter your e-mail message subject and text, and then click the **Send** button.

Send

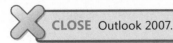 **CLOSE** Outlook 2007.

Viewing SharePoint Calendars Side by Side with Personal Calendars

You can work with multiple calendars when using Outlook 2007, thereby enabling you to create calendars for specific purposes, such as one for work and one for your home life. By using Outlook 2007, you can view several calendars at the same time. When you view and scroll multiple calendars, they all display the same date or time period. This feature is particularly useful if you have connected a SharePoint Calendar list to Outlook 2007. By doing so, you are creating an Outlook 2007 Calendar folder in which a copy of the data from the SharePoint list is stored locally. In this way, you can keep track of any calendar items in a SharePoint list from the Outlook 2007 Calendar folder, even if you are not connected to the network.

> **Tip** In the previous version of Windows SharePoint Services, a Calendar list was called an Events list.

In the following exercise, you will connect to a SharePoint Calendar list and view both your personal Outlook 2007 calendar and a connected SharePoint Calendar list side by side.

 OPEN the SharePoint site in which the Calendar list is located. If prompted, type your user name and password, and then click OK.

BE SURE TO verify that you have sufficient rights to view to the Calendar list. If in doubt, see the Appendix on page 435.

1. On the **Quick Launch**, under **Lists**, click **Calendar**.

2. Click **Actions**, and then select **Connect to Outlook**.

3. An Internet Explorer Security warning dialog box might appear stating: A website wants to open web content using this program on your computer. If so, click **Allow**.

   Outlook 2007 opens, and you might be asked to supply your user name and password.

   A Microsoft Office Outlook dialog box appears, stating you should only connect lists from sources that you know and trust.

4. Click **Advanced**. A SharePoint List Options dialog box appears.

5. In the **Folder Name** textbox, type WideWorldImporters – Calendar and click **OK**.

6. In the **Microsoft Office Outlook** dialog box, click **Yes**.

Your personal Outlook 2007 calendar appears side by side with the connected SharePoint Calendar list. The background color of the Calendar folder name matches the color on the displayed calendar so that you can discern between the two calendars.

Select to view personal calendar.

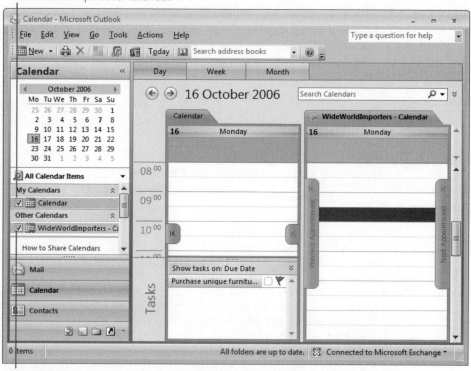

Select to view connected SharePoint calendar list.

> **Tip** Once a Calendar list is connected to Outlook 2007, use the check box to the right of the calendar name to control the number of calendars you wish to view side by side.

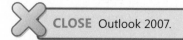
CLOSE Outlook 2007.

Synchronizing SharePoint Tasks List Content

Tasks in the 2007 Microsoft Office suite are integrated across Outlook 2007, Windows SharePoint Services, and Microsoft OneNote 2007, thus enabling you to work between applications smoothly. Connecting a Tasks list in Outlook 2007 enables you to aggregate all of your tasks in one place. You can view all tasks in the Tasks windows, or you can view tasks assigned only to you in the To-Do bar. The To-Do bar is a new feature in Outlook 2007 and includes a calendar and task information. Tasks include regular tasks contained within a Tasks folder as well as e-mail messages flagged for follow up. Daily tasks are also displayed in the Calendar view. As with any connected list or library, it is important to understand the difference between online and offline synchronization.

- **Online** Once a list or library is connected, edits made in Outlook 2007 are automatically synchronized with the master content on the SharePoint site. These changes are also synchronized with other users who are connected to these SharePoint lists and libraries in Outlook 2007.

- **Offline** When you are offline, you can view and edit cached copies of the SharePoint content, but your modifications are not synchronized with the master content on the SharePoint site. To synchronize the content, you must go online.

> **Tip** The Outlook Archive feature cannot be used with the SharePoint List folder, nor with any connected lists or libraries.

In this exercise, you will connect to a Tasks list, make it available offline, and then edit the a task offline.

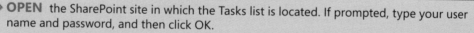

OPEN the SharePoint site in which the Tasks list is located. If prompted, type your user name and password, and then click OK.

BE SURE TO verify that you have sufficient rights to write to the Tasks list. If in doubt, see the Appendix on page 435.

1. On the **Quick Launch**, under **Lists**, click **Tasks**.

2. Click **Actions**, and then select **Connect to Outlook**.

3. An Internet Explorer Security warning dialog box might appear stating: A website wants to open web content using this program on your computer. If so, click **Allow**.

   Outlook 2007 opens, and you might be asked to supply your user name and password.

A Microsoft Office Outlook dialog box appears, stating you should only connect lists from sources that you know and trust.

4. Click **Yes**. Outlook 2007 opens and displays the tasks in the navigation pane.

   The Tasks list appears under Other Tasks. Only the tasks assigned to you are displayed in the To-Do bar Tasks list and the Daily Tasks list.

Offline

5. On the standard toolbar, click **File**, and then select **Work Offline**.

   The Offline icon appears in the lower right corner of the Outlook 2007 window.

6. Click **New.** A new, untitled task form opens.

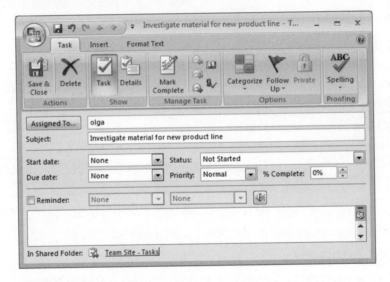

> **Tip** Hover the mouse over the icon, or link to the right of In Shared Folder:. A tool tip appears with the date that the Tasks list was last updated.

7. In the **Assigned To** textbox, type your e-mail addresses. In the **Subject** textbox, type Investigate material for new product line.

Save & Close

8. On the **Task** tab, in the **Actions** group, click the **Save & Close** button. The new task appears in the Detail pane.

9. In the **Tasks** pane, under **Other Tasks**, right-click your Tasks List folder and select **Open in Web Browser**.

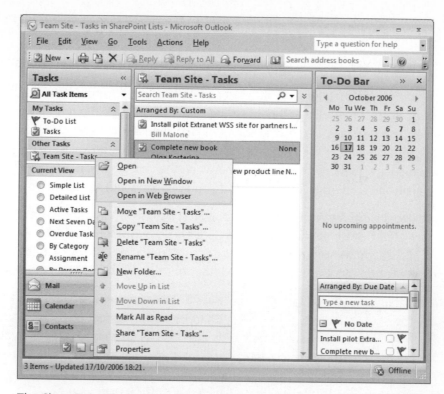

The SharePoint Tasks list is displayed. Notice that the task you added in Outlook 2007 does not appear in the SharePoint Tasks list.

10. Close the browser.

11. On the standard toolbar, click **File** and then select **Work Offline**.

The Offline icon disappears from the lower right corner of the Outlook 2007 window.

12. Press **F9**.

> **Tip** Synchronization between Outlook 2007 and SharePoint occurs periodically. Pressing F9 synchronizes all Outlook 2007 connections immediately.

13. In the **Tasks** pane, under **Other Tasks**, right-click your Tasks List folder and select **Open in Web Browser**.

The SharePoint Tasks list is displayed. The task you added in Outlook 2007 appears in the SharePoint Tasks list.

 CLOSE all Outlook 2007 dialog box windows, and then close Outlook 2007.

Managing SharePoint Alerts in Outlook 2007

When you create an alert for an item, such as a document, list item, document library, list, survey, or search result, you immediately receive a confirmation e-mail message notifying you that the alert was successfully created. This message indicates that the alert process is working. The confirmation message also contains information about the alert and provides links to the SharePoint site where the item is located. When someone makes a change to the item, you receive an e-mail message alert that indicates what was changed, who made the change, and when the change was made. You should create an alert when content has changed and you need (or want) to take notice of it.

To avoid alerts swamping your inbox, you should carefully choose the SharePoint content about which you wish to be alerted. Ideally, you should select only important content that you want to monitor. Consider subscribing to RSS feeds for other SharePoint content that is not as important and does not need your close supervision.

By default, Windows SharePoint Services does not provide an alert aggregation capability for all of your alerts across every SharePoint site. To manage your alerts by using the browser, you would have to visit each site that has an alert set. To help you manage your alerts, you could save the message notifying you that an alert was successfully created because it provides a link to the SharePoint site. You could then use the e-mail message alert to navigate to those sites on which the alerts are set.

In an environment where many SharePoint sites exist, managing your alerts could be a daunting task if they were monitored and organized merely by the links in your e-mail alert messages and by memory. When using Outlook 2007, you can manage the e-mail alerts received from all SharePoint intranet and trusted Web sites from one dialog box.

In the following exercise, you will use Outlook 2007 to create a new alert.

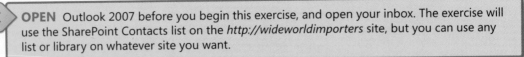

OPEN Outlook 2007 before you begin this exercise, and open your inbox. The exercise will use the SharePoint Contacts list on the *http://wideworldimporters* site, but you can use any list or library on whatever site you want.

1. On the **Outlook 2007** menu, click **Tools**, and then click **Rules and Alerts**. The Rules and Alerts dialog box is displayed.

Troubleshooting If the Rules and Alerts option does not appear on the Tools menu, you are probably viewing your Outlook 2007 calendar. Click the Mail button to view your e-mail messages.

2. Click the **Manage Alerts** tab.

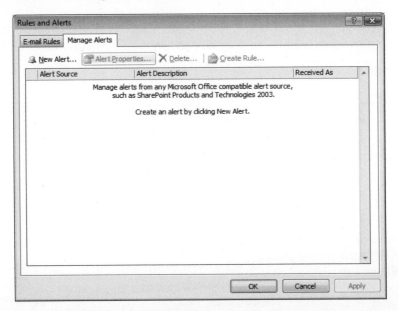

New Alert

3. Click the **New Alert** button. The New Alert dialog box is displayed.

4. In the **Web site Address** textbox, type the URL of a SharePoint site that contains a Contacts list, and then click **Open**.

An Internet Explorer window opens displaying the New Alert Web page.

5. Select the **Contacts** option.

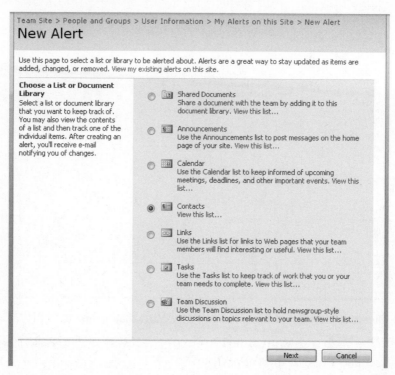

6. Scroll down to the end of the Web page, and then click **Next**. The New Alert page is displayed.

7. In the **Send Alerts To** section, type your e-mail address if it doesn't already appear. Review the other settings.

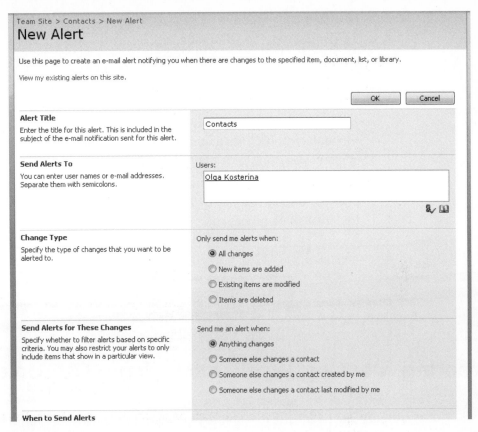

8. Click **OK**.

> **Important** If your SharePoint server is not configured to send e-mail, an Error page will display.

Internet Explorer displays the My Alerts on this Site Web page. Under the Frequency: Immediate area, the alert named Contacts is listed.

9. Close all Internet Explorer windows.

10. Switch to **Outlook 2007** where the Rules and Alerts dialog box should still be visible. A new alert for **Contacts: All items (All Changes)** should be listed.

> **Tip** If the alert does not appear in the Rules and Alerts dialog box, click OK and then close Outlook 2007. Restart Outlook 2007, and then reopen the Rules and Alerts dialog box.

From the Rules and Alerts dialog box, you can:

- Alter the properties of an alert. The Alert Properties dialog box provides a link to the SharePoint site, buttons to "Modify Alert" and "View Item," and a link to the Alerts management page on the SharePoint site.

- Select multiple alerts by using the [Ctrl] or [Shift] key when you click an alert. You can then click the [Del] button to delete all of the alerts you selected. Click Yes to the Microsoft Office Outlook warning dialog box that appears and asks whether you want to delete the selected rows.

- Use Outlook 2007 rules to manage your alerts so that a notification window pops up, a sound is played, the alert e-mail message is moved to a specified folder, or some other action is performed on the alert message.

CLOSE all Outlook 2007 dialog box windows, and then close Outlook 2007.

Both Chapter 4 and Chapter 6, "Working with Library Settings," contain more information about managing alerts on lists and documents from the browser.

Creating Meeting Workspaces from Outlook 2007

When you create an Outlook 2007 meeting request, you can also create a *Meeting Workspace* site or link the meeting to an existing workspace site. You were introduced to Meeting Workspaces in Chapter 8, "Working with Meeting Workspaces." Meeting Workspaces enable you to share your meeting agenda and objectives, publish documents and files, track tasks, and complete other collaborative activities through one central location. By centralizing this information, your meeting attendees have access to the latest information and you avoid sending files through your e-mail system. Three methods can be used to create a Meeting Workspace.

1. Create a page on a SharePoint site.
2. Select the Meeting Workspace check box when you create a Calendar list.
3. Click Meeting Workspace on a new meeting request in Outlook 2007.

In this exercise, you will create a Meeting Workspace from Outlook 2007.

OPEN Outlook 2007 before you begin this exercise.

BE SURE TO verify that you have sufficient rights to create a SharePoint site. If in doubt, see the Appendix on page 435.

1. In Outlook 2007, on the **Standard** toolbar, click the down arrow to the right of **New** and then click **Meeting Request**. A new, untitled meeting form opens.

2. In the **To** textbox, type the e-mail addresses of people you want to invite to the meeting. In the **Subject** textbox, type Product Review.

> **Important** SharePoint uses the Subject of the meeting request as the Meeting Workspace site name. If you create a Meeting Workspace site with a blank meeting request Subject line, Outlook 2007 will create a Meeting Workspace site with the name *UntitledXXX*, where *XXX* is a number based on the number of existing untitled sites.

3. In the **Location** textbox, type The Wide World Importers Main Office.

Meeting
Workspace

4. On the **Meeting** tab, in the **Attendees** group, click the **Meeting Workspace** button. The Meeting Workspace task pane appears to the right of the form.

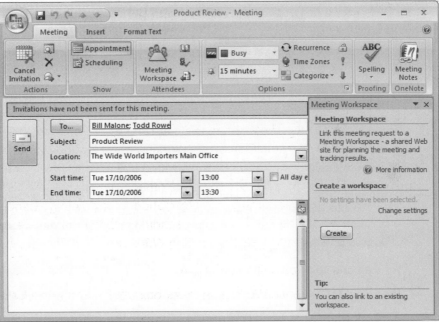

5. In the **Meeting Workspace** task pane, in the **Create a workspace** section, click **Change settings**.

The Meeting Workspace task pane displays the Select a workspace settings.

6. Click the down arrow next to **Select a location**, and then select **Other**. The Other Workspace Server dialog box is displayed.

7. Type the URL of a SharePoint site. The Meeting Workspace site will be a subsite of the SharePoint site that you type here.

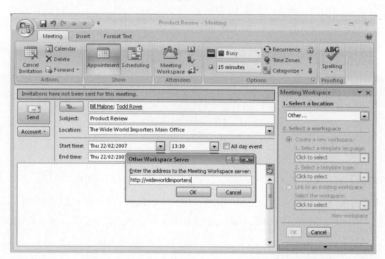

> **Important** You cannot create a new Meeting Workspace site under an existing Meeting Workspace site. You must also be a member of a site group with the Create Subsites permission for the parent site.

8. Click **OK**.

> **Tip** You can select a different language for your site if other language packs are installed on your SharePoint server. You can also choose a different Meeting Workspace template. By default, SharePoint installs five Meeting Workspace templates: Basic Meeting Workspace, Blank Meeting Workspace, Decision Making Workspace, Social Meeting Workspace, and Multipage Meeting Workspace. You can associate a meeting request with an existing Meeting Workspace by selecting the Link to an existing workspace option.

9. In the **Meeting Workspace** task pane, click **OK**, and then click **Create**.

Outlook 2007 connects to the SharePoint Web site and creates the workspace. A meeting request is placed in your Outlook 2007 Calendar that contains the details of the meeting and a URL to the meeting workspace. No corresponding entry exists in the Calendar list for the parent site. The Outlook 2007 meeting request and Meeting Workspace task pane are updated.

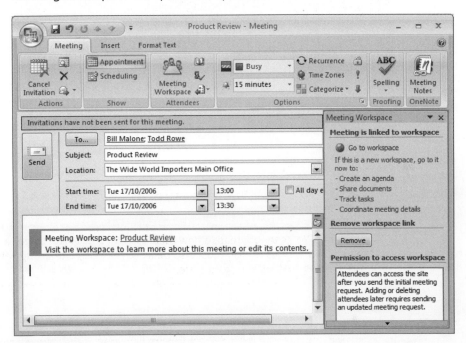

10. Click **Send**.

    Outlook 2007 attempts to add the attendees to the Meeting Workspace site in the Contributor site group. If Outlook 2007 was unable to include the attendees to the site, you will receive a notification.

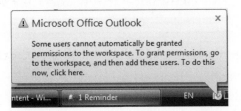

Attendees can access the Meeting Workspace site that you created by clicking the link in the invitation e-mail they receive from you. The following image displays a sample of the invitation e-mail.

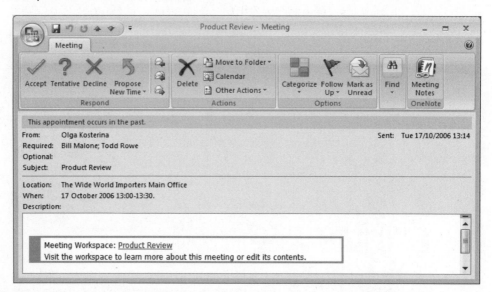

11. Click the **Product Review** link to display the Product Review Meeting Workspace site.

CLOSE Outlook 2007 as well as any open browser windows.

After creating the Meeting Workspace, you can add or remove attendees using the meeting request in Outlook 2007. When you send the meeting request, Outlook 2007 updates the Meeting Workspace.

> **Important** If you change the meeting request and then click Save & Close instead of clicking Send, the updates will not be sent to the Meeting Workspace site.

You can also add and remove attendees through the Meeting Workspace site by clicking Manage Attendees in the Attendees Web Part; however, this does not update the meeting request in Outlook 2007, which you will need to do manually. For this reason, many users prefer to create and manage Meeting Workspaces from within Outlook 2007. If you delete the Meeting Workspace, the meeting request in your calendar contains a broken link pointing to the recently deleted site. Similarly, if you cancel the meeting or delete the meeting request in your Outlook 2007 calendar, the Meeting Workspace still exists and displays a message that this has occurred.

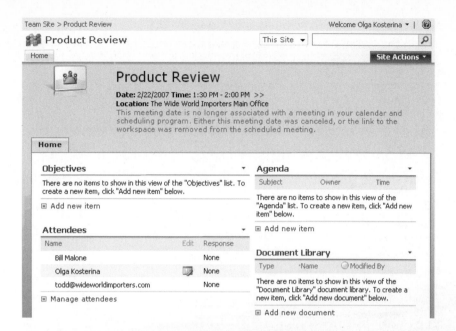

Therefore, do not cancel a meeting to send a new meeting request with changed details. Instead, send an updated meeting request to attendees because this maintains the link between the meeting request and the Meeting Workspace. If you cancel or delete the meeting request in your Outlook 2007 calendar, you may not remember where you created the Meeting Workspace. Consequently, you should save a link to your Meeting Workspace, such as on a SharePoint link list, or delete the Meeting Workspace after saving any important information that the site contained.

Configuring an RSS Feed

Earlier in this chapter, you learned how to manage alerts, which are notifications received via e-mail that notify you when content has changed in a SharePoint list or library. A new feature found in Outlook 2007 is support for Really Simple Syndication (RSS)—previously known as Rich Site Summary—which is another method of notifying you when something has changed or new content is published within a SharePoint site. RSS should be used for tracking content that is regularly updated. It is commonly used to stay up to date with the latest news on Web sites and blogs, but can also be used to distribute pictures, audio, or video content. Sites that expose their content via RSS are said to have a RSS feed. You can create an RSS feed on content stored in a SharePoint list.

In this exercise, you will add a RSS feed to Outlook 2007.

OPEN the SharePoint list or library to which you would like to subscribe to the RSS feed. The exercise will use the *http://wideworldimporters* site and the Shared Documents library, but you can use whatever site and list or library you want. If prompted, type your user name and password, and then click OK.

1. On the **Quick Launch**, under **Documents**, click **Shared Documents**.

2. In the **Shared Documents** library, click **Actions** and then select **View RSS Feed**.

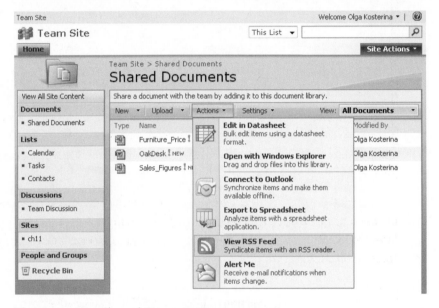

The Team Site: Shared Documents page appears.

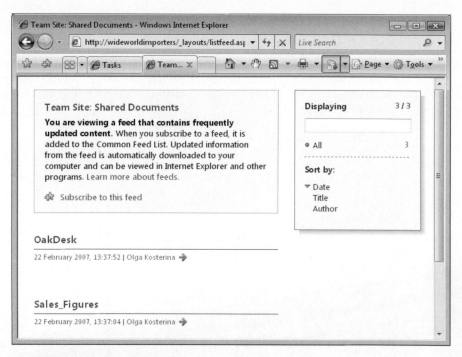

3. Click **Subscribe to this feed**.

   An Internet Explorer dialog window appears from which you can choose the folder in which to place your RSS feed subscription. Your RSS feed subscription is added to Internet Explorer's Favorites Center and is simultaneously added to the RSS Feeds folder in Outlook 2007.

   > **Tip** If you are using a version of Internet Explorer that is earlier than Internet Explorer 7, then Outlook 2007 will open automatically.

4. Open Outlook 2007. In the Outlook 2007 navigation bar, under **Mail Folders**, expand the **RSS Feeds** folder by clicking the + symbol.

   The RSS feeds to which you have subscribed appear as folders.

5. Click **Team site: Shared Documents**. The detail pane displays an entry for each document in the Shared Documents library.

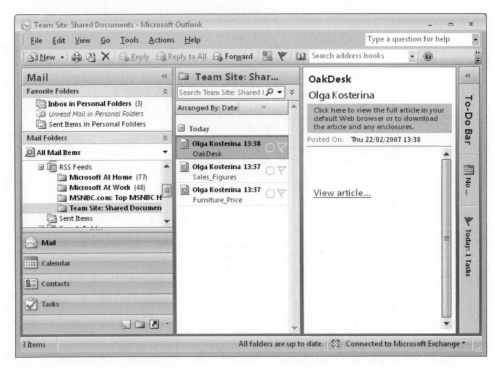

> **Tip** You can add new RSS feeds from within Outlook 2007. Right-click the RSS Feeds folder and select Add A New RSS Feed. To use this method, you must know the URL of the RSS feed.

6. On the standard bar, click **Tools** and then select **Account Settings**. The Account Settings dialog box appears.

7. Click **RSS Feeds**, and then select **Team Site: Shared Documents**.

Change...

Change

8. Click the **Change** button. The RSS Feed Options dialog box appears.

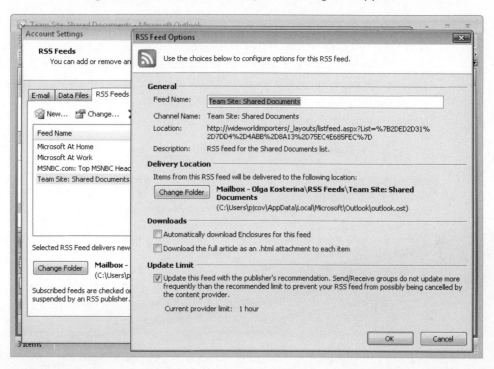

9. In the **General** section, in the **Feed Name** textbox, type WideWorldImporters: Shared Document library and then click **OK**.

10. In the **Account Settings** dialog box, notice that the RSS feed has a new name and then click **Close**.

   In the Outlook 2007 navigation pane, under the RSS Feeds folder, the SharePoint document library to which you subscribed has a new folder name.

 CLOSE Outlook 2007 as well as any open Internet Explorer windows.

For more information on RSS, see Chapter 4.

Work with Workflow in Outlook 2007

You were introduced to workflows in Chapter 5, "Creating and Managing Libraries." By using the browser or SharePoint Designer, workflows can be associated with lists, libraries, or content types to make them available to run on list items or documents. A workflow's progress is recorded in a Workflow History list, and workflow tasks are assigned to participants by using a Tasks list. Outlook 2007 serves as a place to receive workflow-related notifications and complete workflow tasks.

In the following exercise, you will manage workflow tasks in Outlook 2007.

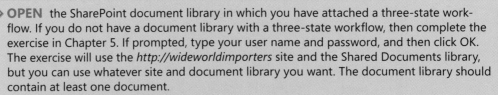

OPEN the SharePoint document library in which you have attached a three-state workflow. If you do not have a document library with a three-state workflow, then complete the exercise in Chapter 5. If prompted, type your user name and password, and then click OK. The exercise will use the *http://wideworldimporters* site and the Shared Documents library, but you can use whatever site and document library you want. The document library should contain at least one document.

BE SURE TO complete the steps in Chapter 5 to create a workflow. Connect the Tasks list you associated with the workflow to Outlook 2007. See the first exercise in this chapter for steps to connect a list to Outlook 2007.

1. On the **Quick Launch**, under **Documents**, click **Shared Documents**.

2. Move your mouse over the document that you want to start a workflow. When an arrow appears to the right of the document name, click the arrow.

A drop-down menu appears.

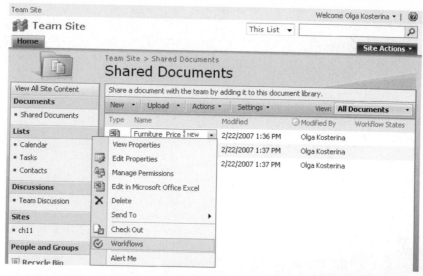

3. Click **Workflows**. The Workflows: <document name> page appears, where <document name> is the name of the document you chose to start the workflow in Step 2.

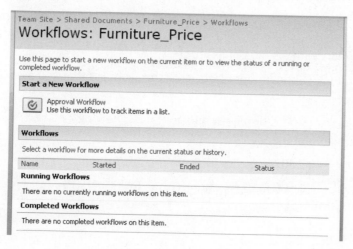

Workflow

4. In the **Start a New Workflow** area, click the workflow icon. The Workflows: <document name> page is redisplayed.

In the Running Workflows section the <workflow name> appears with a status of In Progress, where <workflow name> is the name you typed when you attached the workflow to the document library.

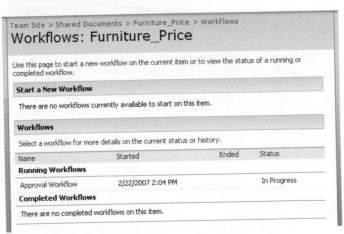

5. In the breadcrumb, click **Shared Documents**. The Shared Documents library is displayed.

The <workflow name> column for the document on which you started the workflow appears with a status of In Progress.

6. On the **Quick Launch**, under **Lists**, click the Tasks list that you associated with your workflow.

The Tasks List page is displayed and contains a new task named "Workflow initiated: <document name>".

Tasks

7. Open **Outlook 2007** and click **Tasks** in the left navigation pane.

8. In the **Tasks** navigation pane, under **Other Tasks**, click the Tasks list that you associated with the workflow.

In the detail pane, the Workflow initiated: <document name> task appears.

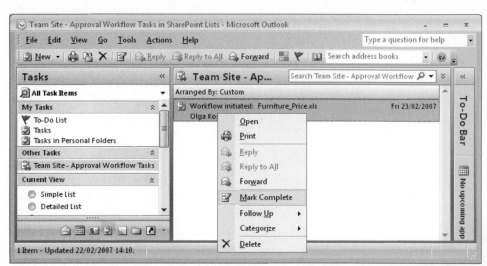

9. Right-click the task, and select **Mark Complete**.

The text of the task, Workflow initiated: <document name>, is struck through, denoting that the task is completed.

10. Press **F9**.

In the detail pane, a second task is added named Review task <document name>.

11. Double-click the task.

The Review task <document name> Task form opens. The task contains two links to the document: the task item in the Tasks list and a link to the Tasks list. By using these links, you can open, review, and modify the document's contents.

Document link

Task item   Task list

> **Important** One or both links to the document may be broken if the site, document library, or document name contains spaces.

12. In the **Status** drop-down list, select **Completed** and close the task.

The text of the Review task: <document name> task is struck through.

13. In the **Tasks** navigation pane, under **Other Tasks**, right-click the **Tasks** list that you associated with the workflow and select **Open** in Web browser.

The Tasks List page is displayed and contains the two completed tasks.

14. On the **Quick Launch** bar, under **Documents**, click **Shared Documents**. The Shared Documents library is displayed.

The <workflow name> column for the document on which you started the workflow appears with a status of Completed.

 CLOSE Outlook 2007 as well as any open Internet Explorer windows.

Key Points

- You can copy contacts listed in your personal Outlook 2007 Contacts folder both to and from a SharePoint Contacts list.

- You can copy and move SharePoint list items both to and from Outlook 2007.

- You can connect any SharePoint Contacts list, Calendar, Tasks list, and discussion board to Outlook 2007. This action creates a folder in Outlook 2007 that you can synchronize with the SharePoint list or that synchronizes automatically every 20 minutes.

- In Outlook 2007, you can view multiple calendars side by side. These calendars can be connected to SharePoint Calendar lists.

- You can aggregate and manage all of your tasks in one place whether you created them within Outlook 2007, in a SharePoint Tasks list, or within Office OneNote 2007.

- You can manage all of your SharePoint alerts from the Outlook 2007 Rules And Alerts dialog box.

- You can create a Meeting Workspace site from Outlook 2007 by using a meeting request. When using this technique, you create a Meeting Workspace as a subsite to a SharePoint Web site.

- You can manage your RSS feeds in Outlook 2007 just like your other mail by flagging them for follow-up, assigning them a specific color, or automating any process by using the Rules.

- You can receive task notification when a workflow requires interaction.

Chapter at a Glance

Import data from an Excel 2007 spreadsheet, **page 330**

Use the Access Web Datasheet, **page 333**

Export a SharePoint list to an Excel 2007 spreadsheet, **page 340**

Export an Excel 2007 table to a SharePoint list, **page 344**

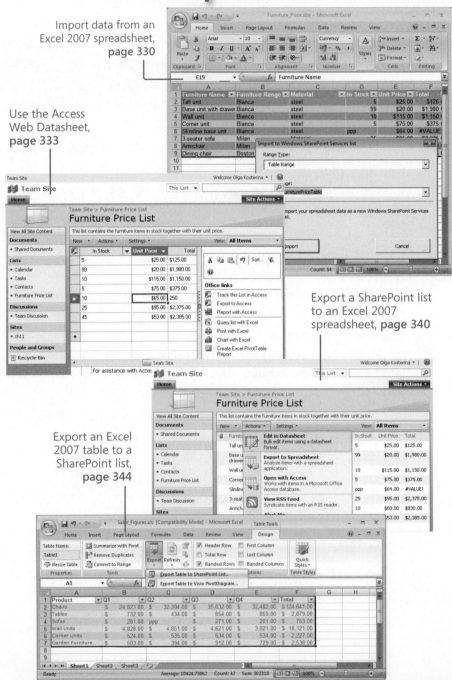

12 Using Windows SharePoint Services with Excel 2007

In this chapter, you will learn to:

✔ Import data from a Microsoft Office Excel 2007 spreadsheet to a list in Microsoft Windows SharePoint Services.

✔ Use the Access Web Datasheet.

✔ Export a SharePoint list to an Office Excel 2007 spreadsheet.

✔ Export an Excel 2007 table to a SharePoint site.

Microsoft Windows SharePoint Services provides the collaborative backbone to the 2007 Microsoft Office System. In Chapter 7, "Working with Document Workspaces," you discovered how to share and manage documents stored in a SharePoint Web site from within the 2007 Microsoft Office suite. You also created SharePoint sites from your 2007 Microsoft Office suite applications.

This chapter focuses on the integration of Windows SharePoint Services with Microsoft Office Excel 2007, which allows you to export and import data to and from SharePoint lists. Office Excel 2007 also provides one-way synchronization from SharePoint lists to Excel 2007 spreadsheets, so you can take the data offline and then synchronize with the SharePoint lists when you reconnect.

Important Before you can use the practice files provided for this chapter, you need to install them from the book's companion CD to their default location. See "Using the Book's CD" on page xix for more information.

Importing Data from an Excel 2007 Spreadsheet to a List in SharePoint

In many situations, you might already have data within a spreadsheet, but later find that you need to share the data with other members of your team. SharePoint provides the ability to import data from an Excel 2007 spreadsheet into a SharePoint list. Those users who have appropriate permissions may read the SharePoint list, while others may even revise the list or enter additional data. You can choose to import all of the data held on a worksheet, a *range* of cells, a *named range*, or an *Excel 2007 table*.

In the following exercise, you will use your browser to create a SharePoint Custom list that contains data imported from an Excel 2007 spreadsheet.

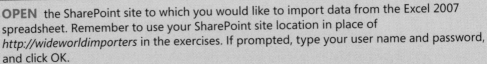

OPEN the SharePoint site to which you would like to import data from the Excel 2007 spreadsheet. Remember to use your SharePoint site location in place of *http://wideworldimporters* in the exercises. If prompted, type your user name and password, and click OK.

USE the Furniture_Price.xlsx document in the practice file folder for this topic. This practice file is located in the *Documents\Microsoft Press\SBS_WSSv3\Chapter 12* folder.

BE SURE TO install and activate the 2007 Microsoft Office suite before beginning any of the exercises in this chapter.

BE SURE TO verify that you have sufficient rights to create a new list. If in doubt, see the Appendix on page 435.

Tip This exercise works when using Microsoft Office Excel 2003 as well as Excel 2007, but you must install the Compatibility Pack for the 2007 Microsoft Office System to import the xlsx file.

1. Click **Site Actions** and then click **Create**. The Create page is displayed.

2. Under the **Custom Lists**, click **Import Spreadsheet**. The New page is displayed.

3. In the **Name** textbox, type FurniturePrice.

Tip Any URL in SharePoint is limited to 260 characters. The Name that you type here is used to create both the URL and the Title of the list. Later in this exercise, you will alter the title with a user-friendly name.

4. In the **Description** textbox, type This list contains the furniture items in stock together with their unit prices.

> **Important** If you import a spreadsheet into a site based on the Meeting Workspace template, an option appears on the New page to share the same items for all meetings. If you choose not to share the same items for all meetings, then each meeting displays the list with only the items added for that date. Once items become series items for a list, you cannot change the setting back to list items for a specific date.

Browse

5. Click the **Browse** button. The Choose file dialog box appears.

The Choose file dialog box displays your Documents folder or the last folder that you accessed.

Documents

6. If the Documents folder is not displayed in the Choose file dialog box, under **Favorite Links**, click the **Documents** icon.

7. Double-click **Microsoft Press, SBS_WSSv3, Chapter 12**, and then double-click the **Furniture_Price.xlsx** file.

Import

Import

8. On the **New** page, click the **Import** button.

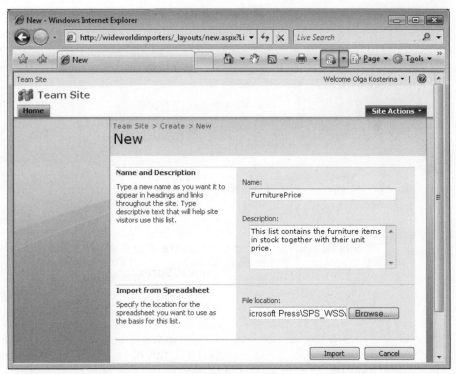

Excel 2007 opens Furniture_Price.xlsx and displays the Import to Windows SharePoint Services List dialog box.

9. From the **Range Type** drop-down list, check that **Table Range** is selected.

10. Click in the **Selected Range** drop-down list, choose **Stock!FurniturePriceTable**, and then click **Import**.

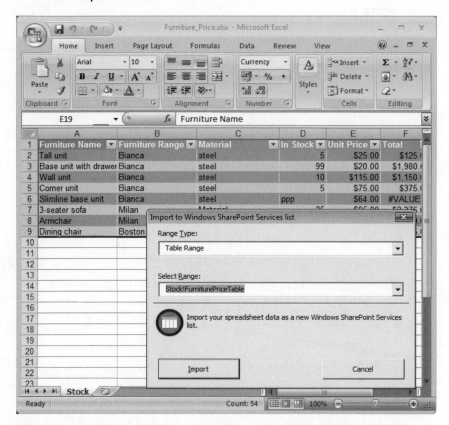

The All Items view of the FurniturePrice list is displayed, and the URL in the Address box is *http://wideworldimporters/Lists/FurniturePrice/AllItems.aspx.*

> Tip If you import a range of cells from an Excel 2007 spreadsheet and want the Excel 2007 column names to become the SharePoint list column names, you should first edit the spreadsheet and convert the range of cells to an Excel 2007 table. See the last exercise in this chapter for instructions on converting a range of cells into an Excel 2007 table.

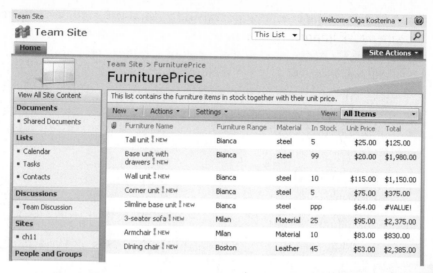

11. To change the title of the list, click **Settings**, and then click **List Settings**. The Customize Furniture page appears.

12. Under **General Settings**, click **Title, description and navigation**. The List General Settings: FurniturePrice page appears.

13. In the **Name and Description** area, in the **Name** textbox, type a user-friendly Furniture Price List.

14. Under the **Navigation** area, click the **Yes** option to display this list on the Quick Launch.

Save

15. Click the **Save** button at the bottom of the Web page. The Customize Furniture Price List page appears.

16. On the breadcrumb, click the **Furniture Price List** link. The All Items view of the Furniture Price List appears.

    The title of the list has changed to Furniture Price List, but the URL remains set as *http://wideworldimporters/Lists/PlantPrice/AllItems.aspx*.

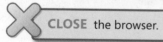
CLOSE the browser.

Using the Access Web Datasheet

If you create a list by importing an Excel 2007 spreadsheet, you might find it convenient to use a spreadsheet-like environment when editing, formatting, or entering data into your newly created list. This spreadsheet-like environment is called the *Access Web Datasheet*, previously known as the Datasheet view, and was introduced in Chapter 4, "Working with Lists."

Using a list or library in a datasheet can be a tremendous productivity booster. However, to make use of this feature, you must have the Microsoft Office 2003 Editions or the 2007 Microsoft Office suite installed on your computer and your browser must support Microsoft ActiveX controls. If these requirements are not met, you will receive a message indicating that the list will be displayed in Standard view. The Explorer view of a document, form, or a wiki page library does not support the Access Web Datasheet, nor does the Calendar view of Calendar lists. The following list types do not support the Access Web Datasheet.

- Discussion board
- Survey
- Picture library
- All galleries such as the Site template, List template, and Web Part galleries
- Data sources
- Inbox

The Access Web Datasheet presents all list items in a grid and facilitates editing across the entire table. A *task pane* on the right edge of the Access Web Datasheet enables powerful integration between Windows SharePoint Services, Office Excel 2003, Excel 2007, Microsoft Office Access 2003, and Microsoft Office Access 2007.

In the following exercise, you will add a new list item, edit an existing list item, remove an existing list item, add a list field, and briefly explore the task pane.

OPEN the SharePoint site to which you imported data from the Excel 2007 spreadsheet. Remember to use your SharePoint site location in place of *http://wideworldimporters* in the following exercises. If prompted, type your user name and password, and click OK.

BE SURE TO verify that you have sufficient rights to contribute to the list. If in doubt, see the Appendix on page 435. Also, complete the first exercise in this chapter before proceeding.

1. On the **Quick Launch**, under **Lists**, click **Furniture Price List**.
2. Click **Actions**.
3. From the drop-down list, click **Edit in Datasheet** to change the display from Standard View.

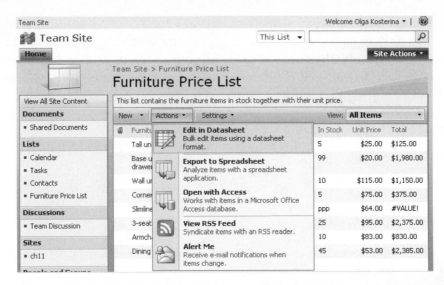

The standard view changes to the Access Web Datasheet.

Access icon

Edit

Saving

New Item

Tip An Access Web Datasheet consists of rows, and each row corresponds to a list item. A column corresponds to a list field. The down arrow in the column headings is used to filter and sort data. Using the Access Web Datasheet is like editing a table in Excel 2007 or Office Access 2007. In the previous version of Windows SharePoint Services, the Access Web Datasheet was based on Office Excel technologies. When using SharePoint 3.0, the Access Web Datasheet is reliant on Access 2007. An Access icon appears in the top left corner of the Access Web Datasheet, and the words Access Web Datasheet display in the status bar.

When you type a value in a cell or choose a value from a drop-down list, an Edit icon displays to the far left indicating that changes have been made to the row. You can use the cursor keys or mouse to move from cell to cell to make changes to any row in the list.

When you leave a row that was changed or navigate away from the Web page, a Saving icon indicates that SharePoint is updating the database with your changes. You can continue making changes to different rows, and SharePoint saves your changes in the background. If your changes result in a conflict or error, the Access Web Datasheet will be updated with information necessary to resolve the conflict or error.

The last row in the Access Web Datasheet is always empty, and there is a New Item icon in the left column. This empty row can be used to add additional list items to the list. The Access Web Datasheet does not display the star (*) row for a document library.

> **Tip** All list items in the list are displayed on one Web page in the Access Web Datasheet regardless of the size of the list. Therefore, it isn't practical to edit extremely large lists by using the Access Web Datasheet. To improve the performance of an Access Web Datasheet, create a view and hide unnecessary columns, but do not remove those columns that are marked as Required. Apply one or more filters to hide rows that are not relevant to the view.

4. In the last row of the list, in the **Furniture Name** column, type Bench and press Tab. Type Woodland, press Tab, and type s.

Like Excel 2007 or Access 2007, the IntelliSense feature displays other values that occur in this column.

5. Press the ↓ to choose **steel**, and then press Enter.

The new item row changes to become the currently edited row, and another new item row is added to the bottom of the list.

> **Tip** As in other 2007 Microsoft Office suite applications, you can use Ctrl + X to cut, Ctrl + C to copy, Ctrl + V to paste, Ctrl + Z to undo the last changes, and Esc to cancel an edit on the current list item.

Vertical I-Beam
Pointer

6. Position the mouse cursor on the boundary between the **Furniture Range** and **Material** columns until the vertical I-beam icon appears.

7. Drag the column boundary to reduce the size of the **Furniture Range** column.

Horizontal
I-Beam Pointer

> **Tip** Rows can be resized in much the same way by using the horizontal I-beam icon between the rows. Both columns and rows can be resized based on their content by double-clicking. You can also reorder columns by simply dragging them to the desired location.

8. Click the far left cell to highlight the entire **Armchair** list item.

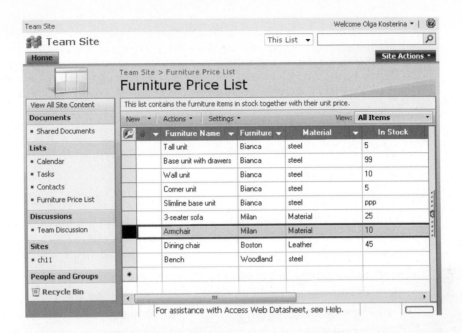

Row Select
Pointer

Column Select
Pointer

List Select
Pointer

Tip By holding down the Shift key while selecting the far left cell so that the row select pointer appears and then clicking the far left cell of another row, you can select all rows between the first row clicked and the second row clicked. Similarly, holding down the Shift key while selecting the top row of a column so that the column select pointer appears and then clicking the top row of another column will select all columns between the two clicks. However, holding down the Ctrl key while selecting does not select and deselect list items regardless of whether they are adjacent, as you might expect. Instead, it exclusively selects the clicked row and abandons all other selections just as if you had clicked the items without holding down the Ctrl key.

9. Press the ⌷Del⌷ key to permanently remove the list item from the list. A delete confirmation dialog box appears.

10. Click **Yes** to finish deleting the list item and redisplay the Access Web Datasheet of the list.

11. Click the fifth cell in the **In Stock** column. Overtype **ppp** with 10, and then press Tab.

12. Replace **$64** with 65, and then press Tab.

The list item is saved to the database, and a dollar ($) sign is placed before the number 65 because the Unit Price column is a Currency type.

13. Replace **#VALUE!** with 250, and then press Enter.

The list item is saved to the database, but no dollar ($) sign is placed before the number 250. When the spreadsheet was imported in the previous exercise, the *Single Line Of Text* column type was used to create the In Stock and Total columns because they did not contain data of one particular type, whereas the *Unit Price* column contained only currency values. In the Excel 2007 spreadsheet, the Total column was a calculated column. To provide the same functionality in the SharePoint list, the column needs to be a Calculated data type. You cannot change the data type of an existing column to a Calculated data type, but must instead create a new column by using the Calculated data type.

14. Right-click the **Total** column, and then click **Add Column** in the context menu.

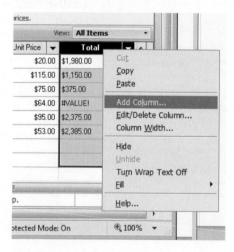

The Create Column: Furniture Price List page appears.

15. In the **Name and Type** area, in the **Column Name** textbox, type Total Cost, and then select the **Calculated (calculation based on other columns)** option.

16. In the **Additional Column Settings** area, under the **Insert Column**, double-click **In Stock**.

17. Scroll to the bottom of the page and click **OK**.

18. Click the first cell in the **Total Cost** column, type =[In Stock]*[Unit Price]*1.1, and then press Enter.

A dialog box appears warning you that the results of your calculation change could take some time.

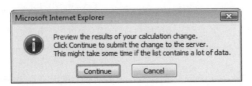

19. Click **Continue**. The Access Web Datasheet status bar displays the formula that you typed.

> **Important** Formulas are equations that perform calculations on values in the list and are similar to the formulas you use in Excel 2007 and Access 2007. They can contain *functions*, *column references*, *operators*, and *constants*. For example, a formula could be =PI()*[In Stock]^2, where PI() is a function, * and ^ are operators, [In Stock] is a column reference, and 2 is a constant.

20. Click the vertical bar on the far right side of the Access Web Datasheet page to expose the task pane, which allows you to quickly integrate with Excel 2007 and Access 2007.

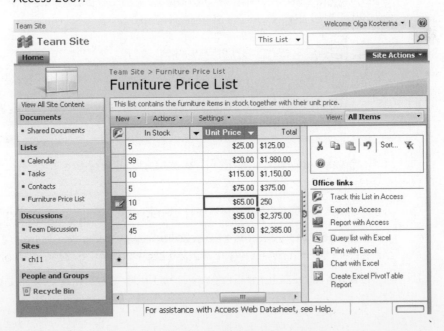

At the top of the task pane is a series of buttons for common commands such as Cut, Copy, Paste, Undo, Custom Sort, Remove Filter/Sort, and Help.

Help

> **Note** More information about the Access Web Datasheet can be found by clicking the Help icon in the task pane, clicking the Help link in the status bar of the Access Web Datasheet, clicking a cell in the Access Web Datasheet and pressing F1, or right-clicking any cell inside the Access Web Datasheet and clicking Help.

CLOSE the browser.

Exporting a SharePoint List to an Excel 2007 Spreadsheet

You can export the contents of SharePoint lists, results of a survey, or document libraries to an Excel 2007 spreadsheet. The exported list or library is a Web query that stays updated with changes to the original list in your SharePoint site. The Excel 2007 spreadsheet maintains a connection to the SharePoint list and therefore becomes a *linked object*.

In this exercise, you will export a list from a SharePoint site to an Excel 2007 spreadsheet. You will add data to the spreadsheet and then synchronize the data in the spreadsheet with the contents of the list on the SharePoint site.

OPEN the SharePoint site on which you have a list from which to export data to an Excel 2007 spreadsheet. This exercise uses the list you created in the first exercise of this chapter. Remember to use your SharePoint site location and your list in place of *http://wideworldimporters* and *Furniture Price List* in the exercises. If prompted, type your user name and password, and click OK.

1. In the **Quick Launch**, under the **Lists** area, click **Furniture Price List**.

> **Tip** The export process exports only the columns and rows contained in the list's current view, which is the All Items view in this exercise. If none of the views contain the data you wish to export, then you must create a new view to meet your needs. Alternatively, you can choose one of the existing views, export the list to a spreadsheet, and then delete the unwanted data.

2. Click **Actions**. From the menu, click **Export to Spreadsheet**.

   SharePoint generates an Excel 2007 query.

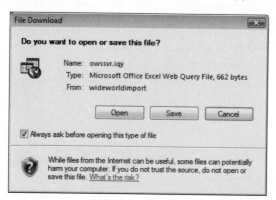

3. When the **File Download** dialog box appears, click the **Open** button.

   Excel 2007 opens a new workbook that contains one worksheet named owssvr(1). A Microsoft Office Excel Security Notice dialog box is displayed warning you that data connections have been blocked.

4. Click **Enable**.

   The Excel 2007 query results are displayed in the owssvr(1) worksheet in an Excel 2007 table. Each column in the list contains an AutoFilter arrow in the header row, and the Design contextual tab is active. Excel 2007 names your Table_owssvr_1.

Tip When you export a SharePoint library, Excel 2007 represents the documents in the list with hyperlinks that point to the documents on the SharePoint site. Similarly, attachments on list items are replaced with a hyperlink. In the Excel 2007 spreadsheet, click the link to open the file.

Tip You should make a habit of renaming your tables so that you recognize the data they contain. This process helps formulas that summarize table data much easier to understand. To rename your table, first ensure that the Design contextual tab is active, and then, in the Properties group, edit the value in the Table Name field.

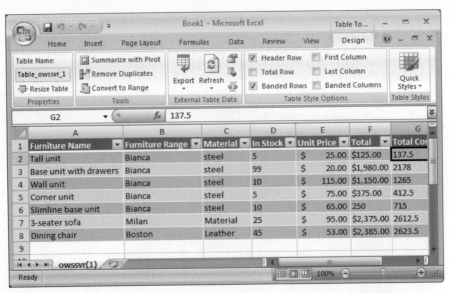

5. Click cell **A9**, type **Antique**, and press `Tab`. Type **Bi**, and press `Tab` again.

   IntelliSense completes the word Bianca for you.

6. Type **wood**, and press `Tab`. Type **5**, and press `Tab`. Type **10**, and then press `Enter`.

   Excel 2007 places a dollar ($) sign before the number 10. However, the Total Cost column will not automatically calculate the data in that column. Although the columns in Excel 2007 retain the data types from the exported SharePoint list, they do not retain the formulas of a calculated column.

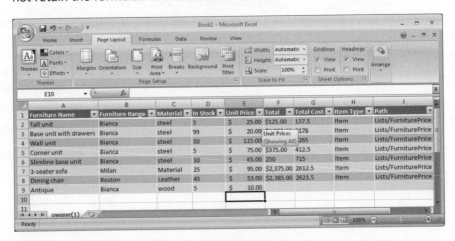

7. Click the **Data** tab, and click the **Refresh All** button.

Refresh All

The spreadsheet is updated with a copy of the data from the Furniture Price List on the SharePoint Web site. Your changes to data in the Excel 2007 spreadsheet are lost, which differs from the behavior of Excel 2003. In Excel 2007, changes that you make to data in your Excel 2007 worksheet do not synchronize with the list on the SharePoint Web site, that is, only a one-way synchronization occurs from the SharePoint site to Excel 2007. When using Excel 2003, two-way synchronization is still available.

8. Click cell **A2** and then, in the **Connections** group, click **Properties**. The External Data Properties dialog box appears.

   You can use this dialog box to alter the behavior of the refresh activity.

9. Click **Cancel**.

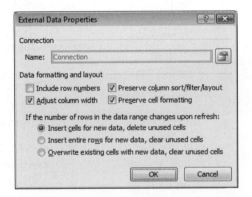

> **Tip** You can also initiate the exporting and linking of a SharePoint list to Excel 2007 by using the Access Web Datasheet task pane, which contains four options: Query list with Excel, Print with Excel, Chart with Excel, and Create Excel PivotTable Report.

 CLOSE the browser and Excel 2007. You do not need to save the spreadsheet.

Exporting an Excel 2007 Table to a SharePoint Site

Creating a SharePoint list from within Excel 2007 is known as exporting an Excel table. In Excel 2003, this was known as publishing an Excel list. Once the table data is placed on the SharePoint site, users can see the Excel 2007 data without opening Excel 2007. As in the first exercise of this chapter, you can maintain a link between the SharePoint list and the Excel 2007 data, but any changes in the Excel 2007 spreadsheet are not reflected in the SharePoint list. You can only synchronize changes in the SharePoint list to the Excel 2007 spreadsheet.

In the following exercise, you will export a spreadsheet to a SharePoint list by using Excel 2007 and a two-step wizard.

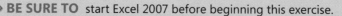

BE SURE TO start Excel 2007 before beginning this exercise.

USE the Sales_Figures.xlsx document in the practice file folder for this topic. This practice file is located in the *Documents\Microsoft Press\SBS_WSSv3\Chapter 12* folder. Remember to use your SharePoint site location in place of *http://wideworldimporters* in the exercise.

OPEN the Sales_Figures.xlsx document.

1. In **Excel 2007**, click any cell within the data.

2. On the **Home** tab, in the **Styles** group, click **Format as Table** and then choose a table style.

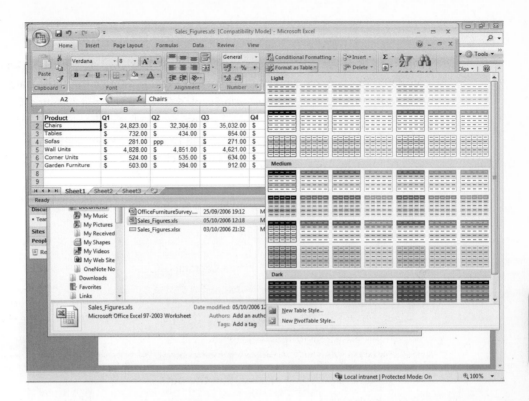

Tip By selecting one cell in the data, Excel 2007 automatically selects a range of cells that contain data; however, you can select a different range of cells to use when creating a table. In addition, if your data does not contain headers, Excel 2007 creates them for you and labels them as Column1, Column2, and so on. If the data you want to export is already found within an Excel 2007 table, you do not need to complete the first three tasks of this exercise.

3. When the **Format As Table** dialog box appears, click **OK**.

Excel 2007 converts the data in the workbook into a table. An Excel 2007 table was previously known as a list in Excel 2003. Each column header contains an AutoFilter arrow and a black border surrounding the data, which means that the table is active on the worksheet.

The Table Tools, Design contextual tab appears.

> **Tip** If the table is not active on the worksheet, then the Design tab disappears. To export a table, it must be active on the worksheet. To make a table active, click any cell in the table.

4. On the **Design** tab, in the **External Table Data** group, click **Export**.

5. From the drop-down menu, click **Export Table to SharePoint List**.

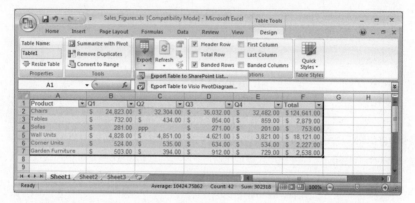

The first step of the two-step Export Table to SharePoint Site Wizard is displayed.

6. In the **Address** textbox, type http://wideworldimporters.

7. Select the **Create a read-only connection to the new SharePoint List** check box.

> **Important** If the "Create A Read-Only Connection To The New SharePoint List" check box is selected, the spreadsheet is linked to the SharePoint list and you can synchronize updates from the SharePoint list to the spreadsheet. However, once the SharePoint list is created, you cannot link the spreadsheet to the SharePoint list. Therefore, if you wish to synchronize updates between the list and the spreadsheet, be sure to select this check box now.

8. In the **Name** textbox, type SalesFigures. In the **Description** text box, type This list contains furniture sales for this year.

9. Click the **Next** button.

Excel 2007 checks the data in each column to ensure that the data belongs to a data type supported by Windows SharePoint Services. If it doesn't, Excel 2007 usually applies the Text data type to each column. Excel 2007 also checks whether each column contains only one type of data. If a column contains a mixture of data types, such as numbers and text, then Excel 2007 chooses Text as the data type. Once Excel 2007 completes its check, the second step of the two-step Export Table to SharePoint Site Wizard is displayed.

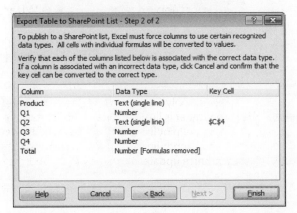

In the Key Cell column, notice that cell C4 in column Q2 contains a different data type from the rest of the cells in this column. Also, the formulas are removed from the Total column.

> **Tip** At this point, you can click the Cancel button, correct the erroneous data, and then restart the export process. Also, because Excel 2007 removes formulas during the export process, you may consider deleting the Total column and creating a calculated column once you have completed the export process and the data is on your SharePoint site.

Finish

10. Click the **Finish** button. A Windows SharePoint Services dialog box is displayed with the URL of your new SharePoint List.

> **Important** The new SharePoint list does not appear on the Quick Launch.

11. Click the **http://wideworldimporters/Lists/SalesFigures/Allitemsg.aspx** link. A new Internet Explorer window opens displaying the new SharePoint list.

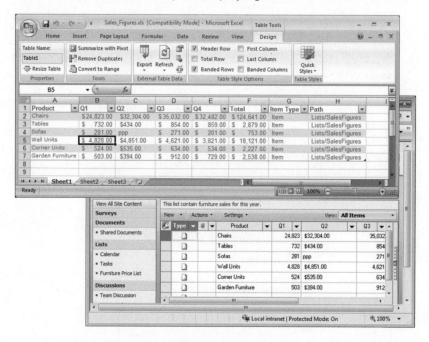

Data Range
Properties

Open in Browser

Unlink

> **Important** Before you close Excel 2007, notice that the spreadsheet contains two extra columns. When you export a spreadsheet that is linked to a SharePoint list, Item Type and Path columns are added to your spreadsheet. On the Design contextual tab, use the External Table data group to alter the properties of a range of cells, open the connected SharePoint list in a browser, or unlink a list.

CLOSE all browser windows.
CLOSE the Windows SharePoint Services dialog box by clicking OK.
CLOSE Excel 2007 and save changes to the spreadsheet.

Key Points

- You can create a Custom List from the browser by importing data from an Excel 2007 spreadsheet.

- You can create an Excel 2007 spreadsheet from the browser and export data into it from a SharePoint list.

- From within Excel 2007, you can export data held within an Excel table into a newly created SharePoint list.

- You can synchronize changes between a SharePoint list and an Excel 2007 spreadsheet, which is a one-way synchronization process.

Chapter at a Glance

Export data from an Access 2007 database to a SharePoint list, **page 353**

Import/link data from a SharePoint list to an Access 2007 table, **page 356**

Move data from an Access 2007 database to a SharePoint site, **page 362**

Work offline, **page 367**

Work with workflow, **page 370**

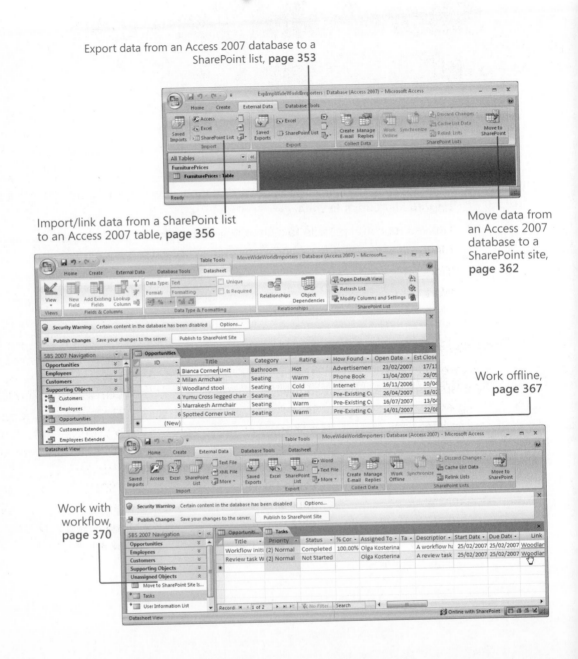

13 Using Windows SharePoint Services with Access 2007

In this chapter, you will learn to:

✔ Export data from a Microsoft Office Access 2007 database to a list in Microsoft Windows SharePoint Services.

✔ Import a list to an Office Access 2007 table.

✔ Link an Access 2007 table to a SharePoint list.

✔ Move data from an Access 2007 database to a SharePoint site.

✔ Work offline.

✔ Work with workflow.

Microsoft Windows SharePoint Services provides the collaborative backbone to the 2007 Microsoft Office System, which we explored in Chapter 7, "Working with Document Workspaces," Chapter 11, "Using Windows SharePoint Services with Outlook 2007," and Chapter 12, "Using Windows SharePoint Services with Excel 2007." This chapter focuses on the integration of Windows SharePoint Services with Microsoft Office Access 2007. This combination of Windows SharePoint Services and Office Access 2007 makes it easy for you to build client–server databases against Windows SharePoint Services. In doing so, users who do not possess the skills or privileges to be an SQL Server Database Administrator can still obtain the manageability and stability benefits of storing data on the server while retaining the ease of use of Access 2007. The level of server functionality integrated into Access 2007 can be expected to continue to grow in the future.

Access 2007, like Microsoft Office Excel 2007, allows you to export and import data both to and from SharePoint lists. Access 2007 also provides two-way synchronization between Access databases and SharePoint lists so you can work with lists offline and then synchronize the changes when you reconnect.

Access 2007 consists of a number of tabs, many of which provide a quick way to work with SharePoint Web sites and lists, as summarized in the following table.

Tab	Group	Description
Create	Tables	Use the SharePoint Lists drop-down menu to create a list on a SharePoint site and a table in the current database that links to the newly created list. You can also the drop-down menu found on an existing list.
External Data	Import	Use the SharePoint List command to import from or link to data on a SharePoint list.
	Export	Use the SharePoint List command to export the selected object as a SharePoint list.
	SharePoint Lists	Use this group to work offline, synchronize, discard changes, cache list data, relink lists, and migrate some or all parts of a database to a new or existing SharePoint Web site.
Datasheet	SharePoint List	Use this group when the database is linked to a SharePoint site or a table is linked with a SharePoint list. The icons provided in this group can be used to open the corresponding SharePoint list in the default view, refresh data shown in the linked table with the data stored on the SharePoint list, modify the list's columns and settings, create an alert on the SharePoint list, modify the workflow associated with the linked SharePoint list, and change the permissions of the linked SharePoint list.

Important Before you can use the practice files in this chapter, you need to install them from the book's companion CD to their default locations. See "Using the Book's CD" on page xix for more information.

Important Remember to use your SharePoint site location in place of *http://wideworldimporters* in the following exercises.

Exporting Data from an Access 2007 Database to a SharePoint List

Access 2007 allows you to export a table or other database objects to a number of formats such as an external file, Lotus 1-2-3, Paradox or dBase database, Office Excel 2007 workbook, Microsoft Office Word 2007 Rich Text Format (RTF) file, text file, eXtensible Markup Language (XML) document, Open DataBase Connectivity (ODBC) data source, or HyperText Markup Language (HTML) document. Beginning with Microsoft Office Access 2003, you can also export a table to a SharePoint site where a new list is created.

In the following exercise, you will export a table from within an Access 2007 database into a SharePoint site by creating a new SharePoint list.

> **USE** the ExpImpWideWorldImporters.accdb database located in the *Documents\Microsoft Press\SBS_WSSv3\Chapter 13* folder. Remember to use your SharePoint site location in place of *http://wideworldimporters* in the following exercise.
>
> **BE SURE TO** start Access 2007 before beginning this exercise.
>
> **OPEN** the ExpImpWideworldImporters.accdb database.

1. In the **ExpImpWideWorldImporters**: database window, click the **External Data** tab.

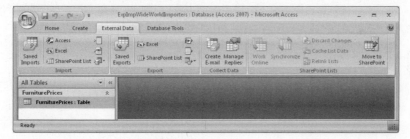

2. In the **Export** group, click **SharePoint List**. The Export – SharePoint Site dialog box is displayed.

> **Troubleshooting** If the SharePoint List link is not active, under All Tables, click the FurniturePrices: Table.

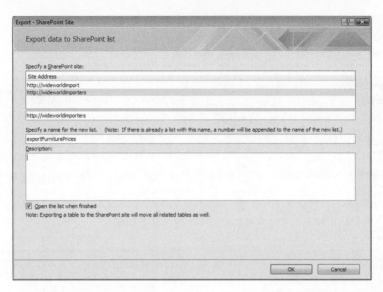

3. In the **Specify SharePoint site** area, choose **http://wideworldimporters**.

> **Troubleshooting** If the URL for the Wide World Importers Web site does not appear, type the URL in the textbox.

4. In the **Specify a name for the new list** textbox, type exportFurniturePrices.

5. Leave the **Open the list when finished** check box selected.

6. Click **OK**. A dialog box opens displaying the progress of the import.

7. Internet Explorer displays the newly created list, **exportFurniturePrices**, in All Items view.

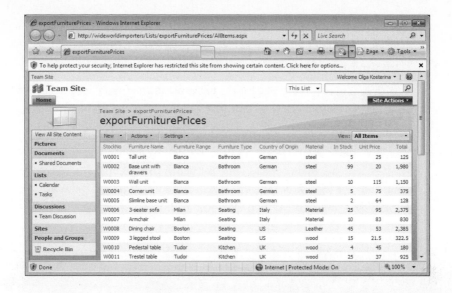

> **Tip** If you mistype the Web site name in the Site textbox, Access 2007 displays a warning dialog box stating that it can't find the Web site. If this occurs, verify the Web site address and try again.

8. Return to the Save Export Steps page of the Export – SharePoint Site dialog box in Access 2007.

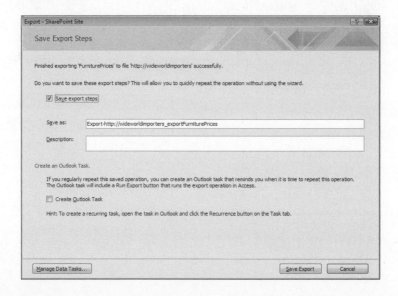

9. Select the **Save export steps** check box. The Save As and Description textboxes as well as the Create an Outlook Task area appear.

Save Export

10. Click the **Save Export** button. The Export – SharePoint Site dialog box closes.

A Move to SharePoint Site Issues table appears in the Access 2007 navigation pane that details aspects of the data that couldn't be applied to the SharePoint list.

To export the data to a SharePoint list, Access queries the Access table for data, which it then copies to the SharePoint list. By saving the export query, you can now repeat the above steps without using the wizard. Your saved exports can be found under the External Data tab in the Export group. Similarly, you can save your export as a Microsoft Office Outlook 2007 task, which you can then configure to remind you to run the export query.

 CLOSE the ExpImpWideWorldImporters.accdb database and close the browser. Choose No if prompted to save changes.

Importing a List to an Access 2007 Table

By using Access 2007, you can create a new table by importing data from an external data source such as Lotus 1-2-3, a Paradox or dBase database, Excel 2007 workbook, Office Outlook 2007 or Microsoft Exchange folder, XML document, ODBC data source, and SharePoint Web site. The new table becomes an integral part of your database, and the data are not affected by subsequent changes made to the data source after they are imported.

In this exercise, you will import data from a SharePoint list.

USE the ExpImpWideWorldImporters.accdb database located in the *Documents\Microsoft Press\SBS_WSSv3\Chapter 13* folder. Remember to use your SharePoint site location in place of *http://wideworldimporters* in the following exercise. This exercise uses the Price of Furniture SharePoint list that you created in first exercise of this chapter. You can also use your own list if you wish.

BE SURE TO start Access 2007 before beginning this exercise.

OPEN the ExpImpWideWorldImporters.accdb database.

1. In the **ExpImpWideWorldImporters**: database window, click the **External Data** tab.

2. In the **Import** group, click **SharePoint List**. The Get External Data – SharePoint Site dialog box appears.

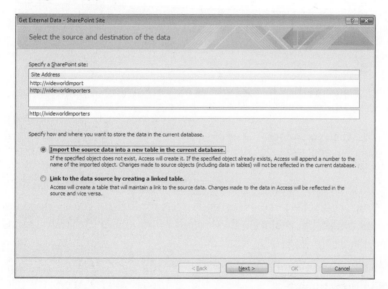

3. In the **Specify a SharePoint site** area, choose **http://wideworldimporters**.

> **Troubleshooting** If the URL for the Wide World Importers Web site does not appear, type the URL in the textbox.

4. Select the **Import the source data into a new table in the current database** option.

Next

5. Click the **Next** button. The Import data from list page of the Get External Data – SharePoint Site dialog box appears.

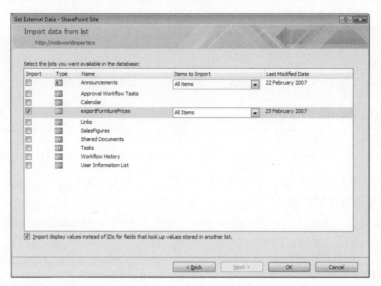

6. Select the check box to the right of **exportFurniturePrices**.

> **Tip** When you import data from a SharePoint list, the imported data are based on a view, and only those columns and rows shown in the view are imported. You can select the required view from the Items To Import drop-down list.

The Import displays values instead of IDs for lookup values stored in another list and allows you to maintain the lookup *relationship* that this list may have with other SharePoint lists.

7. Click **OK**. The Save Import Steps page of the Get External Data – SharePoint Site dialog box appears.

8. Click **Close**. The Get External Data – SharePoint Site dialog box closes and the exportFurniturePrices table appears in the Access 2007 navigation pane.

9. Double-click the **exportFurniturePrices** table. Access 2007 opens the exportFurniturePrices table in Datasheet view.

You can now edit the value in the cells of the table. Such changes will not be reflected back in the Furniture Price list on the SharePoint Web site.

> **Important** Changes to the SharePoint list are not copied back to the Access 2007 table, nor are changes to the Access 2007 table reflected back in the SharePoint list. A linked object is not created as part of this process.

CLOSE the ExpImpWideWorldImporters.accdb database and any open browser windows.

Linking an Access 2007 Table to a SharePoint List

Data were copied in the previous two sections so that the same data could be stored in both an Access 2007 database and on a list on a SharePoint site. However, no data synchronization between these two data locations occurred. If you do not want to maintain two copies of that data but do need to refer to the data within Access 2007, then Access 2007 provides methods of accessing external data that are physically located outside an Access 2007 database. The easiest way to externally reference a SharePoint list is to use linked tables, which were known as attached tables prior to Microsoft Access 95. A linked table stores only a connection to the SharePoint list. You should use linking rather than importing if the data are maintained by either a user or a separate application on the SharePoint Web site.

In this exercise, you will link a table to a SharePoint list.

USE the ExpImpWideWorldImporters.accdb database located in the *Documents\Microsoft Press\SBS_WSSv3\Chapter 13* folder. Remember to use your SharePoint site location in place of *http://wideworldimporters* in the following exercise. This exercise uses the exportFurniturePrices SharePoint list that you created in the first exercise of this chapter. You can also use your own list if you wish.

BE SURE TO start Access 2007 before beginning this exercise.

OPEN the ExpImpWideWorldImporters.accdb database.

1. In the **ExpImpWideWorldImporters**: database window, click the **External Data** tab.

2. In the **Import** group, click **SharePoint List**. The Get External Data – **SharePoint Site** dialog box appears.

3. In the **Specify a SharePoint site** area, choose **http://wideworldimporters**.

> **Troubleshooting** If the URL for the Wide World Importers Web site does not appear, type the URL in the textbox.

4. Check that the **Link to the data source by creating a linked table** option is select-ed and then click **Next**.

The Choose the SharePoint lists you want to link to page of the Get External Data – SharePoint site dialog box is displayed.

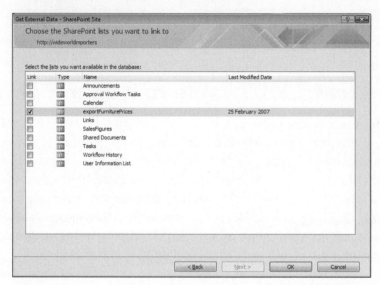

5. Select the check box to the right of **exportFurniturePrices**.

6. Click **OK**.

The Get External Data – SharePoint site dialog box closes. Access 2007 now has two linked tables: exportFurniturePrices1 and User Information List. The exportFur-niturePrices SharePoint list contains columns named Created By and Modified By. These lookup columns point to the User Information List.

7. Right-click the linked **exportFurniturePrices1** table, and then select **SharePoint List Options**.

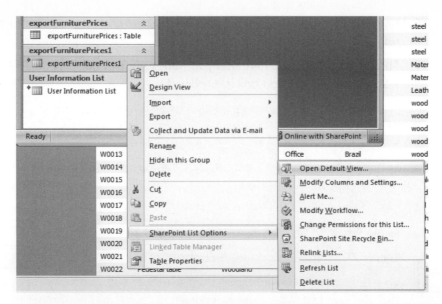

A context-sensitive menu is displayed that provides a quick way to manage the SharePoint list from within Access 2007.

8. Under **All Tables**, in the **exportFurniturePrices1** group, double-click **exportFurniturePrices1**.

Access 2007 opens the linked exportFurniturePrices1 table in Datasheet view.

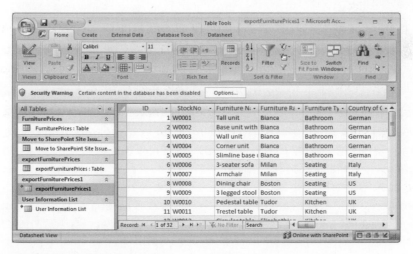

9. Click the **Datasheet** tab.

10. In the **SharePoint List** group, click Open **Default View**.

Internet Explorer opens and displays the exportFurniturePrices list in All Items view.

11. Switch back to Access 2007. In the exportFurniturePrices1 Datasheet view, click the cell in the first row under the **Furniture Name** column, and type Base Unit.

12. Click the cell in the second row under the **Furniture Name** column.

> **Important** By moving to another row, Access 2007 automatically synchronizes changes to the SharePoint list.

Refresh

13. Switch back to Internet Explorer, click the **Refresh** button, and then verify that the first row has been modified.

14. Click the **New** button. The exportFurniturePrices: New Item page is displayed.

New

15. In the **StockNo** textbox, type W0033, and then click **OK**.

The W0033 item is added to the bottom of the exportFurniturePrices list.

Refresh List

16. Switch back to Access 2007. On the **Datasheet** tab, in the **SharePoint List** group, click **Refresh List**. Alternatively, you can press [F5] and verify that the W0033 item has been added to the bottom of the table.

 CLOSE the ExpImpWideWorldImporters.accdb database and any open browser windows.

Moving Data from an Access 2007 Database to a SharePoint Site

Many Access 2007 applications grow from the need to manage and aggregate data. These data-centric applications often prove useful to more than one person in an organization, and thus the need to share them increases. However, Access 2007 is not truly meant for concurrent use. As Access 2007 database applications grow and become more complex, it is necessary to consider upsizing them to a data repository that can support more users while increasing availability, reliability, and manageability. Beginning with Microsoft Office Access 2000, various tools and wizards have helped with this process. With Access 2007, you can now upsize your Access database to Windows SharePoint Services, which is known as moving or publishing your Access 2007 database.

When you move data from an Access 2007 database to a SharePoint site, this process creates a SharePoint list for each Access 2007 table. Data from Access 2007 tables move into these SharePoint lists, and each data row becomes a list item in a SharePoint list. Tables in the Access 2007 database are replaced with linked tables that point to the newly created SharePoint list(s). Optionally, the Access 2007 database can then be loaded into a SharePoint document library. The Access 2007 database now becomes a user interface to the data by retaining views, reports, and relationships between tables. Access 2007 views also appear as SharePoint list views.

Because the data are now in SharePoint, you can use SharePoint functionality. For example, you can restore deleted list items from the Recycle Bin and apply workflow rules to data items. Changes to the list are versioned by default. If you choose to save the database in the document library, users who wish to use the database can navigate to the document library in their browser, where the database can be opened in Access 2007.

Prior to Access 2007, multiple users kept their own copy of an Access database and amended it separately, often not viewing others' amendments until they were included in official documents and the need to amalgamate the changes was recognized. To allow users to keep their own copy of a database, a business process would need to be introduced to maintain the data integrity of the database and distribute updates to the appropriate users. By using the process outlined in the previous paragraph, Access 2007 users can add and modify data by using either SharePoint or the linked tables within the Access 2007 database. New views, data relationships, and reports maintained in the Access 2007 database file can be managed as any other document when saved in SharePoint, including check-in and check-out facilities. Security on the data and the Access 2007 database can be maintained using SharePoint security. To take advantage of these new features, you must move your data from within your Access database to SharePoint.

In the following exercise, you will move data from within an Access 2007 database to a SharePoint site by uploading the Access 2007 database into a document library.

USE the MoveWideWorldImporters.accdb database located in the *Documents\Microsoft Press\SBS_WSSv3\Chapter 13* folder. Remember to use your SharePoint site location in place of *http://wideworldimporters* in the following exercise.

BE SURE TO start Access 2007 before beginning this exercise.

OPEN the MoveWideWorldiImporters.accdb database.

1. In the **MoveWideWorldImporters**: database window, click the **External Data** tab.

2. In the **SharePoint Lists** group, click **Move to SharePoint**. The Move to SharePoint Site Wizard dialog box is displayed.

3. In the **What SharePoint site do you want to use?** textbox, type http://wideworldimporters.

Browse

4. Click the **Browse** button. The **Location** dialog box is displayed.

5. Click **Browse Folders**. The Favorites and Site Content areas of the dialog box appear.

6. Double click **Shared Documents**. The contents of the Shared Document library are displayed.

7. Click **OK**. The URL of the document library is displayed in the Move to SharePoint Site Wizard dialog box.

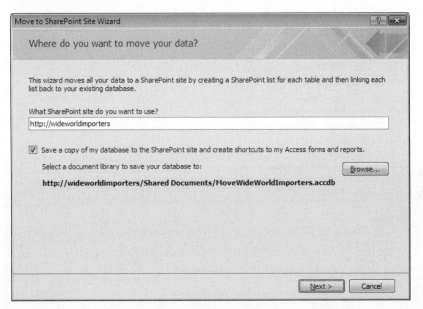

8. Click **Next**.

   The Move to SharePoint Site Wizard dialog box then displays the progress of the move operation, eventually stating that the tables are successfully shared and noting whether any issues were encountered.

9. Select the **Show Details** check box.

The Move to SharePoint Site Wizard dialog box displays the tasks it completed during the move operation. Note that a backup of the database is made.

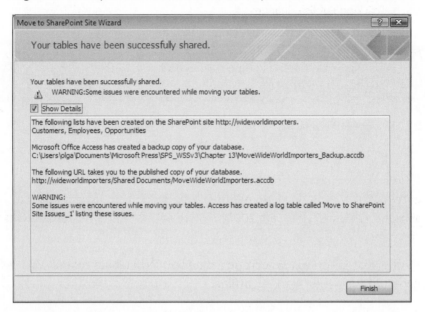

10. Click **Finish**. The three Access 2007 tables—Customers, Employees, and Opportunities—are now linked tables.

11. Under **SBS 2007 Navigation**, in the **Unassigned Objects** group, double-click the **Move to SharePoint Site Issues** table.

Access 2007 opens the Move to SharePoint Site Issues table in Datasheet view, where you can view the issues that Access 2007 encountered during the move.

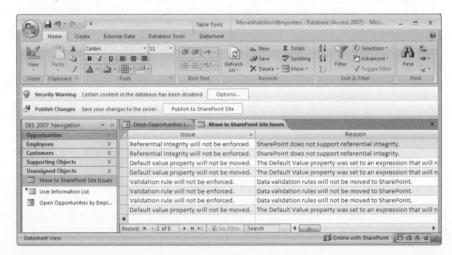

> **Tip** If you make changes to the Access 2007 database, such as creating a new view or report, then the database file can be saved to the document library on the server by clicking Publish Changes.

 CLOSE the MoveWideWorldImporters.accdb database and the browser. Choose Yes if prompted to save changes.

Working Offline

In the previous section, you moved an Access 2007 data-centric application to a SharePoint site. However, you might still like to access the data in a disconnected environment. When using Access 2007, you are able to cache SharePoint list data locally and synchronize changes back to the server.

In this exercise, you will synchronize data and a metadata column with a table linked to a SharePoint List when working offline.

 USE the MoveWideWorldImporters.accdb database located in the *Documents\Microsoft Press\SBS_WSSv3\Chapter 13* folder. Remember to use your SharePoint site location in place of *http://wideworldimporters* in the exercise. This exercise uses the linked tables that were created during the move operation in the previous exercise. You can also use your own tables that are linked to a SharePoint list if you wish.

BE SURE TO start Access 2007 before beginning this exercise.

OPEN the MoveWideWorldImporters.accdb database.

1. In the **MoveWideWorldImporters**: database window, click the **External Data** tab.

2. In the **SharePoint Lists** group, click **Work Offline**.

Synchronize

Synchronize

Discard Changes

Discard Changes

   The text, Offline with SharePoint, appears on the status bar. In the SharePoint Lists group, the Synchronize and Discard Changes icons become active. All data are cached within the Access 2007database and links to the SharePoint lists are temporarily cut.

> **Important** If you share this Access 2007 database, the data are then visible to users who do not have permissions to view them on the SharePoint site.

3. Under **SBS 2007 Navigation**, in the **Supporting Objects** group, double-click **Opportunities**.

Access 2007 opens the linked Opportunities table in Datasheet view. The application behaves much like it did online.

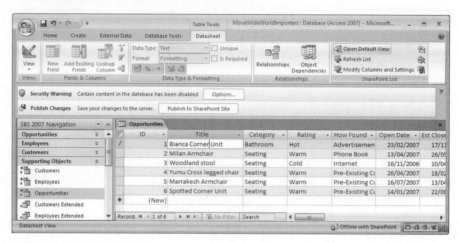

4. Click the **Datasheet** tab.

5. In the **SharePoint List** group, click **Open Default View**. Internet Explorer opens and displays the Opportunities list in All Items view.

6. Switch back to Access 2007. In Datasheet view of the **Opportunities** table, click the cell in the first row under the **Title** column and type Bianca Corner Unit.

7. Click a cell in the second row.

Pencil icon

A grayed pencil icon in the first column of the first row indicates that you have made changes to this row. When you are online with the SharePoint Web site, moving from the row you are editing causes Access 2007 to synchronize changes. This has not occurred here.

8. Switch back to Internet Explorer. Click **Refresh**, and then verify that the first row has not been modified.

9. Click the cell in first row under **Title**, type Woodland Bench, and then click a cell in the second row.

10. Switch back to **Access 2007**. On the **External Data** tab, in the **SharePoint Lists** group, click **Synchronize**.

Access 2007 temporarily connects to the SharePoint list to synchronize changes. The Resolve Conflicts dialog box appears.

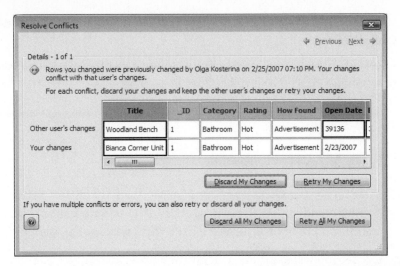

11. Click **Discard My Changes**. The Access 2007 database remains offline and the Datasheet view of the Opportunities table closes.

12. Under **SBS 2007 Navigation**, in the **Supporting Objects** group, double-click **Opportunities**.

    Access 2007 opens the linked Opportunities table in Datasheet view, and the Title column of the first row contains the text Woodland Bench.

13. In Datasheet view of the **Opportunities** table, click the cell in the first row under the **Title** column and type Bianca Corner Unit.

14. Click a cell in the second row.

15. On the **External Data** tab, in the **SharePoint Lists** group, click **Work Online.**

    The text, Online with SharePoint, appears in the status bar and the Datasheet view of the Opportunities table closes.

16. Switch back to Internet Explorer. Click the **Refresh**, and then verify that the first row contains Bianca Corner Unit.

17. Click **Settings** and then click **Create Column.**

18. In the **Name and Type** area, in the **Column Name** textbox, type Advertisement and select the **Yes/No** option.

19. Click **OK**. The Opportunities page is displayed with the Advertisement column at the end of the list.

20. Switch back to Access 2007. On the **External Data** tab, in the **SharePoint Lists** group, click **Synchronize.**

21. Open the **Opportunities** table if necessary and check that the **Advertisement** column is visible.

CLOSE the MoveWideWorldImporters.accdb database and the browser. Choose Yes if prompted to save changes.

Working with Workflow

Access 2007 can use the workflows found in Windows SharePoint Services. You can use workflow routing and approval, build business logic to automatically assign tasks to other users, report on project status, and ensure that tasks are completed on time.

In this exercise, you will associate a workflow with a table linked to a SharePoint list to assign tasks automatically when a new item is added to a SharePoint list.

USE the MoveWideWorldImporters.accdb located in the *Documents\Microsoft Press\SBS_WSSv3\Chapter 13* folder. Remember to use your SharePoint site location in place of *http://wideworldimporters* in the exercise. This exercise uses the linked tables that were created during a previous exercise of this chapter. You can also use your own tables that are linked to a SharePoint list if you wish.

BE SURE TO start Access 2007 before beginning this exercise.

OPEN the MoveWideWorldImporters.accdb database.

1. In the **MoveWideWorldImporters**: database window, under **SBS 2007 Navigation** in the **Supporting Objects** group, right-click **Opportunities**.

2. Click **SharePoint List Options**, and then click **Modify Workflow**.

   Internet Explorer opens and the Change Workflow Settings: Opportunities page is displayed. No workflows are currently associated with the Opportunities list.

   Team Site > Opportunities > Settings > Workflow settings
   ## Change Workflow Settings: Opportunities

   Use this page to view or change the workflow settings for this list. You can also add or remove workflows. Changes to existing workflows will not be applied to workflows already in progress.

   Workflows

   There are no workflows currently associated with this list.

   ▫ Add a workflow

3. Click **Add a workflow**. The Add a Workflow: Opportunities page is displayed.

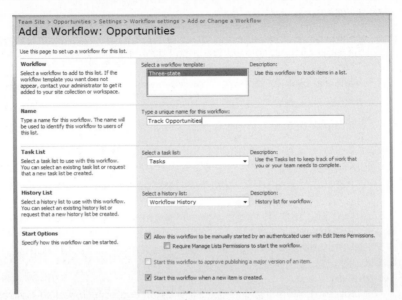

4. In the **Workflow** area, choose **Three-state**.

5. In the **Name** area, type Track Opportunities.

6. Accept the default values for the **Task List** and **History List**.

7. In the **Start Options** area, select the **Start this workflow when a new item is created** check box and then click **Next**. The Customize the Three-state Workflow page is displayed.

8. In the **Workflow States** area, under **Select a 'Choice' field**, click **Rating**.

9. Accept the default setting, scroll to the bottom of the page, and click **OK**. The Opportunities page is displayed.

> **Tip** In the Specify What You Want To Happen When A Workflow Is Initiated check box, the default action is to assign the task to the person who created the list item, which in this instance is you.

10. Switch back to Access 2007. Enter a new Opportunities item by opening the **Opportunities** table if necessary.

11. In the last row of the table in the **Title** column, type Woodland Stool. Press [Tab], and type S.

    As is done in Excel 2007, the IntelliSense feature completes the word based on other values in this column.

12. Press ⁅Tab⁆ to choose **Seating** and type H. Press ⁅Tab⁆ to choose **Hot**.

13. Click in any cell in the first row.

14. Click the **External Data** tab and then, in the **Import** group, click **SharePoint List**. The Get External Data – SharePoint Site dialog box appears.

15. Verify that the **Link to the data source by creating a linked table** option is selected and then click **Next**.

16. Click the check box to the right of **Tasks** and then click **OK**.

Access 2007 now has two additional tables: Tasks and User Information List under Unassigned Objects.

17. Double-click **Tasks**. Access 2007 open the Tasks table in Datasheet view.

Notice that one task item is assigned to you, titled Workflow initiated: Woodland Stool.

18. In the task item assigned to you, click the cell in the **Status** column and click **Completed**.

19. Press ⁅F5⁆. The Tasks table is refreshed and a second task appears titled Review Task Woodland Stool.

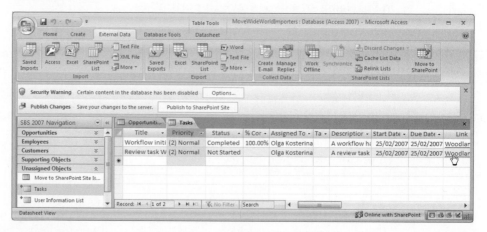

20. In the **Link** column, click **Woodland Stool**. You might need to scroll to the right to see this column.

Internet Explorer opens and displays the Opportunities: Woodland Stool page. Notice that the Rating is now Warm.

21. Return to Access 2007 and repeat Steps 18 to 20. The **Rating** should now be **Cold**.

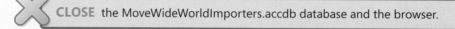

CLOSE the MoveWideWorldImporters.accdb database and the browser.

Key Points

- Integration with Windows SharePoint Services makes Access 2007 a great collaboration tool while enabling data to be stored on enterprise servers for better manageability.

- Access 2007 allows you to export and import data to and from SharePoint lists. Data in the Access 2007 table are not affected by subsequent changes made to the SharePoint list because there is no synchronization process between Access 2007 and a SharePoint site.

- When using Access 2007, you should create a new table that's linked to a SharePoint list where data are maintained by users on the SharePoint Web site and you want Access 2007 to use the most current data. You can use Access 2007 to enter data into these SharePoint Lists, where two-way synchronization is provided, and you can maintain an offline cache when working offline.

- In Access 2007, you can move a database to a SharePoint site. Data are moved into SharePoint lists, and the Access 2007 database is stored in a document library. This functions well for data-centric applications that are shared between people and enables you to take advantage of SharePoint features such as workflow, security, and search.

Chapter at a Glance

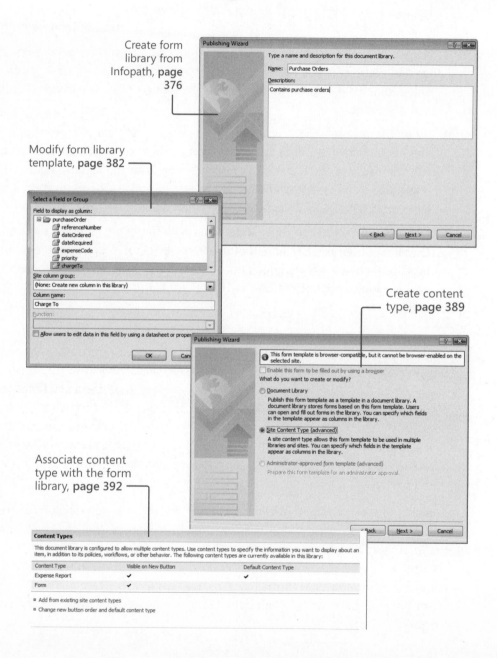

Create form library from Infopath, **page 376**

Modify form library template, **page 382**

Create content type, **page 389**

Associate content type with the form library, **page 392**

14 Using Windows SharePoint Services with InfoPath 2007

In this chapter, you will learn to:

- ✔ Create a form library from Microsoft Office InfoPath 2007.
- ✔ Modify an existing form library.
- ✔ Fill out a form.
- ✔ Edit an existing form.
- ✔ Create a content type from Office InfoPath 2007.
- ✔ Associate a content type with a form library.
- ✔ Modify a content type.

Microsoft Windows SharePoint Services contains many features to help you more fully utilize Microsoft Office InfoPath 2007. In particular, SharePoint form libraries provide the primary integration point between Windows SharePoint Services and Office InfoPath 2007. *Form libraries* allow you to use and share InfoPath 2007 forms. An *InfoPath form* collects information from a user in a structured way. Form libraries provide a central location where users can fill out and store forms based on the same template. For example, you can use InfoPath 2007 to create purchase orders and subsequently store them in a SharePoint form library.

In this chapter, you will learn how to use InfoPath 2007 so as to work with SharePoint form libraries and the forms stored within these libraries. You will create a SharePoint form library and modify an existing form library from InfoPath 2007. You will then use InfoPath 2007 to create new forms based on a form library's template as well as edit existing forms stored in the form library. In addition, you will create and modify a site content type based on an InfoPath 2007 template and associate this site content with a form library.

> **Important** Before you can use the practice files in this chapter, you need to install them from the book's companion CD to their default location. See "Using the Book's CD" on page xix for more information.

> **Important** Remember to use your SharePoint site location in place of *http://wideworldimporters* in the following exercises.

Creating a Form Library from InfoPath 2007

A SharePoint form library stores forms that are based on the same form template. An *InfoPath form template* is a file that defines the appearance, structure, and behavior of an InfoPath 2007 form. Form templates allow form designers to create the look, feel, and functionality of the form. After the form template is created, users create new forms by filling out the fields provided by the template.

InfoPath 2007 operates in two different modes: Design mode and Fill out a form mode.

- Design This mode allows designers to create form templates. For example, a template used for purchase orders is created in Design mode.

- Fill out a form This mode provides users with a familiar Microsoft Office suite environment in which they create new forms by filling out the fields provided for them. For example, a new purchase order is created in Fill out a form mode.

When you create a new SharePoint form library from InfoPath 2007, you publish a form template into a newly created library. The library is then associated with this template, and every form in this library has the same appearance and structure.

You can also create a form library from a SharePoint site. For detailed instructions, refer to Chapter 5, "Creating and Managing Libraries."

In the following exercise, you will use InfoPath 2007 to create a new SharePoint form library named Purchase Orders.

USE the Purchase Order Template.xsn form template located in the *Documents\Microsoft Press\SBS_WSSv3\Chapter 14* practice folder.

BE SURE TO open InfoPath 2007 before beginning this exercise. Close the Getting Started window if it appears.

1. From the **File** menu, choose **Design a Form Template**. The Design a Form Template window appears.

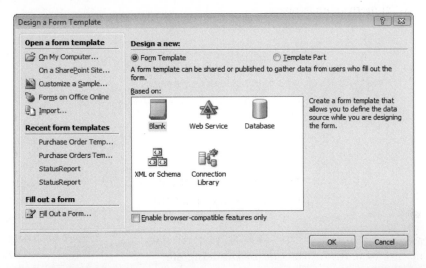

2. In the **Design a Form Template** window, under **Open a form template**, click **On My Computer**.

3. Navigate to the **Documents\Microsoft Press\SBS_WSSv3\Chapter 14** folder, choose **Purchase Order Template.xsn**, and click **Open**.

If the dialog box with the publishing location warning appears, click OK.

The Purchase Order template opens in Design mode. Note the Design Tasks pane that appears.

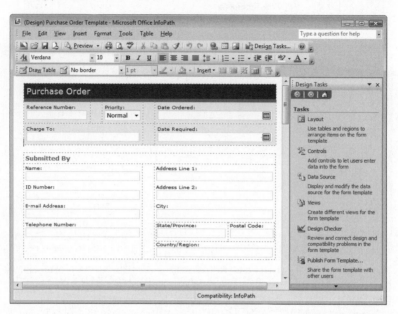

4. On the **File** menu, choose **Publish**. The InfoPath Publishing Wizard opens.

> **Tip** You can also click Publish Form Template in the Design Tasks pane.

5. On the page listing the options for publishing location, select the first bullet point: **To a SharePoint server with or without InfoPath Forms Services**, and click **Next**.

6. On the next page, in the **Enter the location of your SharePoint or InfoPath Forms Services site**, type the URL of the SharePoint site in which you want to create the form library, such as http://wideworldimporters. Click **Next**.

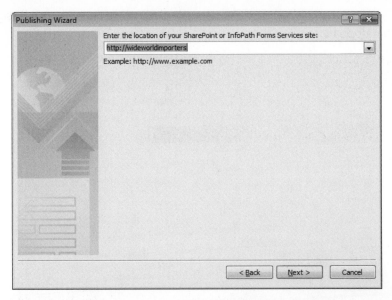

7. If prompted, type your user name and password for the SharePoint site, and click **OK**.

8. On the next page, choose **Document library** and click **Next**.

9. On the next page, choose **Create a new document library and click** Next.

10. On the next page, in the **Name** box, type the name for the form library, such as Purchase Orders. In the **Description** box, type a description of the information in the form library you are creating, such as Contains purchase orders. Click **Next**.

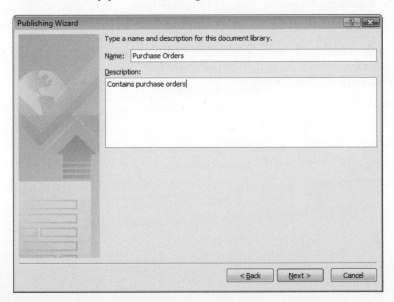

> **Tip** While you do need to provide a name for your new library, a description is optional.

11. The next page in the Publishing Wizard allows you to define the table layout for the Form Library page. The form data on the SharePoint Form Library page are displayed in a table. Data in the table columns come from the forms fields. You create the table layout by specifying the form fields that you want to become the table columns.

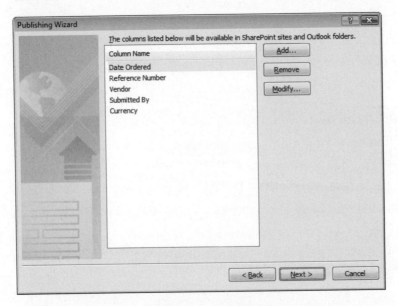

> **Tip** After the library is created, this table is displayed on the form library page in the library's default All Documents view.

The table columns for this form library are listed in the Column Name list. Five form fields will become columns after the library is created: Date Ordered, Reference Number, Vendor, Submitted By, and Currency. Since the majority of orders for Wide World Importers use the same currency, the owner has decided not to display the currency used in the purchase orders on the site.

12. To prevent the Currency column from appearing in the form library, choose **Currency**, and then click **Remove**.

The Currency column is removed for the Column Name list.

13. Click **Next**.

> **Tip** Table contents on the Form Library page can be searched on a SharePoint site. Therefore, if you want to make particular form data searchable, make sure the field that contains the data becomes a table column.

14. On the next page, verify the form information that you provided, and then click **Publish**. The form library is created.

15. On the confirmation page, choose **Open this document library**, and click **Close**.

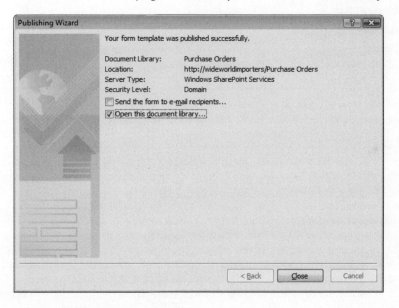

The Purchase Orders library page appears in the browser. The library is empty. Note that the name of the library appears on the Quick Launch in the left navigation panel under Documents.

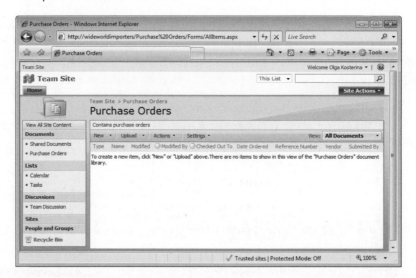

 CLOSE InfoPath 2007 and close the browser.

> **Tip** When the form template is published to the SharePoint site, it is stored in the Forms folder within this library under the default name template.xsn. If you want to verify that your template has been published, start the browser and go to the site to which you published a template, such as *http://wideworldimporters*. Click *All Site Content* in the left navigation panel. Under *Document Libraries*, click *Purchase Orders* library. On the Form Library page, from the *View* menu, select *Explorer View*. The *Forms* folder is displayed, and your form template is stored inside this folder. Double-click the *Forms* folder to verify that template.xsn is inside this folder. After locating the form template, close the browser.

Modifying an Existing Form Library

To modify an existing form library, you can change the form template on which the library is based. Care must be used when changing a form template because your changes might result in the loss of data within the existing forms stored in the form library that are based on this template. For example, if you remove a field from a form template, this field no longer appears in the existing forms that are based on that form template; consequently, the data in this field is lost. However, if you are making additions to the form or changing its appearance, you shouldn't lose any data.

> **Tip** If in doubt, do not modify the existing library. Instead, publish the changed form template to a new form library.

In this exercise, you will modify the existing form library from InfoPath 2007. In the Purchase Orders form library template, you will change the form title to Wide World Importers Purchase Orders and then add the Charge To column to the table layout of the Form Library page.

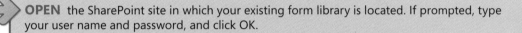

OPEN the SharePoint site in which your existing form library is located. If prompted, type your user name and password, and click OK.

1. In the left navigation panel, click **View All Site Content**.

2. Under **Document Libraries**, click the **Purchase Orders** library.

3. On the **Purchase Orders** form library page, from the **Settings** menu, choose **Form Library Settings**.

4. On the **Customize Purchase Orders** page, in the **General Settings** area, choose **Advanced Settings**.

5. On the **Form Library Advanced Setting** page, in the **Document Template** area, under **Template URL**, click **(Edit Template)**.

6. If prompted, type your user name and password for the SharePoint site, and click **OK**.

7. If a dialog box appears that asks whether you want to continue, click **Yes**.

    The Purchase Orders form template opens in InfoPath 2007 in Design mode.

8. Position your cursor to the left of the **Purchase Order** heading. Type Wide World Importers so that the heading reads Wide World Importers Purchase Order.

9. From the **File** menu, choose **Publish**. The InfoPath Publishing Wizard opens.

10. On the page that lists the options for publishing location, select the first bullet point: **To a SharePoint server with or without InfoPath Forms Services**, and click **Next**.

11. On the next page, in the **Enter the location of your SharePoint or InfoPath Forms Services site**, type the URL of the SharePoint site on which you want to create the form library, such as http://wideworldimporters. Click **Next**.

12. On the next page, choose **Document Library**, and click **Next**.

13. On the next page, click **Update the form template in an existing document library**, and then choose the **Purchase Orders** library from the list of existing libraries. Click **Next**.

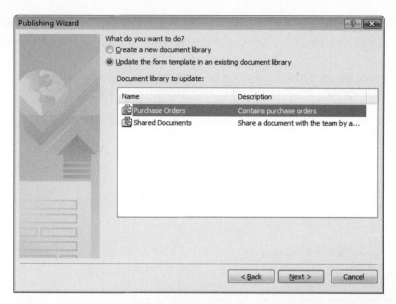

You will now modify the table layout for the form library page by adding a Charge To column.

14. On the page that lists column names, click **Add**. The **Select a Field or Group** dialog box appears.

15. Select the **chargeTo** field. In the **Column name** box, edit the field so that it reads Charge To. Click **OK**.

Charge To is added to the list of column names.

16. Click **Next**.

17. On the next page, verify that the form information is correct, and then click **Publish**. The modified template has been published to the SharePoint site.

18. On the confirmation page, click **Close**.

 CLOSE InfoPath 2007, and then close the browser.

Filling Out a New Form

After a form library is created, the users can fill out new forms and edit existing forms in the library.

In the following exercise, you will create a new form and save it to the SharePoint form library.

 OPEN the SharePoint site in which the form library is located. If prompted, type your user name and password, and click OK.

1. In the left navigation panel, click **All Site Content**.

2. Under **Document Libraries**, click the **Purchase Orders** library.

3. On the **Purchase Orders** form library page, click **New**. Alternatively, you can open the **New** menu and choose **New Document**.

InfoPath 2007 opens in Fill out a form mode and displays a new form based on the Purchase Order template. You will now fill out the form.

4. In the **Reference Number** field, type 12345. Under **Vendor Information**, in the **Company name** field, type Contoso. Fill out other form fields with fictitious data.

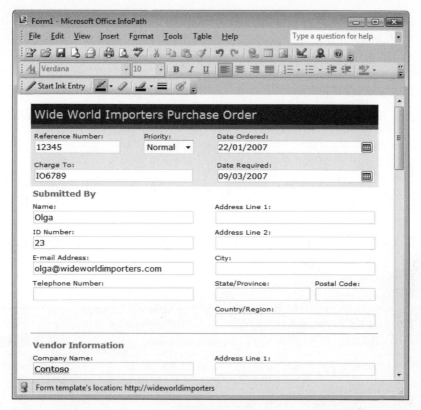

5. From the **File** menu, choose **Save As**. The Save As dialog box appears.

6. In the **File Name** box, type ContosoPO.

7. Click **Save**. The form is saved to the Purchase Orders form library.

8. On the Windows taskbar, select the browser that points to the Purchase Orders form library.

9. Refresh the browser and verify that the ContosoPO form is listed in the library.

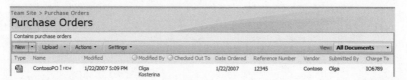

 CLOSE InfoPath 2007, and then close the browser.

Editing an Existing Form

You might often find yourself in a situation in which you need to edit an existing form that is stored in the SharePoint form library, such as correcting mistyped data. The existing form is edited in InfoPath 2007 and then saved to the form library.

In this exercise, you will edit the existing form and save it back to the form library.

OPEN the SharePoint site in which the form library is located. If prompted, type your user name and password, and click OK.

1. Navigate to the **Purchase Orders** library.

2. On the **Purchase Orders** page, hover the mouse over the **ContosoPO** name so that the arrow appears to the right. Click the arrow and choose **Edit in Microsoft Office InfoPath**.

   > **Tip** You can also simply click the ContosoPO name. If the File Download dialog box appears, click Open.

   InfoPath 2007 opens the ContosoPO form in Fill out a form mode.

3. Change the **Reference Number** to 12346.

4. From the **File** menu, choose **Save**. The form is saved to the Purchase Orders form library.

5. On the Windows taskbar, select the browser that points to the Purchase Orders form library.

6. Refresh the browser and verify that the edited form with reference number 12346 is listed in the library.

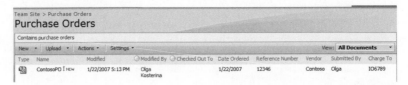

You will now edit the ContosoPO form and save it under a different name.

7. On the **Purchase Orders** form library page, hover the mouse over the **ContosoPO** name so that the arrow appears to the right. Click the arrow and then choose **Edit in Microsoft Office InfoPath**. InfoPath 2007 opens the ContosoPO form in Fill out a form mode.

8. Change the **Reference Number** to 12347.

9. Under **Vendor Information**, change the **Company name** to Northwind Traders. Make other changes to form data if you like.

10. From the **File** menu, choose **Save As**. The Save As dialog box appears.

11. In the **File Name** box, type NorthwindPO, and then click **Save**. The form is saved to the Purchase Orders form library.

12. On the Windows taskbar, select the browser that points to the Purchase Orders form library.

13. Refresh the browser and verify that the NorthwindPO form is listed in the library.

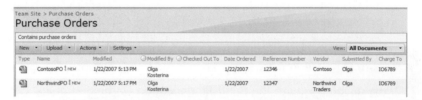

 CLOSE InfoPath 2007, and then close the browser.

Creating a Content Type from InfoPath 2007

When a standard form is used throughout an organization, you repeatedly need to create form libraries based on the same form. These libraries might be located in different sites within a site collection. Instead of creating numerous libraries based on the same template, you can create a content type based on that form template and then associate this content type with as many libraries as needed, thereby making the template reusable across your site collection. All content types for a site collection are located within the Site Content Type gallery and are accessible from all libraries on all sites in this site collection.

You can create a new content type and modify an existing content type from within InfoPath 2007. When you create a new content type from InfoPath 2007, you first publish a form template for this content type into any document library within the site collection and then associate the new content type with this template.

In the following exercise, you will use InfoPath 2007 to create a new content type based on a form template named Expense Report Template.xsn.

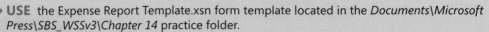

USE the Expense Report Template.xsn form template located in the *Documents\Microsoft Press\SBS_WSSv3\Chapter 14* practice folder.

BE SURE TO open InfoPath 2007 before beginning this exercise. Close the Getting Started window if it appears.

1. From the **File** menu, choose **Design a Form Template**. The Design a Form Template windows appears.

2. In the **Design a Form Template** window, under **Open a form template**, click **On My Computer**.

3. Navigate to the **Documents\Microsoft Press\SBS_WSSv3\Chapter 14** folder, choose **Expense Report Template.xsn**, and click **Open**.

4. If the dialog box with the publishing location warning appears, click **OK**.

   The Expense Report template opens in Design mode.

5. On the **File** menu, choose **Publish**. The InfoPath Publishing Wizard opens.

6. On the page that lists the options for publishing location, select the first bullet point: **To a SharePoint server with or without InfoPath Forms Services**, and click **Next**.

7. On the next page, in the **Enter the location of your SharePoint or InfoPath Forms Services site**, type the URL of the SharePoint site in which you want to create the content type, such as http://wideworldimporters. Click **Next**.

8. On the next page, choose **Site Content Type (advanced)** and click **Next**.

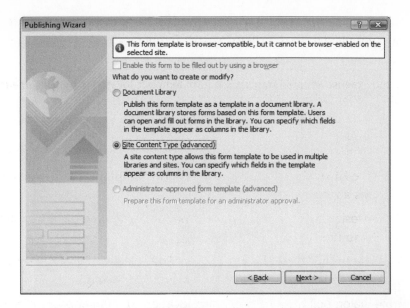

> **Important** The Expense Report template in this exercise is browser compatible. To enable browser-compatible templates, InfoPath Form Services must be installed on your server. InfoPath Form Services is available within Microsoft Office SharePoint Server 2007 and Microsoft Office Form Server 2007. Windows SharePoint Services does not include InfoPath Form Services.

> **Note** A detailed comparison between different editions of Office SharePoint Server 2007 and Windows SharePoint Services is provided in the SharePointProductsComparison.xls file on the book's companion CD.

9. On the next page, choose **Create a new content type** and click **Next**.

10. On the next page, in the **Name** box, type the name for the content type, such as Expense Report. In the **Description** box, type a description of the content type you are creating, such as Expense report form v1.0. Click **Next**.

> **Tip** While you do need to provide a name for your new content type, a description is optional.

On the next page, you must specify a document library where the template is to be stored, which can be any document library within the site collection. In the Wide World Importers site, a library called Templates has been created to store content type templates, but you can use any document library you wish.

11. Type the location of the library where the template is to be stored as well as the file name under which you'd like it to be stored, such as http://wideworldimporters/ templates/ExpenseReport.xsn. Click **Next**.

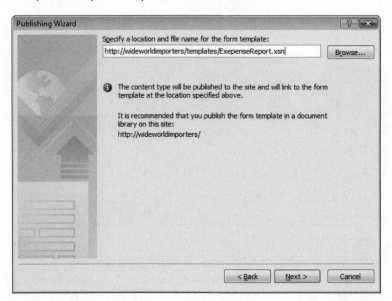

12. Keep the existing table layout. Click **Next**.

13. On the next page, verify the form information, and then click **Publish**.

14. The form template is published into the designated document library, and the associated content type is created. On the confirmation page, click **Close**.

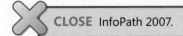 **CLOSE** InfoPath 2007.

Associating a Content Type with a Form Library

After the content type has been created, you can associate it with a form library. Associating a content type with a form library means that the form library contains items of that content type and that the New command in that library allows users to create new items of that type.

In this exercise, you will create a new form library for January Expense Reports, associate it with the custom Expense Report content type that you created in the previous exercise, and then configure this content type as a default content type for that library.

OPEN a SharePoint site in which you'd like to associate a library with a content type. If prompted, type your user name and password, and then click OK.

1. To create a new form library, from the **Site Actions** menu, choose **Create**.

2. On the **Create** page, under **Libraries**, click **Form Library**.

3. On the **New** page, in the **Name** box, type a name for the new library, such as January Expense Reports. Type a description for the new library, such as Contains January expense reports, and click **Create**.

4. On the new form library page, under the **Settings** menu, choose **Form Library Settings**. The **Customize** page appears.

5. On the **Customize** page, under **General Settings**, click **Advanced settings**.

6. On the **Advanced Settings** page, in the **Content Types** area, choose **Yes** to allow management of content types, and click **OK**.

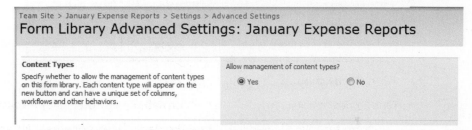

7. On the **Customize** page, under **Content Types**, click **Add from existing site content types**.

8. On the **Add Content Types** page, on the **Available Site Content Types** list, choose the content type you'd like to associate with this library, such as **Expense Report**, and click **Add**. The content type appears in the Content types to add box.

9. Click **OK**.

   You will now make the new content type a default for this library.

10. On the **Customize** page, under **Content Types**, click **Change new button order and default content type**.

11. On the **Change new button order and default content type** page, in the **Content type Order** area, in the line that contains the **Expense Report** content type, select **1** in the **Position from Top** drop-down list. Click **OK**.

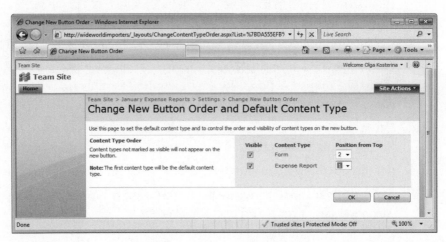

> **Tip** The first content type is the default content type for a library.

12. On the **Customize** page, under **Content Types**, verify that the Expense Report content type is listed as the default content type.

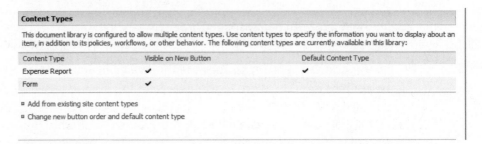

13. Navigate to the form library by clicking its link in the site navigation breadcrumb above the page title.

14. On the form library page, click **New**.

InfoPath 2007 opens in Fill out a form mode and displays a new form based on the Expense Report content type that, in turn, is based on the Expense Report Template.xsn template.

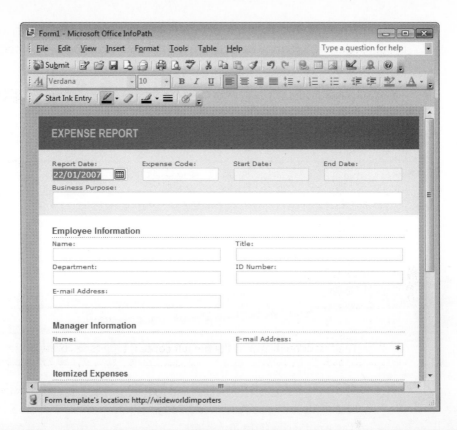

CLOSE InfoPath 2007, and then close the browser.

Modifying a Content Type

By using InfoPath 2007, you can modify a form template on which existing content type is based. Similar to modifying the form template for a single library, it's important to be careful when changing a content type form template because you might lose data in the existing forms stored in all form libraries that are based on this content type. For example, if you remove a field from a form template, this field no longer appears in all existing forms in all libraries associated with the content type based on this template; consequently, the data in this field are lost. However, if you are making additions to the content type form template or changing its appearance, you shouldn't lose any data.

> **Tip** If in doubt, do not modify the existing content type. Instead, create a new content type based on the modified form template.

In the following exercise, you will modify the existing content type. You will add the Wide World Importers subtitle to the form template on which the Expense Report content type is based.

 OPEN a SharePoint site in which you'd like to modify a content type. If prompted, type your user name and password, and then click OK.

1. From the **Site Actions** menu, choose **Site Settings**.

   If you are in the top-level site in the site collection, move to Step 2. If you are not in the top-level site, under Site Collection Administration, choose Go to the top level site settings.

2. On the top-level site **Site Settings** page, under **Galleries**, click **Site content types**.

3. In the **Site Content Type Gallery**, scroll down to the **Microsoft Office InfoPath** area and click the content type you'd like to modify, such as **Expense Report**.

4. On the **Site Content Type** page, under **Settings**, click **Advanced Settings**.

5. On the **Site Content Type Advanced Settings** page, in the **Document Template** area on the right, click **(Edit Template)**.

   The Expense Report template opens in InfoPath 2007 in the Design mode.

6. Position your cursor at the end of the Expense Report title and press the ⌷Enter⌷ key on the keyboard to create a new line. In this new line, type the subtitle Wide World Importers.

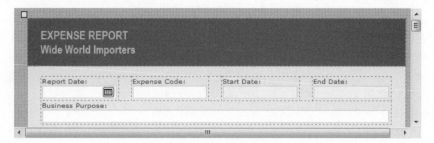

7. On the **File** menu, choose **Publish**. The InfoPath Publishing Wizard opens.

8. On the page that lists the options for publishing location, choose **To a SharePoint server with or without InfoPath Forms Services**, and click **Next**.

9. On the next page, in the **Enter the location of your SharePoint or InfoPath Forms Services site**, type the URL of the top-level site in which you want to modify the content type, such as http://wideworldimporters. Click **Next**.

10. On the next page, choose **Site content type (advanced)** and click **Next**.

11. On the next page, choose **Update an existing site content type.** Select the name of the site content type you'd like to modify and click **Next**.

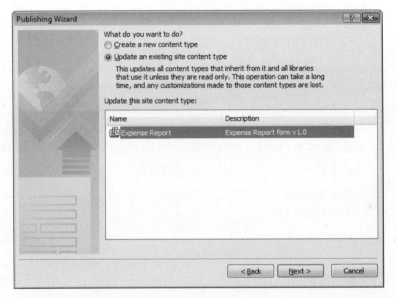

12. On the next page, verify the document library in which the template is stored as well as the file name of template, such as http://wideworldimporters/templates/ExpenseReport.xsn. Click **Next**.

13. Keep the existing column layout. Click **Next**.

14. On the next page, verify the form information, and then click **Publish**.

    The modified form template is published into the designated document library.

15. On the confirmation page, click **Close**.

You will now verify that the changes to the content type have been made.

16. On the Windows taskbar, select the browser that points to the Site Content Type Advanced Settings page. Click **Home** to go to the top-level site home page.

17. Navigate to a form library that is based on the modified content type, such as **January Expense Reports**.

18. In the **January Expense Reports** Form Library page, click **New**. The modified form opens in InfoPath 2007 in Fill Out Form view.

19. Verify that the changes to the content type form template have been made. Fill in the form with fictitious data, and then save the form to the form library.

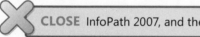 **CLOSE** InfoPath 2007, and then close the browser.

Key Points

- SharePoint form libraries provide the primary integration point between Windows SharePoint Services and InfoPath 2007.

- Form libraries can be created from within InfoPath 2007 as well as from the SharePoint site.

- When you create a new SharePoint form library from InfoPath 2007, you publish a form template into a newly created library.

- You can define a table layout on the Form Library page when you publish the form template into this library.

- After the form library has been created, you can modify its template by using InfoPath 2007.

- To make the form template reusable across your site collection, create a content type based on that form template by using InfoPath 2007. You can then associate this content type with as many libraries as necessary.

- After the content type is created, you can modify its underlying template by using InfoPath 2007.

- To create a new form based on a library template, click New on the Form Library page. The empty form opens in InfoPath 2007. Fill out the form data, and then save the new form to the library.

- To edit an existing form, click the form on the library's page. The form opens in InfoPath 2007. Edit the form data, and then save the form to the library.

Chapter at a Glance

Remove a Web Part, page 405

Add a Web Part from a Web Part Gallery, page 407

Customize a Web Part by using the Web Part tool pane, page 414

Create a New Web Part Page by using a browser, page 422

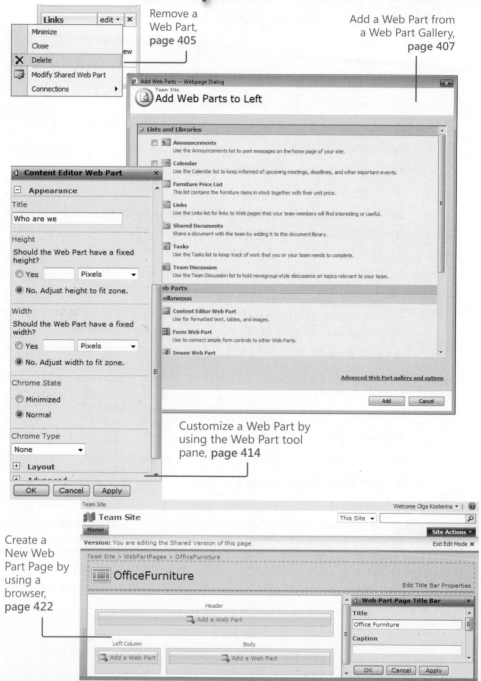

15 Working with Web Parts

In this chapter, you will learn to:

✔ Understand Web Parts and Web Part Pages.

✔ Remove a Web Part.

✔ Add a Web Part from a Web Part Gallery.

✔ Customize a Web Part using the Web Part tool pane.

✔ Customize a home page using Web Parts.

✔ Create a New Web Part Page by using a browser.

Web sites based on Microsoft Windows SharePoint Services use a technology known as *Web Part Pages*, which are special Web pages that contain one or more Web Parts. *Web Parts* are reusable components that can contain any type of Web-based information including analytical, collaborative, and database information. This technology enables Web sites to be flexible and highly customizable. To customize these sites, you can use three types of tools.

● A browser

● A Windows SharePoint Services–compatible Web page editing tool, such as Microsoft Office SharePoint Designer 2007

● Programmatically, a tool such as Microsoft Visual Studio .NET 2005

No one tool can do everything, and therefore it is likely that in any deployment of Windows SharePoint Services, all three tools will be used at some period of time.

This chapter introduces the basic concepts of Web Part Pages and Web Parts. By using the browser, you will learn how to view Web Part Pages in different ways, as well as how to change the appearance of Web Part Pages by adding and removing Web Parts and by tailoring a site by adding Web Part Pages.

> **Important** Before you can use the practice files in this chapter, you need to install them from the book's companion CD to their default locations. See "Using the Book's CD" on page xix for more information.

> **Important** Remember to use your SharePoint site location in place of *http://wideworldimporters* in the following exercises.

Web Parts and Web Part Pages

Before discussing the customization of any of the portal sites, certain basic concepts must be addressed. A SharePoint site contains one or more Web Part Pages. Web Part Pages contain Web Parts that can display the contents held in the site's lists or document libraries, as well as Web Parts that display other content. There are two versions, also known as views, of a Web Part Page.

- *Shared Version* This version is the Web Part Page that every user with the appropriate permissions on a site can view.

- *Personal Version* This version of a Web Part Page is available only to you and not to others.

To customize the Shared Version of any Web Part Page within a Web site, you must have the following rights, all of which are included in the Design and Full Control permission levels by default.

- Manage Lists
- Add and Customize Pages
- Apply Themes and Borders
- Apply Style Sheets

A member of a Web site's Site Owners group has Full Control permissions and therefore is able to customize the Shared Version of Web Part Pages.

To customize the Personal View of any Web Part Page, the Web Part Page must be designed to be personalized. You must have the following rights, all of which are included in the Contribute, Design, and Full Control permission levels by default.

● Manage Personal Views

● Add/Remove Personal Web Parts

● Update Personal Web Parts

A member of a Web site's Members group has Contribute permission and therefore is able to customize the Personal Version of Web Part Pages if they are designed to be personalized.

In the following exercise, you will familiarize yourself with the customization capabilities of Windows SharePoint Services.

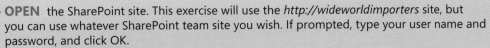

OPEN the SharePoint site. This exercise will use the *http://wideworldimporters* site, but you can use whatever SharePoint team site you wish. If prompted, type your user name and password, and click OK.

BE SURE TO verify that you have sufficient rights to add contacts to a Contacts list. If in doubt, see the Appendix on page 435.

1. On the right of the top link bar, click **Site Actions**.

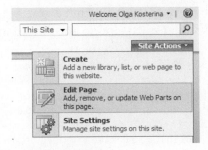

2. Click **Edit Page**.

Internet Explorer redisplays the Web Part Page in edit mode and states that this is the Shared Version of the page. Any changes that you make to the Web Part Page are visible to all users of the site. The Web Part Page is displayed in a grid-like manner, displaying two *Web Part Page zones* denoted by two blue borders labeled at the top as Left and Right. At the top of each Web Part Page zone is an orange rectangle containing the text Add a Web Part.

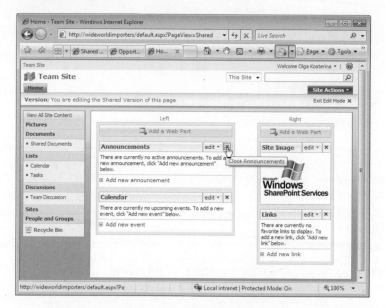

Close

> **Tip** Web Part Page zones are containers for Web Parts. Therefore, on a SharePoint team site, the *Left* zone contains the Web Parts named *Announcements* and *Calendar*, whereas the *Right* zone contains the Web Parts named *Site Image* and *Links*. In edit mode, these Web Parts contain the word edit followed by a down arrow on their title bar and a Close button. The *Announcements*, *Calendar*, and *Links* Web Parts display information held within the *Announcements*, *Calendar*, and *Links* lists, whereas the *Site Image* Web Part is a built-in Web Part that displays the Windows SharePoint Services image.
>
> Other Web Part Pages might be comprised of more or less than two zones, depending on the Web Part Page template used when creating the Web Part Page. You can also add or remove zones from a Web Part Page by using a tool, such as Office SharePoint Designer.

2. Below **Site Actions**, click **Exit Edit Mode**.

The Web Part Page is displayed in normal mode, in which the zones are no longer visible. In addition, the word edit and the Close button in the title bar of the Announcements, Calendar, and Links Web Parts are no longer visible. The title bar of the Site Image Web Part does not appear.

3. In the upper right corner of the page, click the arrow next to the **Welcome <your name>** message.

4. Click **Personalize this Page**.

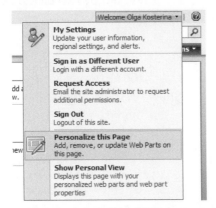

Internet Explorer redisplays the Web Part Page in edit mode and states that this is the Personal Version of the page. Any changes that you make to the Web Part Page only affect your view of the Web page.

> **Tip** When a Web page is not in edit mode, there is no visible indication as to whether the page shows the Shared Version or the Personal Version of the page. If the Show Personal View option is displayed on the Welcome drop-down menu, you are viewing the Shared Version of the page. If the Show Shared View option appears, you are viewing the Personal Version of the page. As an Administrator or Web designer, you cannot customize the personal views of specific users; you can only customize the shared view and your own personal view.

5. Below **Site Actions**, click **Exit Edit Mode**. The Web Part Page is displayed in normal mode.

CLOSE Internet Explorer.

Removing a Web Part

When created, SharePoint sites can contain a number of libraries, lists, and one or more Web Part Pages composed of one or more Web Parts. As you customize your site, you might decide that you do not need all of the Web Parts on these Web Part Pages and might want to remove them.

In this exercise, you will delete and close Web Parts to remove them from a Web site's home page.

 OPEN a SharePoint team site. The exercise will use the http://wideworldimporters site, but you can use whatever site you wish. If prompted, type your user name and password, and click OK.

1. In the upper right corner of the page, click the arrow next to the **Welcome <your name>** message and check that the **Show Personal View** menu option is displayed. This indicates that the Web Part Page is in *Shared View*.

> **Troubleshooting** If the Show Shared View option is displayed, the Web Part Page is in *Personal View*. To switch to *Shared View*, click the arrow to the right of the Welcome message, and click Show Shared View on the drop-down menu.
>
> If the Web Part Page does not contain the Site Actions link, you do not have Full Control or Design permission levels on this Web site; therefore, when you complete this exercise, you are personalizing the Web Part Page. You will be shown Web Part Pages in Shared View until you personalize them, at which time the Personal View becomes your default view for that Web Part Page. You can reset the Personal View back to the Shared View values by clicking Reset Page Content from the Welcome menu.

2. Click the down arrow on the **Announcements** Web Part title bar. From the Web Part drop-down menu, click **Close**, which temporarily removes the Announcements Web Part from the Web page.

> **Tip** You can also close Web Parts when a Web Page is displayed in edit mode by either clicking Close from the Web Part drop-down menu or clicking the cross in the Web Part title bar.

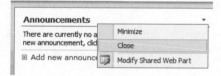

Internet Explorer redisplays the Web page with only three Web Parts.

3. Click **Site Actions**, and then click **Edit Page**.

Internet Explorer displays the Shared Version Web page in edit mode with the zones clearly visible.

4. On the **Links** Web Part title bar, click **edit**.

5. From the Web Part drop-down menu, click **Delete**.

An Internet Explorer question dialog box is displayed.

6. Click **OK** to delete the Web Part.

7. Below **Site Actions**, click **Exit Edit Mode**. Internet Explorer redisplays the Web Part Page in normal mode.

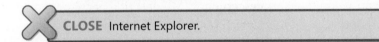

CLOSE Internet Explorer.

Adding a Web Part from a Web Part Gallery

As you customize your site, you might decide to add other information as well as remove some of the Web Parts on the Web Part Pages. This you can do by adding additional Web Parts. You can insert Web Parts on multiple pages and also insert a Web Part multiple times on the same Web page. Windows SharePoint Services provides built-in Web Parts for each Web site created Two types of Web Parts are most commonly use via the browser.

- *List View Web Parts (LVWP)* Web Parts that display the contents of libraries and lists. Each time data in the list or library changes, the changes are reflected in the LVWP.

- *Built-in Web Parts* Web Parts that display other content. There are eight built-in Web Parts.

The eight built-in Web Parts available on Web sites created from the Team site, Blank site, or Document Workspace templates are summarized in the following table.

Web Part	Description
Content Editor Web Part	Use this Web Part to add content to a Web Part Page such as formatted text, tables, and images. This Web Part allows you to add content by using a Rich Text Editor or HyperText Markup Language (HTML) source editor. The HTML <FORM> element is not allowed in the Content Editor Web Part. If you need to add a Web Part that uses the <FORM> element, consider using the Page Viewer or Form Web Parts.
Form Web Part	Use this Web Part if you want to send data to another Web Part via a Web Part connection. The content displayed in the other Web Part is dependent on the data it receives.
Image Web Part	Use this Web Part to display pictures and photos. This Web Part is included by default on the home Web Part Page of many sites to display a logo.
Page Viewer Web Part	Use this Web Part to display the content of a linked resource such as a Web site, Web pages, files, or folders. In this way, you can display an entire Web page within a Web Part. The linked content is isolated from other content on the Web Part Page, and hence the content is displayed asynchronously from the rest of the page. This means that you can view and use other content in other Web Parts on the page even if the link in this Web Part happens to take a long time to return its content. Also use this Web Part if you want to retrieve data from a server that requires authentication.
Relevant Documents	Use this Web Part to display documents that are relevant to the current user. This Web Part generates a personalized view of documents checked out by, created by, or last modified by the current user. You can configure the Web Part to use more than one criterion. To improve the performance of the Relevant Documents Web Part in a large-scale document management environment, use Column indexing on the Modified By, Created By, or Checked Out By columns. Make sure that the Show Items From The Entire Site Collection check box is not selected when configuring the Web Part.
Site Users	Use this Web Part to view a list of the site users and their online status.
User Tasks	Use this Web Part to display tasks that are assigned to the current user.
XML Web Part	Use this Web Part for Extensible Markup Language (XML) with Extensible Stylesheet Language (XSL) to define how the XML is displayed. You might use the XML Web Part to display structured data from database tables or queries as well as XML-based documents.

> **Tip** In addition to built-in Web Parts, you can create your own Web Parts by using tools, such as SharePoint Designer and Visual Studio .NET 2005. You can also import custom Web Parts.
>
> SharePoint Designer allows you to add a *Data Form Web Part (DFWP)*. In the previous version of Windows SharePoint Services, the DFWP was known as the Data View Web Part (DVWP) because it only allowed you to view data. The DFWP not only allows you to view data, but it can provide you with a form to write data to a variety of data sources such as Microsoft SQL Server databases, XML files, and Web services, as well as data held in SharePoint lists and libraries. SharePoint Designer provides a "What You See Is What You Get" (WYSIWYG) *Extensible Stylesheet Language Transformation* (XSLT) editor that the developer uses to format the Data Form Web Part. For example, you can create a DFWP that applies a style to a selected HTML tag or data values when the data meet specified criteria. If you use SharePoint Designer 2007 with the Furniture Sales List, you could highlight items when there are no units in stock.

In this exercise, you will customize the home page of a SharePoint site. You will add the *Content Editor and List View Web Part*s and restore a Web Part from the Web Part Page Gallery.

OPEN a SharePoint site. This exercise will use the *http://wideworldimporters* site, but you can use whatever site you wish. If prompted, type your user name and password, and click OK.

BE SURE TO complete the second exercise in this chapter before beginning this exercise. You must also have a list that contains data, such as the Furniture Price list created in Chapter 12, "Using Windows SharePoint Services with Excel 2007." Alternatively, you can create a practice site for this chapter based on the Chapter 15 Starter.stp site template located in the *Documents\Microsoft Press\SBS_WSSv3\Chapter 15* folder.

See "Using the Book's CD" on page xix for instructions on how to create a practice site.

1. Click **Site Actions** and then click **Edit Page**. Internet Explorer displays the Web Part Page in edit mode.

2. In the **Left** Web Part Page zone, click **Add a Web Part**.

The Add Web Parts – Webpage Dialog box appears, which categorizes the Web Parts into either Lists and Libraries or All Web Parts.

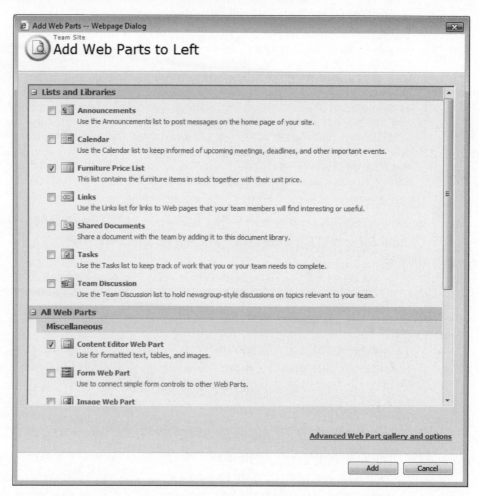

3. In the **Lists and Libraries** area, choose **Furniture Price List**. In the **All Web Parts** area, under **Miscellaneous**, choose **Content Editor Web Part**.

4. Click **Add**.

5. Scroll down the page and hover over the icon to the left of **Content Editor Web Part** so that the mouse pointer changes to a four-way arrow.

Four-Way Arrow Pointer

6. While holding down the mouse button, drag the Web Part to the area above the **Furniture Price List** Web Part.

As you move the Web Part, an orange rectangle containing the words Content Editor Web Part appears, and a dark orange horizontal line shows you where the Content Editor Web Part will be added.

> **Tip** When using a browser, Web Parts can only be added to Web Part Page zones and are subsequently called *dynamic Web Parts*. When using a tool, such as SharePoint Designer, Web Parts can be added outside Web Part Page zones and are subsequently called *static Web Parts*. Using a static Web Part allows users to view the Web Part, but prevents them from interacting with or modifying the Web Part through the browser. This is helpful if you do not want users to be able to make any changes to either the Web Part or the way it is displayed on the page.

Internet Explorer redisplays the Web Part Page in edit mode with the Content Editor Web Part placed above the Furniture Price List Web Part.

7. In the **Left** Web Part Page zone, click **Add a Web Part**. The Add Web Parts – Webpage dialog box appears.

8. At the bottom of the dialog box, click **Advanced Web Part gallery and options**.

   The Add Web Parts – Webpage Dialog box closes, and the Add Web Part tool pane appears displaying three Web Part Galleries: Closed Web Parts, <Site Name> Gallery and Server Gallery. You might need to scroll to the right to see the tool pane.

Web Part Galleries are containers in which Web Parts and Web Part templates are stored. The number in the bracket to the right of each gallery states the number of Web Parts contained in each gallery. The orange box around the *Team Site Gallery* indicates that you are viewing the contents of that gallery, and the *Web Part List* area lists those Web Parts that are held in the *Team Site Gallery*. This gallery contains a Web Part for each list or document library created for this site, plus the eight built-in Web Parts described earlier in this chapter.

9. In the **Add Web Parts** tool pane, click **Closed Web Parts**.

   The Add Web Parts tool pane now lists the contents of the Closed Web Parts gallery. This gallery holds Web Parts that are temporarily removed from a Web Part Page by using the Close option. Currently, the Close Web Parts gallery contains only one Web Part—the Announcements List View Web Part that you removed in the second exercise of this chapter.

Add

10. At the bottom of the **Add Web Parts** tool pane, click the arrow to the right of **Add to:**. From the drop-down list, click **Right**, and then click the **Add** button.

    When you use this method to add Web Parts to a Web Part Page, the Web Part is added to the top of the zone.

> **Tip** The Closed Web Parts Gallery now contains no Web Parts because you have placed the Announcements List View Web Part back onto the Web Part Page. The Closed Web Parts gallery differs from other galleries in that it is a temporary storage space for Web Parts removed from a Web Part Page. You can liken the Closed Web Parts Gallery to the Recycle Bin; however, Web Parts are only placed here when the Close option is used. When the Delete option is used, the Web Part is permanently deleted from a Web Part Page.
>
> Web Parts placed in other galleries act like templates. Web Parts from the other two galleries can be placed on a Web Part Page multiple times. Once a Web Part is placed on a Web Part Page, it can be uniquely customized, but the template from which the Web Part is created remains in the Web Part Gallery.

Close

11. On the **Add Web Parts** tool pane title bar, click the **Close** button.

The Add Web Parts tool pane closes and the Web page is displayed in edit mode.

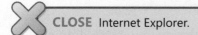

CLOSE Internet Explorer.

> **Tip** Web Parts can be badly written. If they are not thoroughly tested, you might find that a Web Part Page does not display when you add a Web Part to it. In such situations, append ?Contents=1 to the URL of the Web Part Page, such as *http://wideworldimporters/default. aspx?contents=1*. The Web Part Maintenance Page is displayed from which you can delete the offending Web Part.

Customizing a Web Part by Using the Web Part Tool Pane

Once you add a Web Part to the Web Part Page, you might find that you have to customize it to display the content that you wish users to your Web site to see. You might also have to tailor the Web Part's properties for it to take on the look and feel you require.

In the following exercise, you will customize the *Content Editor Web Part* and a SharePoint List View Web Part.

BE SURE TO complete the second and third exercises in this chapter before you begin this exercise. Also, you must have created and populated a Picture library, such as the *Employee Photos* Picture library created in Chapter 5, "Creating and Managing Libraries." Alternatively, you can create a practice site for this chapter based on the Chapter 15 Starter.stp site template located in the *Documents\Microsoft Press\SBS_WSSv3\Chapter 15* folder.

OPEN a SharePoint site. This exercise will use the *http://wideworldimporters* site, but you can use whatever site you wish. If prompted, type your user name and password, and click OK.

See "Using the Book's CD" on page xix for instructions on how to create a practice site.

1. Click the down arrow on the title bar of the **Content Editor Web Part**, and then click **Modify Shared Web Part**.

Internet Explorer displays the Web page in edit mode, with the Content Editor Web Part outlined with an orange dotted line and its tool pane visible.

2. In the **Content Editor Web Part** tool pane, click the **Rich Text Editor** button.

   The Rich Text Editor – Web Page Dialog box is displayed. You can use this editor in a very similar fashion to entering text using Microsoft Office Word. You can enter text, change styles, insert hyperlinks, insert pictures, cut, copy, paste, undo, redo, remove formatting, and so on. The shortcut keys that you use in Office Word will also work with this editor.

3. In the **Rich Text Editor – Webpage Dialog** box, type Welcome to Wide World Importers., and then press ⌨Enter to move the cursor to a new line.

4. Select the sentence you just typed, and click the **Font Size** button. A window appears displaying the range of Font Sizes available.

5. Click **5 – Example Text**. The Font Size window closes.

6. On a new line, type Wide World Importers is one of the leading Importers, Exporters and Distributors of unique pieces of art and furniture from around the world. On a second new line, type Who are we? and then press ⌨Enter.

7. Format Who are we? as font size **4 – Example Text**, and then click the **Underline** button.

8. Place the cursor on a new line, and click the **Insert Image** button. The Insert Image – Webpage Dialog box is displayed.

9. In the **Alternate Text:** textbox, type Olga Kosterina.

10. In the **Address** textbox, type http://wideworldimporters/Employee Photos/pjcov. jpg. You need to adjust the URL for your SharePoint site location.

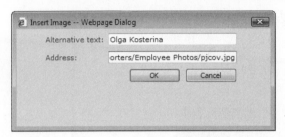

> **Important** Do not refer to an image that is stored on a hard drive, such as c:/SBS_WSS/Olga.jpg, because, in most cases, the image displays as a broken link. Internet Explorer tries to resolve the reference to the image file by accessing the user's local hard drive, which does not contain the folder or the image. You should upload all images into picture or document libraries within the site where the Web Part Page resides and then refer to the image by its URL.

11. Click **OK**.

12. On a new line beneath the picture, type Olga Kosterina, Owner.

Insert Hyperlink

13. Select the text Olga Kosterina, and then click the **Insert Hyperlink** button. The Insert Hyperlink – Webpage Dialog box is displayed.

14. In the **Address** textbox, type mailto:.olga@wideworldimporters.com.

When a user clicks the name Olga Kosterina on your Web page, your mail program opens a new message dialog box to send an e-mail to Olga Kosterina.

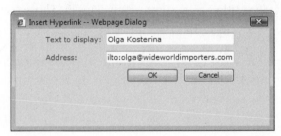

15. Click **OK**.

Center

16. Press Ctrl + Del to select all of the content you just entered, and then click the **Center** alignment button.

Save

17. In the lower right corner, click the **Save** button.

The Rich Text Editor – Web Page Dialog box closes, and the typed content is displayed in the Content Editor Web Part.

> **Troubleshooting** If an Error page displays indicating that the security validation for the page has timed out, click the Refresh page link to try the operation again.

18. Verify that the Content Editor Web Part tool pane is open. If not, click edit on the **Content Editor Web Part** title bar, and then click **Modify Shared Web Part**.

19. In the **Content Editor Web Part** tool pane, click the expand (+) icon next to **Appearance** to expand the Appearance area.

20. In the **Appearance** area, in the **Title** textbox, type Who are we.

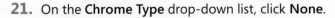

21. On the **Chrome Type** drop-down list, click **None**.

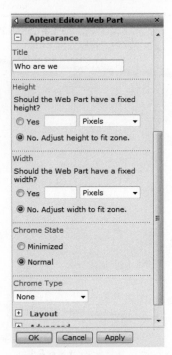

22. Click **OK** to close the Content Editor Web Part tool pane.

23. On the title bar of the **Furniture Price List** Web Part, click **edit** and then click **Modify Shared Web Part**.

Internet Explorer displays the Web page in edit mode, with the Furniture Price List Web Part outlined with an orange dotted line and its tool pane visible.

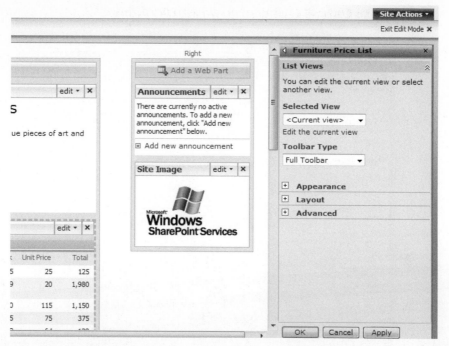

24. In the **Furniture Price List** tool pane, below the **Selected View** drop-down list, click the **Edit the current view** link. The Edit View: Furniture Price List Web page is displayed.

25. In the **Columns** area, clear the **Attachments**, **In Stock**, **Unit Price**, **Total**, and **Total Cost** (if shown) check boxes.

> **Tip** In this exercise, you will only display office furniture; therefore, you will use the Furniture Type column to filter data. In the LVWP, the Furniture Type column always contains the text Office. Hence, you could choose not to display the Furniture Type column. However, when you first customize a view, it is good practice to leave the filter column, such as the Furniture Type column, in place so you can check that the filter is configured correctly.

26. Scroll down the page until the **Filter** area is visible. Select the **Show items only when the following is true** option.

27. On the **Show the items when column** drop-down list, click **Furniture Type**. In the **Value** text box, type Office.

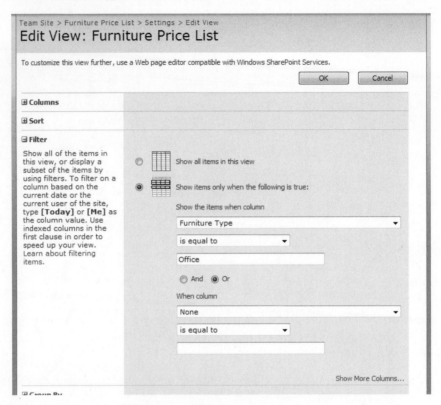

28. At the bottom of the page, click **OK**.

Your Web page is displayed. The Furniture Price List tool pane is no longer visible.

29. On the title bar of the **Furniture Price List** Web Part, click **edit** and then click **Modify Shared Web Part**. The Furniture Price List tool pane is displayed.

30. On the **Toolbar Type** drop-down list, click **Summary Toolbar**.

31. Click the expand (+) icon for the **Appearance** area, and in the **Title** textbox, type Sale – Office Furniture at half price.

32. Click the expand (+) icon for the **Advanced** area and clear the **Allow Minimize**, **Allow Close**, and **Allow Editing in Personal View** check boxes so that a user to this Web page cannot personalize or accidentally close or minimize this Web Part.

33. At the bottom of the **Furniture Price List** tool pane, click **OK**.

34. On the title bar of the **Furniture List Price** Web Part, click **edit** and notice that the Minimize and Close options are no longer available.

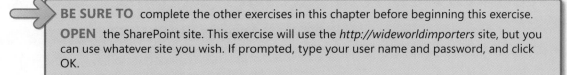

CLOSE Internet Explorer.

Customizing a Home Page by Using Web Parts

As you customize your Web Part Page by adding and removing Web Parts, you might find that the Web Parts are not located where you would like them to be. In this situation, you can move the Web Parts around on the page to obtain the layout you want.

In this exercise, you will move Web Parts on the home page of a SharePoint site.

BE SURE TO complete the other exercises in this chapter before beginning this exercise.

OPEN the SharePoint site. This exercise will use the *http://wideworldimporters* site, but you can use whatever site you wish. If prompted, type your user name and password, and click OK.

1. Click **Site Actions**, and then click **Edit Page**.

   Internet Explorer displays the Web Part Page in edit mode with the zones clearly visible.

2. Move the mouse pointer over the title bar of the **Who are we** Web Part so that the pointer changes to a four-way arrow. While holding down the mouse button, drag the Web Part below the **Site Image** Web Part.

As you move the Web Part, an orange horizontal line moves from the Web Part's current location to where the Web Part is being moved.

3. Move the mouse pointer over the title bar of the **Announcements** Web Part so that the pointer changes to a four-way arrow. While holding down the mouse button, drag the Web Part above the **Sale – Office Furniture at half price** Web Part.

4. Below **Site Actions**, click **Exit Edit Mode**.

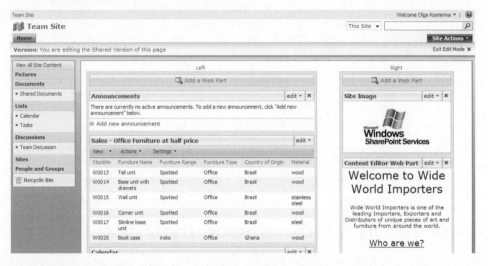

 CLOSE Internet Explorer.

Creating a New Web Part Page by Using a Browser

SharePoint sites are provisioned with one or more Web Part Pages. Users can create additional Web pages that can be stored and accessed via document libraries.

In the following exercise, you will create a document library to store Web Part Pages. You will then create a Web Part Page and provide a link to the Web Part Page from your home page so the rest of your team can view it.

OPEN the SharePoint site in which you would like to create Web Part Pages. This exercise will use the *http://wideworldimporters* site, but you can use whatever site you wish. If prompted, type your user name and password, and click OK.

BE SURE TO verify that you have sufficient rights to create a document library. If in doubt, see the Appendix on page 435.

1. Click **Site Actions**, and then click **Create**. The Create Page Web page is displayed.

2. Under **Libraries**, click **Document Library**. The New page is displayed.

3. In the **Name** textbox, type **WebPartPages**.

> **Tip** Any URL in SharePoint is limited to 260 characters and must not contain the characters /\ : * ? " < > | # { } % & ~ or tab characters and multiple periods. Spaces in URLs should be avoided because they are replaced by the characters %20 and therefore take up three characters. The Name that you type in the Name textbox is used to create the URL as well as the Title of the document library and therefore should be short but meaningful. You can alter the title with a user-friendly name at a later date.

4. In the **Document Template** area, on the **Document template:** drop-down list, select **Web Part page**.

New

> **Tip** You do not need to create a special document library to store your Web Part Pages. You can instead store them in the Shared Documents document library that is created when you create a team Web site. However, if you plan to create a number of Web Part Pages, you can place them all in their own document library. By creating a document library that uses the Web Part Page document template, you can also create Web Part Pages by clicking the New button.

Team Site > Create > New

New

Name and Description

Type a new name as you want it to appear in headings and links throughout the site. Type descriptive text that will help site visitors use this document library.

Name:

WebPartPages

Description:

Navigation

Specify whether a link to this document library appears in the Quick Launch.

Display this document library on the Quick Launch?

◉ Yes   ◯ No

Document Version History

Specify whether a version is created each time you edit a file in this document library. Learn about versions.

Create a version each time you edit a file in this document library?

◯ Yes   ◉ No

Document Template

Select a document template to determine the default for all new files created in this document library.

Document Template:

Web Part page

Create   Cancel

Create

5. At the bottom of the page, click the **Create** button. The All Documents view of the new Web Part Pages document library is displayed.

6. Click the **New** button. The New Web Part Page page is displayed.

7. In the **Name** textbox, type **OfficeFurniture**.

> **Tip** Any URL in SharePoint is limited to 260 characters. Like SharePoint lists and libraries, the Name that you type in the Name textbox is used to create the URL as well as the Title of the Web page. Later in this exercise, you will alter the title with a user-friendly name.

8. In the **Layout** area, on the **Choose a Layout Template** list, click **Header, Left Column, Body**.

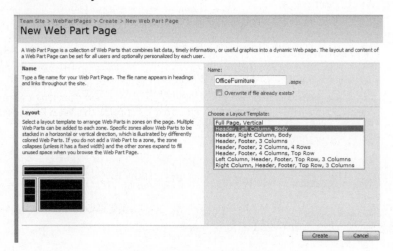

9. At the bottom of the Web page, click **Create**.

After a few moments, the new Web Part Page is displayed with three distinct Web Part Page zones: Header, Left Column, and Body. The page is currently empty except for the top link bar and the Site Actions link. No Web Parts are placed within the Web Part Page zones.

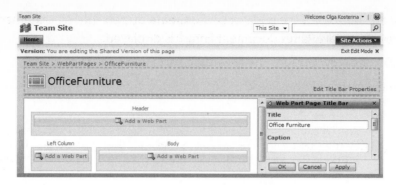

10. Click **Edit Title Bar Properties**. The Web Part Page Title Bar appears.

11. Under **Title**, type Office Furniture and click **OK**. The Web Part Page Title Bar closes.

> **Tip** Because you created this Web Part Page within the SharePoint team site, the Team Web Site Gallery contains a Web Part for each list or document library created in the WideWorldImporters team site plus the eight built-in Web Parts described earlier in this chapter. If you completed all of the exercises in this chapter, the number of Web Parts in the Team Web Site Galley should be one more than the number at the end of the previous exercise because you created a new document library in this exercise called Web Part Pages. You can now customize this Web Part Page by using the techniques described earlier in this chapter; such as changing the position of the Web Parts and modifying the Web Part titles.

12. Click **Site Actions**, and then click **Site Settings**. The Site Settings page is displayed.

13. In the **Look and Feel** area, click **Top link bar**. The Top Link Bar page is displayed.

14. Click **New Link**. The New Link page is displayed.

15. In the **Type the Web address** textbox, type http://wideworldimporters/
WebPartPages/OfficeFurniture.aspx. You need to adjust the URL for your
SharePoint site and document library location.

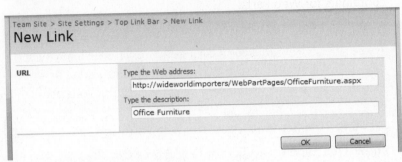

16. In the **Type the description** textbox, type Office Furniture and then click **OK**.

The Top Link Bar page is displayed, and a second tab labeled Office Furniture appears to the right of the Home tab.

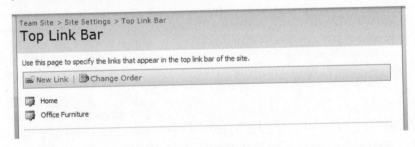

> **Tip** Alternative methods used to make the new Web Part Page visible are to have the Web Part Page document library appear on the Quick Launch, to place a List View Web Part of the document library on the home page, or to add a link item that points to the new Web Part Page if you have a links list.

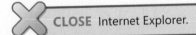

CLOSE Internet Explorer.

Key Points

- Windows SharePoint Services use a technology known as Web Part Pages that are containers for Web Parts.

- A Web Part Page contains Web Part Page zones in which Web Parts can be placed.

- Web Parts are reusable components that can contain any type of Web-based content. They can display the contents of lists and libraries, as well as other content such as the results of database queries, Web sites, Web pages, files, and folders.

- To customize a Web site, you must either have certain permissions or be a member of the Team Owners group.

- A Web Part Page can have two versions: a Shared Version and a Personal Version. All users can see changes made to the Shared View. Changes made to the Personal View are visible only to the user who altered their Personal View of the Web Part Page. A user can reset their Personal View back to the Shared View setting if desired.

- Web Parts are placed in one of three Web Part Galleries: Closed Web Parts, Team Site Gallery, and Server Gallery.

- The Closed Web Parts Gallery is a temporary storage space for Web Parts removed from a Web page by using the Close button.

- The Team Web Site Gallery contains a List View Web Part for each list or library created in the team site, plus eight built-in Web Parts: Content Editor Web Part, Form Web Part, Image Web Part, Page Viewer Web Part, Relevant Documents, Site Users, User Tasks, and XML Web Part.

- By using the browser, you can create additional Web Part Pages that are stored within a document library.

Chapter at a Glance

Understand how search works, **page 430**

Execute a simple search query, **page 432**

Execute a complex search query, **page 433**

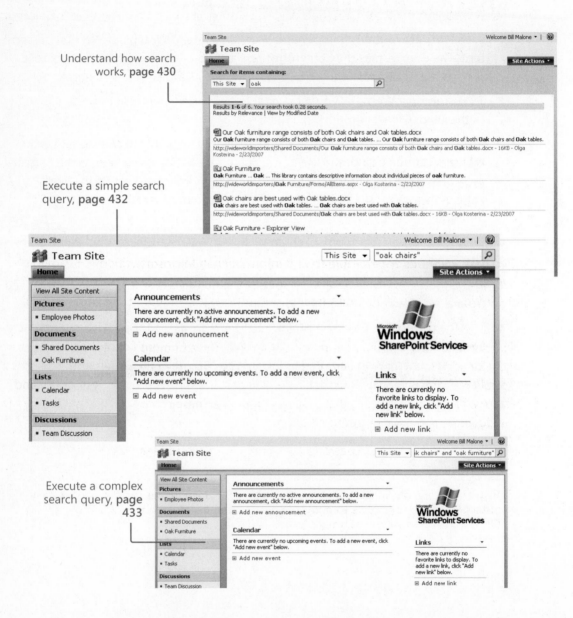

16 Finding Information on the SharePoint Site

In this chapter, you will learn to:

✔ Understand how search works.

✔ Execute a simple search query.

✔ Execute a complex search query.

Two basic methods are available to find information in Microsoft Windows SharePoint Services. The first method is to browse a hierarchical structure of links and pages to find the information you need. The second—and often faster—method of finding information is to search for it.

Searching for information is the process of entering one or more words in the search web part to form a search query that is executed against the index built on the SharePoint servers by your System Administrators. The servers process your *query* and return a set of content items that match your query. These *content items* contain links to the documents that you want to find.

This chapter introduces the basic concepts of how to execute search queries.

> **Important** Before you can use the practice sites provided for this chapter, you need to install them from the book's companion CD to their default locations. See "Using the Book's CD" on page xix for more information.

> **Important** Remember to use your SharePoint site location in place of *http://wideworldmporters* in the following exercises.

Understanding How Search Works

Before discussing the execution of a search query, certain basic concepts must be covered. A search query contains one or more words that represent the content you are trying to find. Search scopes help you focus your search query so that only a portion of the overall index is queried. Your SharePoint Administrators build or create the index by crawling the content you want to find. When executing a query, SharePoint returns a set of content items that form a result set. If you query to locate information that you know exists and it doesn't appear in your result set, contact your SharePoint Administrator for assistance.

In the following exercise, you will familiarize yourself with the interface of the search Web Parts.

OPEN the SharePoint site. This exercise will use the *http://wideworldmporters* site, but you can use whatever SharePoint team site you want. If prompted, type your user name and password, and then click OK.

BE SURE TO verify that you have sufficient permissions to execute a query in the site you are using. If in doubt, see the Appendix on page 436.

1. In the upper right corner of the **home** page, find the **search** Web Part.

   This Web Part contains a scope drop-down list whose default setting is \This Site, a query input box, and a magnifying glass icon that executes the query.

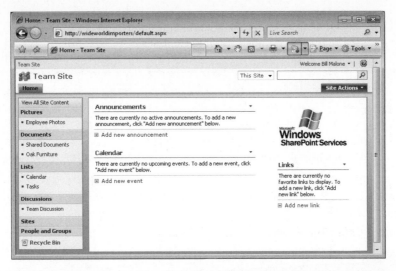

2. Enter a query term that can be found in at least one document in your site, such as oak.

The result set contains items that match your query term, including documents and folders. Note that you can sort the result set by either relevance or modified date. If more than one page of content items matches your query, the total number of pages in the result set appears, with each page number representing a link to that page of the overall result set.

 CLOSE the browser.

Executing a Search Query

In the last exercise, you executed a search query to familiarize yourself with search-specific interfaces. However, there is more to executing a query than entering a single word. To find the information you really need, you might need to enter more than one query term. It stands to reason that the more query terms you enter, the more discriminating your query becomes, thereby producing a more focused result set.

Search queries can be comprised of any of the following items.

- Single word
- Multiple words
- Single phrase in quotes
- Multiple phrases in quotes

For example, if you search the phrase oak furniture, the result set contains only those content items containing the words *oak furniture*. If a document contains the words *oak chest* but not *oak furniture*, that document will not appear in the result set.

If you search two phrases and separate them by the word AND, then both phrases must appear in the document for that document to appear in the result set.

In this exercise, you will enter a query phrase to observe how the results are more focused when multiple phrases are entered in the search Web Part.

OPEN the SharePoint site. This exercise will use the *http://wideworldmporters* site, but you can use whatever SharePoint team site you want. If prompted, type your user name and password, and then click OK.

BE SURE TO verify that you have permissions to the site in which you want to execute your query. If in doubt, see the Appendix on page 435.

1. In the **search** Web Part, type a phrase encapsulated in quotation marks, such as oak chairs.

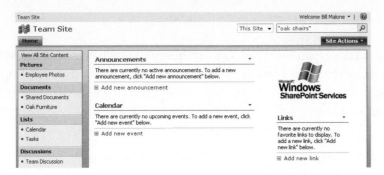

Notice that two items from the index are returned back in the result set: the document containing the phrase oak chairs and the folder hosting the document containing the phrase oak chairs.

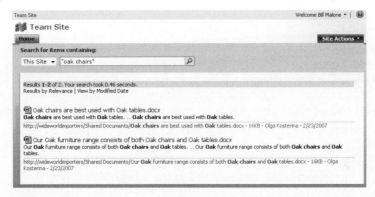

2. Add another phrase, such as oak furniture, to help focus your query. Separate both phrases with the AND operator.

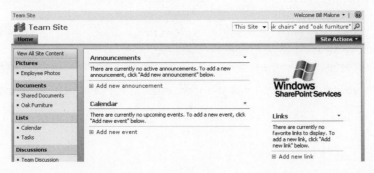

Note that the result set is more focused, containing the only item in the site that contains both phrases.

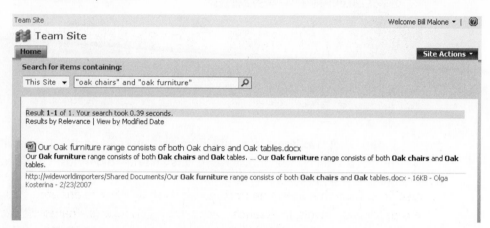

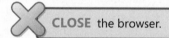 **CLOSE** the browser.

Key Points

- You can find information by actively searching for it instead of browsing for it.
- You can enter any combination of words and phrases to help you find the document of your choice.

Appendix: Windows SharePoint Services Permissions

Microsoft Windows SharePoint Services includes 32 user permissions that determine the specific actions that users can perform on the site. Permissions are grouped together into permission levels. In essence, each permission level is a named collection of permissions that can be assigned to SharePoint users and groups. Five default permission levels are available on every site: Read, Contribute, Design, Full Control, and Limited Access. The following table lists default permission levels along with their corresponding permissions in Windows SharePoint Services.

Permission Level	Description	Permissions Included by Default
Limited Access	Allows access to shared resources in the Web site so that users can access an item within the site. Designed to be combined with fine-grained permissions to provide users with access to a specific list, document library, item, or document without giving users access to the entire site. Cannot be customized or deleted.	View Application Pages, Browse User Information, Use Remote Interfaces, Use Client Integration Features, Open
Read	Allows read-only access to the Web site.	View Application Pages, Browse User Information, Use Remote Interfaces, Use Client Integration Features, Open, View Items, Open Items, View Versions, Create Alerts, Use Self-Service Site Creation, View Pages

Contribute	Allows users to create and edit items in existing lists and document libraries.	View Application Pages, Browse User Information, Use Remote Interfaces, Use Client Integration Features, Open, View Items, Open Items, View Versions, Create Alerts, Use Self-Service Site Creation, View Pages, Add Items, Edit Items, Delete Items, Delete Versions, Browse Directories, Edit Personal User Information, Manage Personal Views, Add/Remove Personal Web Parts, Update Personal Web Parts
Design	Allows user to create lists and document libraries as well as edit pages in the Web site.	View Application Pages, Browse User Information, Use Remote Interfaces, Use Client Integration Features, Open, View Items, Open Items, View Versions, Create Alerts, Use Self-Service Site Creation, View Pages, Add Items, Edit Items, Delete Items, Delete Versions, Browse Directories, Edit Personal User Information, Manage Personal Views, Add/Remove Personal Web Parts, Update Personal Web Parts Manage Lists, Override Check Out, Approve Items, Add and Customize Pages, Apply Themes and Borders, Apply Style Sheets
Full Control	Allows full control	All permissions

You can create new permission levels that contain specific permissions as well as change which permssions are included in the default permissions levels, with a few exceptions. While it is not possible to remove permissions from the Limited Access and Full Control permission levels, your SharePoint administrator can make specific permissions unavailable for the entire Web application by using SharePoint Central Administration. If you are a SharePoint administrator and wish to do this, in SharePoint Central Administration from the Application Management tab, select User Permissions for Web Application, choose the Web application, and then clear the check boxes for those permissions you'd like to disable.

Depending on the scope, user permissions in Windows SharePoint Services can be grouped into three categories: list permissions, site permissions, and personal user permissions. The following table lists user permissions in Windows SharePoint Services, detailing their scope, permission dependencies, and the permissions levels that they are included into by default.

Permission	Description	Scope	Dependent Permissions	Included in These Permission Levels by Default
Add and Customize Pages	Add, change, or delete HTML pages or Web Part Pages; edit the Web site by using a Windows SharePoint Services–compatible editor.	Site	View Items, Browse Directories, View Pages, Open	Design, Full Control
Add Items	Add items to lists, documents to document libraries, and Web discussion comments.	List	View Items, View Pages, Open	Contribute, Design, Full Control
Add/Remove Personal Web Parts	Add or remove personal Web Parts on a Web Part Page.	Personal Permissions	View Items, View Pages, Open	Contribute, Design, Full Control
Apply Style Sheets	Apply a style sheet (.css file) to the Web site.	Site	View Pages, Open	Design, Full Control
Apply Themes and Borders	Apply a theme or borders to the entire Web site.	Site	View Pages, Open	Design, Full Control
Approve Items	Approve minor versions of list items or documents.	List	Edit Items, View Items, View Pages, Open	Design, Full Control

Browse Directories	Enumerate files and folders in a Web site by using Microsoft Office SharePoint Designer and Web DAV interfaces.	Site	View Pages, Open	Contribute, Design, Full Control
Browse User Information	View information about users of the Web site.	Site	Open	All
Create Alerts	Create e-mail alerts.	List	View Items, View Pages, Open	Read, Contribute, Design, Full Control
Create Groups	Create a group of users that can be used anywhere within the site collection.	Site	View Pages, Browse User Information, Open	Full Control
Create Subsites	Create subsites such as team, Meeting Workspace, and Document Workspace sites.	Site	View Pages, Browse User Information, Open	Full Control
Delete Items	Delete items from a list, documents from a document library, and Web discussion comments in documents.	List	View Items, View Pages, Open	Contribute, Design, Full Control
Delete Versions	Delete past versions of list items or documents.	List	View Items, View Versions, View Pages, Open	Contribute, Design, Full Control

Edit Items	Edit items in lists, documents in document libraries, and Web discussion comments in documents; customize Web Part Pages in document libraries.	List	View Items, View Pages, Open	Contribute, Design, Full Control
Edit Personal User Information	Users can change their own user information, such as adding a picture.	Site	Browse User Information, Open	Contribute, Design
Enumerate Permissions	Enumerate permissions in the Web site, list, folder, document, or list item.	Site	Browse Directories, View Pages, Browse User Information, Open	Full Control
Manage Alerts	Manage alerts for all users of the Web site.	Site	View Items, View Pages, Open	Full Control
Manage Lists	Create and delete lists, add or remove columns in a list, and add or remove public views of a list.	List	View Items, View Pages, Open, Manage Personal Views	Design, Full Control
Manage Permissions	Create and change permission levels on the Web site; assign permissions to users and groups.	Site	View Items, Open Items, View Versions, Browse Directories, View Pages, Enumerate Permissions, Browse User Information, Open	Full Control
Manage Personal Views	Create, change, and delete personal views of lists.	Personal Permissions	View Items, View Pages, Open	Contribute, Design, Full Control

Manage Web Site	Perform all administration tasks and manage content for the Web site.	Site	View Items, Add and Customize Pages, Browse Directories, View Pages, Enumerate Permissions, Browse User Information, Open	Full Control
Open	Open a Web site, list, or folder to access items inside that container.	Site	None	All
Open Items	View the source of documents with server-side file handlers.	List	View Items, View Pages, Open	Read, Contribute, Design, Full Control
Override Check Out	Discard or check in a document that is checked out to another user without saving the current changes.	List	View Items, View Pages, Open	Design, Full Control
Update Personal Web Parts	Update Web Parts to display personalized information.	Personal Permissions	View Items, View Pages, Open	Contribute, Design, Full Control
Use Client Integration Features	Use features that launch client applications; without this permission, users must work on documents locally and then upload their changes.	Site	Use Remote Interfaces, Open	All
Use Remote Interfaces	Use SOAP, Web DAV, or Office SharePoint Designer interfaces to access the Web site.	Site	Open	All

Use Self-Service Site Creation	Create a Web site by using Self-Service Site Creation.		View Pages, Browse User Information, Open	Read, Contribute, Design, Full Control
View Application Pages	View forms, views, and application pages; enumerate lists.	List	Open	All
View Items	View items in lists, documents in document libraries, and Web discussion comments.	List	View Pages, Open	Read, Contribute, Design, Full Control
View Pages	View pages in a Web site.	Site	Open	Read, Contribute, Design, Full Control
View Usage Data	View reports on Web site usage.	Site	View Pages, Open	Full Control
View Versions	View past versions of list items or documents.	List	View Items, Open Items, View Pages, Open	Read, Contribute, Design, Full Control

Index

A

Access 2007, 96, 350–373
  offline work in, 367–370
  SharePoint list exported to, 356–358
  SharePoint list linked to, 359–362
  SharePoint site data from, 362–367
  workflows and, 370–372
Access Web Datasheet, 333–340
Alerts
  of library changes, 155–157
  of list changes, 117–119
  in Outlook 2007, 308–312
Approval process, for documents, 153–155

B

Blank Site template, 80
Blogs. See also Wikis
  Blog template for, 48, 81
  comments to, 284–285
  creating, 275–278
  posts to, 278–283
  RSS feeds to, 286–288
Breadcrumbs, for navigation, 23, 88
Built-in Web Parts, 407–408
Business intelligence (BI), 12

C

Calendar events, 207–211
Calendars, 303–304
Call center knowledge bases, 47
Child workspaces, 45, 60–62
Collaboration
  Microsoft Office functions for, 9
  SharePoint Server 2007 and, 11
  SharePoint services for, 2–7
  Team Collaboration Lists for, 69
Contact lists, SharePoint. See Outlook 2007
Content syndication, 71–72
Content types
  form library association with, 392–395
  from InfoPath 2007, 389–392
  InfoPath 2007 modification of, 395–398
  in libraries, 169–172
Creating SharePoint sites. See Management
Cunningham, Ward, 264
Current best approach (CBA) documents, 47
Customizing
  home pages, 421–422
  left navigation panel, 30–35
  top navigation, 27–30
  Web Parts, 414–421

D

Databases. See Access 2007
Delegate controls, 68
Deleting
  Document Workspaces, 199–201
  libraries, 182
  lists, 130
  sites, 73–74
Design permission, 7
Discussion boards, 16. See also Surveys
  creating, 250–255
  e-mail to, 256–257

Outlook 2007 for, 258–260
purpose of, 230
Document Information Panel (DIP),
165, 179
Document libraries. See also Libraries
adding documents to, 143–144
checking documents in and out of,
147–149
creating, 134–137
deleting documents in, 152–153
Document Workspaces and, 186,
198–199
Meeting Workspaces and, 213
Microsoft Office functions and,
149–150
offline documents and, 157–162
for Web Part Pages, 422
Document management, 194–198
Document Workspaces, 184–201
accessing, 192–193
on child site, 60–62
creating, 186–188
deleting, 199–201
document libraries and, 198–199
Microsoft Office functions and
for creating workspaces, 9, 44,
188–192
for document management,
194–198
template for, 80
Dynamic Web Parts, 411

E

E-mail
to discussion boards, 256–257
to lists, 123–129
from SharePoint contacts, 302–303
Enterprise Content Management, in
SharePoint Server 2007, 11

Enterprise Search components, in
SharePoint Server 2007, 11
Excel 2007, 329–349
Access Web Datasheet and, 333–340
SharePoint list exported to, 340–343
SharePoint list imported from,
330–333
SharePoint site imported from,
344–349

F

Farm level features, 68
Files, as list attachments, 98–101
Form libraries, 137–141. See also
InfoPath 2007; Libraries
Frequently asked questions (FAQs), 47
Full control permission, 7, 55

G

Global navigation breadcrumb, 23

H

Help desk knowledge bases, 47
Hierarchy of site, 21–24
Home pages
customizing, 421–422
of Meeting Workspaces, 212–217
navigation of, 16–21

I

InfoPath 2007, 375–399
content types and, 389–398
creation of, 389–392
form library association with,
392–395
modification of, 395–398

forms and
  editing, 388–389
  filling out, 386–387
  library of, 376–382
  modification of, 382–386
Inherited permission, 54

K
Knowledge bases, 47

L
Layouts directory, 45
Libraries, 132–163. See also InfoPath
  2007
  adding documents to, 143–144
  alerts and, 155–157
  on All Site Content page, 21
  checking documents in and out of,
    147–149
  creating, 134–137
  deleting documents in, 152–153
  folders for, 145–146
  form, 137–141
  Microsoft Office functions and,
    149–150
  navigation of, 26–27
  offline documents and, 157–162
  picture, 141–142, 145
  site collection site gallery, 65
  version history and, 151–152
  wiki page, 264–269
  workflows and, 153–155
Library settings, 164–183
  columns and content types in,
    169–172
  configuring, 166–169
  deleting library as, 182

Document Information Panel for,
    165, 179
  securing, 179–181
  using, 174–178
  views as, 172–174
Limited permission, 7, 55
Links, 17–19, 68, 271–273
Lists, 76–131. See also Access 2007;
  Excel 2007; Outlook 2007
  adding, editing, and deleting
    columns of, 101–109
      column types and, 102–103
      priority columns and, 107–109
      site columns and, 104–107
  adding, editing, and deleting items
    on, 89–94
  alerts of changes to, 117–119
  browsing, 15, 25–26
  creating, 83–88
  datasheet view of, 96–97
  default, 78–83
  deleting, 130
  e-mails to, 123–129
  file attachment to, 98–101
  restoring from Recycle Bin, 95–96
  RSS feeds and, 119–123
  sorting and filtering, 110–112
  Team Collaboration, 69
  Things to Bring, 224–226
  viewing types for, 112–117
List View Web Parts (LVWP), 407

M
Management, 42–75
  of child workspace, 60–62
  of content syndication, 71–72
  creating sites and, 44–52
    permissions for, 49–50

SharePoint Central Administration for, 45–46
steps for, 50–52
templates for, 47–49
deleting sites and, 73–74
of documents, 194–198
of features, 68–70
of templates, 65–67
of themes, 63–64
of users and permissions, 53–60
Meeting Workspaces, 202–229
agenda for, 219–221
attendees of, 221–224
for calendar event, 207–211
as child site, 60–61
home pages of, 212–217
lists and, 78–80
objectives of, 217–219
from Outlook 2007, 312–317
templates for, 48, 81, 204–206
Things to Bring list for, 224–226
Web Parts for More Page tab of, 226–228
Microsoft Office functions. See also Access 2007; Excel 2007
for creating workspaces, 9, 44, 188–192
for document management, 194–198
libraries and, 149–150
SharePoint services integration with, 8–10

N

Navigation, 14–41
customizing left panel for, 30–35
customizing top, 27–30
of document libraries, 26–27

of home page and SharePoint site, 16–21
of lists, 25–26
of Recycle Bin, 38–40
of site hierarchy, 21–24
of Web Part Pages, 35–37

O

Office functions. See Microsoft Office functions
"Open editing," of wikis, 264
Outlook 2007, 290–327
discussion boards in, 258–260
e-mail from SharePoint contacts by, 302–303
Meeting Workspaces from, 312–317
RSS feeds and, 317–321
SharePoint alerts in, 308–312
SharePoint calendars and, 303–304
SharePoint contact list connected to, 292–296
SharePoint contact moved from, 297–299
SharePoint contacts copied to, 299–301
SharePoint Task List and, 305–307
workflow in, 322–326

P

Permissions
creating sites and, 49–50
levels of, 435–436
list, 437–441
management of, 53–60
in SharePoint services, 7
in surveys, 245
Personal version of Web Parts, 402

Picture libraries, 141–142, 145. See also Libraries
Portal component, of SharePoint Server 2007, 11
Portland Pattern Repository, 264
Priority columns of lists, 107–109
Productivity, 96

Q

Queries. See Searching SharePoint sites
Quick Launch links, 18–20, 31–33

R

Read permission, 7
Recurring events, Meeting Workspaces from, 213
Recycle Bin, 16, 38–40, 95–96
Rich-Text Editor, 415
Rollup summaries, in blogs, 48
RSS (Really Simple Syndication) feeds, 48, 71
  to blogs, 286–288
  lists and, 119–123
  Outlook 2007 and, 292, 317–321

S

Searching SharePoint sites, 428–434
Security of library settings, 179–181
Settings. See Library settings
Shared version of Web Parts, 402
SharePoint Central Administration, 45–46, 56
SharePoint Designer 2007, 12, 409
SharePoint Server 2007, 11

SharePoint services, 1–13
  Microsoft Office integration with, 8–10
  permissions in, 7
  team collaboration in, 2–7
  technology of, 11–12
  versions of, 8
Site collection level features, 65, 68
Site column gallery, 104
Site columns, of lists, 104–107
Site gallery document library, 65
Site level features, 68
Spreadsheets. See Excel 2007
Surveys, 16, 230–249. See also Discussion boards
  format of, 230
  question types for, 232–234
  responding to, 241–244
  results of, 245–249
  steps in creating, 234–241
Syndication of content, 71–72

T

Teams. See Collaboration
Team Sites template, 80–81
Templates
  for creating sites, 44, 47–49
  InfoPath form, 376–377
  list, 78–80
  management of, 65–67
  Meeting Workspaces, 204–206
Themes, management of, 44, 63–64
Things to Bring list, 224–226
Tool Pane, Web Part, 414–421
Troubleshooting
  contact lists, 301
  recurring events, 297
  surveys, 244
  Web Part versions, 406

U

Unique permission, 49, 54
URLs (universal resource locator), 45

V

Versioning
  as library setting, 151–152, 176–177
  of Web Parts, 402
  of wikis, 273–275
View All Site Content link, 18–19

W

Web application level features, 68
Web Part Galleries, 407–413
Web Parts, 400–427
  browser creation of Web Part Pages
    with, 422–426
  customizing, 414–421
  home pages from, 421–422
  for Meeting Workspaces, 226–228
  navigation of, 35–37
  removing, 405–407
    from Web Part Gallery, 407–413
    on Web Part Pages, 402–405
Wikimedia Foundation, Inc., 264
Wikipedia, 264
Wikis, 262–275. See also Blogs
  creating pages for, 269–271
  history of, 264
  library for, 264–269
  linking, 271–273
  versioning of, 273–275
  Wiki Site template for, 47, 81
WikiWikiWeb, 264
Windows Groups, permissions and,
    54
Workflows
  Access 2007 and, 370–372
  libraries and, 153–155
  Outlook 2007 and, 322–326
Workspaces. See Child workspaces;
    Document workspaces; Meeting
    workspaces

About the Authors

Olga Londer is an Infrastructure Architect at Microsoft where she works across countries and geographies to help IT Professionals to take the best advantage of Microsoft's products and technologies. She is an author of several books, a winner of the British Computer Society IT Trainer Award, a frequent speaker at numerous conferences, and a technical content lead for many international Microsoft events including TechEd and IT Forum. Olga is based in London, UK.

Bill English, MVP, is co-owner of Mindsharp, a company specializing in SharePoint training and consulting. English is also the Principle Author for Microsoft Press's Administrator's Companion for SharePoint Server 2007. Bill resides in Minnesota with his wife and two children, where they say summer is the six best days of the year!

Early in his career, **Todd C. Bleeker**, Ph.D., built shrewd customer service solutions for P&G, pioneered new technologies to revolutionize the transportation logistics systems for Fingerhut, shaped the disease management tools for United Healthcare, drove the human capital procurement vision to an internationalized, commercial-grade, global solution for itiliti (now PeopleClick), and as the CTO for IPCS, managed all offshore software development operations in New Delhi, India while actively participating in various stateside and Canadian projects. In 2004, Todd joined forces with Bill English to grow Mindsharp (http://Mindsharp.com), a high-quality training company.

With over a decade of Microsoft-centric software development in his wake, Todd is regarded as an innovative, resourceful, and competitive technologist with an intense desire to excel. In his spare time, Todd loves to soak up whatever technology Microsoft is churning out and spend countless hours in Minnesota with his wife, Kathryn, and six "high energy" children: Landis, Lake, Lissa, Logan, Lawson, and Lexa.

Penelope Coventry is an independent consultant based in the UK, with more than 25 years of industry experience. She currently focuses on the design, implementation and development of SharePoint Technology-based solutions. Penny has co-authored a number of books, including Microsoft Office SharePoint Server 2007 Administrator's Companion, Microsoft SharePoint Products and Technologies Resource Kit, and the previous version of this book, Microsoft Windows SharePoint Services Step-by-Step v2. Penny is frequently seen at TechEd and IT Forum, either as a Technical Learning guide or on the SharePoint Ask-the-Expert stands. Penny lives in Hinckley, Leicestershire, England with her husband, Peter and dog, Poppy.

What do you think of this book?

We want to hear from you!

Do you have a few minutes to participate in a brief online survey?

Microsoft is interested in hearing your feedback so we can continually improve our books and learning resources for you.

To participate in our survey, please visit:

www.microsoft.com/learning/booksurvey/

...and enter this book's ISBN-10 number (appears above barcode on back cover*). As a thank-you to survey participants in the United States and Canada, each month we'll randomly select five respondents to win one of five $100 gift certificates from a leading online merchant. At the conclusion of the survey, you can enter the drawing by providing your e-mail address, which will be used for prize notification only.

Thanks in advance for your input. Your opinion counts!

Microsoft
Press